Captain Chaos

Navy Cross Recipient Warner W. Tyler, Carrier Air Group Nineteen, and the Battle for Leyte Gulf

by

Steven E. Maffeo

FOCSLE
Annapolis, Maryland

Published by Focsle, LLC
20 Highland Drive
Millersville, Maryland 21108

ISBN: 979-8-9860857-1-5 (Paperback Edition)
ISBN: 979-8-9860857-0-8 (Hardcover Edition)
ISBN: 979-8-9860857-2-2 (Ebook Edition)

Library of Congress Cataloging-in-Publication Data

Maffeo, Steven E.
"Captain Chaos": Navy Cross Recipient Warner W. Tyler, Carrier Air Group Nineteen, and the Battle for Leyte Gulf /
Capt. Steven E. Maffeo, U.S.N., Ret.
Includes bibliographical references, photographs, and maps.
1. Battle for Leyte Gulf, 1944. 2. Second Battle of the Philippine Sea, 1944. 3. Battle off Cape Engaño, 1944. 4. United States. Navy – Biography. 5. World War, 1939-1945—Campaigns—Japan. 6. United States. Navy. Carrier Air Group Nineteen—History. 7. U.S. Naval Reserve Intelligence Command. 8. Tyler, Warner W. 9. Tyler, Mavis A.

"Captain Chaos": Navy Cross Recipient Warner W. Tyler, Carrier Air Group Nineteen, and the Battle for Leyte Gulf /
Steven E. Maffeo.
387 pages

Interior design: Steven E. Maffeo and Stephanee Killen, Integrative Ink

Cover: Tony Mauro Illustration and Design

Back cover painting: "Ensign Warner Tyler at the Battle for Cape Engaño" by Bruce A. Black; used with kind permission. Currently in the collection of the USS Lexington Museum, Corpus Christi, Texas; also used with kind permission.

Praise for Steven Maffeo's Books

Most Secret and Confidential: Intelligence in the Age of Nelson

A thoughtful, insightful, magnificent history, exquisitely researched and brilliantly written.

— Mr. Stephen Coonts, 17-times *NY Times* best-selling author

One of the top three naval / maritime books of the year 2000.

— Mr. Norman Polmar in the U.S. Navy League's *Seapower* magazine

What a joy it is to review a book that is well-researched, well-written, and put together with loving care.

— Professor Carl Christie in the *Journal of Military History*

An exceptional study…a "must read."

— Mr. Michael Riggle in the *U.S. Naval War College Review*

C.S. Forester and Patrick O'Brian aficionados will want this valuable volume on their shelves.

— Emeritus Professor John W. Huston, U.S. Naval Academy

Seize, Burn, or Sink: The Thoughts and Words of Admiral Lord Horatio Nelson

Monumental ... magnificent ... what an achievement! .... Here is Nelson at work, as well as Nelson as a private person, with his concerns and anxieties, his care and thoughtfulness for others, and his ruthless streak.

— Captain Richard Woodman, LVO, FRHistS, FNI

It's a gold mine for everyone who wants to find a way into the man and his mind....if only I had had this at my elbow in 2003!

— Professor Andrew Lambert, King's College, London

I found numerous delightful gems as I perused the pages .... for any serious student of Lord Nelson it is an invaluable reference tool.

— Lieutenant Commander Julian Stockwin, M.B.E.

This book [is] the best of Nelson, or, if you will, Nelson unexpurgated. You will find this book a great read and a reference you will return to often ... when you need just the right phrase.

— Mr. Stephen Coonts

The Perfect Wreck: "Old Ironsides" *and* *HMS* Java *— A Story of 1812*

A highly recommended "must-read" for every naval enthusiast—indeed, for every American!

— Mr. Stephen Coonts

This ripping yarn fascinates, educates, and entertains .... This terrific account is a "must-read."

— Colonel Phillip Meilinger in the *U.S. Naval War College Review*

The author does a fine job in writing for the expert and layman alike. The actual battle is superbly written ... in all its bloody and very sad details.

— Professor Wade G. Dudley in the U.S. Naval Institute's *Naval History* magazine

Maffeo [has a] sense of the epic....he writes convincingly, his characters live, and his frigates swim through a world in which the weather dominates and the sea is, in true Melvillian form, quite indifferent.

— Captain Richard Woodman, LVO, FRHistS, FNI

U.S. Navy Codebreakers, Linguists, and Intelligence Officers against Japan, 1910 - 1941

Captain Maffeo's book is a great contribution to naval history.

— Vice Admiral John M. Poindexter, USN, Ret., Ph.D., Assistant for National Security Affairs to President Reagan

This volume will remain the standard reference for information about the Navy's intelligence personnel before and during World War II.

— Mr. Elliott Carlson in the U.S. Naval Institute *Proceedings*

A scholarly monument to [those that] contributed mightily to the U.S. victory in World War II over Japan—and helped lay the foundations for today's National Security Agency.

— Mr. Stephen Coonts

This book ... will entertain and enlighten today's readers, and perhaps inspire some among them.

— Professor Roger Dingman in the *Journal of Military History*

Absolutely fascinating...These dedicated people—who were underfunded, undermanned, and usually underappreciated—crucially helped in winning the eventual war against Japan.

— General Stephen Lorenz, USAF, Ret.

The Russian Who Saved the World —
A Novel of the Cuban Missile Crisis

This is a riveting fictional version of what might well have happened....In reality, the world dodged a bullet.

— Vice Admiral John M. Poindexter, USN, Ph.D., Ret.

The book is well-researched and told with the help of experts....[It] is a compelling story, richly told, full of historical fact, and entertaining.

— Captain William Hamblet in the U.S.
Naval Institute *Proceedings*

This thrilling ... novel is a fictionalized account of ... the most critical moment of the 20th century. [Maffeo's] expertise and in-depth research make this work authentic and suspenseful, revealing much about the Soviet submarine service of the Cold War.

— Mr. Christopher Miskimon in the
Military Heritage Magazine

One Russian almost killed us all. Another Russian saved us. A frightening story—solidly based on fact.

— Rear Admiral Richard E. Young, USN, Ret.

Steven Maffeo's books: naval history and historical fiction

Most Secret and Confidential:
Intelligence in the Age of Nelson

Seize, Burn, or Sink
The Thoughts and Words of Admiral Lord Horatio Nelson

The Perfect Wreck: "Old Ironsides" *and*
HMS Java *— A Story of 1812*

U.S. Navy Codebreakers, Linguists, and Intelligence Officers
against Japan, 1910-1941 — A Biographical Dictionary

The Russian Who Saved the World —
A Novel of the Cuban Missile Crisis

Captain Chaos
Navy Cross Recipient Warner W. Tyler, Carrier Air
Group Nineteen, and the Battle for Leyte Gulf

Dedicated to

Captain Warner William Tyler

November 30, 1922 – September 9, 1998

and

Mrs. Mavis Ann Lorenzen Tyler

July 16, 1923 – October 16, 2016

And also to Ensign Tyler's squadron mates, in U.S. Navy Torpedo Squadron Nineteen, who did not come back:

Lieutenant, junior grade, Robert H. Goforth,
Arlington, Virginia
Lieutenant, junior grade, John Middleton, Jr.,
Amarillo, Texas
Lieutenant, junior grade, Robert L. Sinclair,
Dallas, Texas
Lieutenant, junior grade, Charles E. Wendt,
Watseka, Illinois
Ensign Alton W. Hallowell,
Federalsburg, Maryland
Aviation Radioman 1st Class William W. Finger,
Sunnyside, New York
Aviation Ordnanceman 2nd Class LaMark Dees,
San Francisco, California
Aviation Radioman 2nd Class William L. Martin,
Holyoke, Massachusetts

Aviation Ordnanceman 2nd Class Jack C. Mitchell,
Pell City, Alabama
Aviation Ordnanceman 2nd Class James C. Reese,
Mesena, Georgia
Aviation Radioman 2nd Class Orville F. Jasper,
Washington, Missouri
Aviation Radioman 2nd Class Bernard F. Murphy,
Haydenville, Massachusetts
Aviation Machinist's Mate 2nd Class Frank J. Caka, Jr.,
Astoria, New York
Aviation Radioman 3rd Class Phillip D. Largo,
Phoenix, Arizona
Aviation Radioman 3rd Class William C. Lyde,
Houston, Texas

***

"A man is not dead while his name is still spoken."

— Sir Terence Pratchett, OBE

"The greatest thing you can do to respect the dead is to remember them, to keep them in your mind so that they do not slip away into that cold, dark infinity that awaits us all."

— Craig Johnson

Quaeque ipse miserrima vidi, et quorum pars magna fui.

(These most lamentable events I witnessed,
and a great part of them I was.)

— *Æneas*, in Virgil's *The Æneid*

"Where do we *get* such men?

They leave this ship and they do their job. Then they
must find this speck lost somewhere on the sea.

When they find it they have to land on its pitching deck.

Where *do* we get such men?"

— Fictional Rear Adm. George Tarrant, in
James A. Michener's *The Bridges at Toko-ri*

"Don't think that we weren't scared, oh just
most of the time!"

— T. Hugh Winters, Commander,
Air Group Nineteen

Table of Contents

Forewords

Reading Captain Steve Maffeo's wonderfully detailed and meticulously researched account of Carrier Air Group Nineteen's combat pilots (flying off the USS *Lexington* before and during the Battle for Leyte Gulf in World War II) brought to focus for me—as nothing ever has before—the reality of what those young naval aviators had accomplished. As a private pilot myself, I long ago realized that I could never really know what those intrepid young men had felt, done, seen—and indeed the enormity of what they had been through. As a result of reading this book, I have now come as close as I ever will to knowing and experiencing an aircraft-carrier pilot's feelings and thoughts while in mortal combat in the air and on the sea.

Weaving through the events of those critical summer and fall months of 1944, Steve has infused numerous actual accounts of the thoughts, briefings, conversations, log books, and the pilots' own written accounts as recorded by those men of Carrier Air Group Nineteen themselves.

Immersed in the book, this old sailor's imagination could smell the salt and feel the rush of air in the cockpits; I could feel the anticipation and, yes, the trepidation and even some deep-seated fear. Fear as the pilot waits for the launch officer to drop his arm (or in some cases waits for the jolt of the hydraulic catapult, praying that the force will be neither too weak nor too strong). The launch will send him and his maximum-loaded airplane off the end of a heaving deck into a humid and pitch-black dawn. He will fly out to try his best to find an enemy who, once found, will be intent on killing him. And these young men did this time after time, day after day—unless, of course, they encountered that one time that they would not come back. My God—those young men were brave!

Steve's book is particularly meaningful to me because it largely focuses upon one of the three sailors I have personally been privileged—no—*honored*, to know who were involved in, fought in, and survived the greatest naval battle the world has ever known: Leyte Gulf.

These men are Henry F. "Doc" Manget, Jr., Marlo L. Webb, and Warner W. Tyler.

So, one day in 1957, on one of my first dates with the beautiful girl who would eventually be my wife Margie (in a wonderful marriage of what is now 62 years and ongoing), she took me to meet her sister Toy and her brother-in-law Doc Manget. Toy's and Doc's entry hall was decorated with photos of World War II and Korean War navy aircraft: *Hellcats*, *Corsairs*, and *Panthers*. As we sat on the couch, and with no prior knowledge of Doc's background, I boldly proceeded to tell him how I myself was learning to fly, and to tell him all about how to fly. Finally, after incessant nudging in my side from Margie, I finally shut up.

Well, when we left, and to my great chagrin, Margie told me that Doc had been a fighter pilot in the U.S. Navy in World War II and the Korean War, and had flown all of the planes in the pictures on his wall. Margie informed me that Doc, on October 24, 1944, had just landed on board the carrier USS *Princeton*—returning from a strike with Torpedo Squadron-27 during the Battle for Leyte Gulf—when the *Princeton* was hit by a Japanese dive bomber. Doc was one of the survivors who jumped off of the flight deck into the Pacific Ocean as the carrier went down. He later, fortuitously, was picked up by a destroyer. Wow, was I humbled. Lesson learned—keep your mouth shut and find out with whom you're talking before you make a fool of yourself!

For many years we all had plenty of laughs, at my expense, over that incident. Later, when Doc was the manager of the DeKalb-Peachtree Airport, Margie and I would fly our little *Cessna* down to Atlanta to visit her relatives. Doc would always be up in the control tower when I called in to approach control. He would also be sure to come on the air and politely ask me if I were really confident that I knew how to land my *Cessna 175*. Talk about rubbing it in!

It's also been my continuing honor to personally know and call 97-year-old Marlo Webb my friend, and to see and talk to him occasionally in his home town of Farmington, New Mexico, where we both live. In World War II, Marlo was a young officer—a lieutenant, (junior grade)—and communications officer on board the destroyer USS *Hailey*. His ship was in Task Unit 77.4.2 ("Taffy 2") during the engagement called the Battle off Samar—which was a part of the huge four-day clash now referred to as the Battle for Leyte Gulf. It's a little unlikely, because of the great distances involved, but Marlo might well have seen (or heard radio chatter from) Warner Tyler's Carrier Air Group-19 aircraft flying from the *Lexington*.

Captain Warner Tyler is the other veteran of that great battle that I have been honored to know and with whom I've enjoyed a close personal and working relationship. Our acquaintance goes back at least to 1970 when, in Denver, Captain Tyler was the commanding officer of Naval Reserve Air Intelligence Unit (NAIRU) D-2, in which I served as intelligence production department head.

I'm not exactly sure why we all affectionately called him "Captain Chaos" and still refer to him as such even to the present day, but I think it was probably based on a nickname he had earned from his World War II flying days in the Pacific, and some of the "chaos" that he and people like Doc Manget had unleashed on the Japanese Navy during the Battle for Leyte Gulf and the months preceding it. Of course, Warner's frequent hi-jinx during the many navy social occasions he attended (often with his delightful wife Mavis), after his retirement from the navy, helped sustain this reputation among all of us who admired the man he was.

The day after Doc had ended up bobbing up and down in the Pacific when the *Princeton* sank, Warner was still "milling about smartly" (one of his favorite sayings), striking the Japanese in an attack that would earn him the Navy Cross—the Navy's second-highest combat medal. Later on, prior to his retirement, it was truly a double honor for me to have one of Warner's sterling silver Captain's eagle insignias pinned on my collar—by him—when I made Captain myself.

I like to paint occasionally, but I've only painted three aircraft pictures in my life. One was of a Navy *Panther* jet depicting Doc's airplane in the Korean War—which I then gave to Doc. The second was of my little *Cessna 175* trailing smoke from a blown engine as I was making a forced landing. The third painting was of Warner Tyler's TBM *Avenger* on his torpedo run against the hybrid Japanese battleship/carrier *Ise.* I had the distinct honor to present that oil painting to Warner at his navy retirement ceremony in 1981. That picture now hangs in the captain's cabin on board the decommissioned USS *Lexington* at Corpus Christi, Texas. I'm also honored that Steve has chosen that painting to grace the cover of this book.

This writer was just a small eight-year old boy when those three young men, and thousands just like them, were putting their lives and their futures on the line for families and children like me—and for their Country. They truly are part of "The Greatest Generation" and were typical of the men and women who made it so. What an honor to have known them. All true, modest gentlemen to whom we owe so much.

So, it is with much pleasure that I write this foreword, and in particular because it gives me the opportunity to describe Warner William Tyler—the man I was fortunate to know and work with, and whom I've so admired.

You know, respect and admiration are not inherited. They are earned. This is particularly true in the military services. I don't know if Warner's character was primarily honed by his wartime experiences, or if it were already in place and just part of his natural bent. Some people are natural leaders, though most of us have to learn by experience.

As I mentioned above, I first met Warner and had the privilege to work for him in the early 1970s when he was commanding officer of reserve unit NAIRU D-2 and I a department head in that unit. Later, I worked for him when he was Reserve Intelligence Area Coordinator—Area Five (RIAC-5), in Denver, and I was subordinate to him as, first, the commanding officer of Naval Air Intelligence Reserve Unit "Armed Forces Air Intelligence Training Center (AFAITC) 0171," and then later as commanding officer of NAIRU "Fleet Intelligence Rapid Support Team Pacific (FIRSTPAC) 0571."

From the day I first met him, and then throughout our later years working together, it was strikingly apparent that here was a *true* leader. I say that for a number of reasons: he was extremely competent, energetic, knowledgeable, fair, down-to-earth—well, I could go on-and-on. He had the imaginative attention to detail common to many great commanders. In addition, there was just something about him that made every person want to do the best they could for this wonderful man.

We all knew that he was a veteran of World War II, but when we first met it took several months before I could get out of him some of his background and what he had done in the Pacific War. He was not a braggart; indeed, he was very modest. But neither was he overly self-effacing. When you asked him a question about his past he would answer and would simply tell you the truth. But you usually did have to dig a bit to get details. If you did get him to talk about the mission where he earned the Navy Cross, he would, but then he'd shrug, smile, and say, "Well, that was a long time ago, and like the admiral says, 'so, what have you done for us lately?'"

I can't emphasize enough that all who worked under him greatly respected him. But it was not out of fear because he was the boss; rather, it was because he was a good man and you wanted to do good work for him. He had a great personality and his "troops" just wanted to be with him and work with him.

In the years I knew and worked with Warner I never saw him get upset or rattled in the least about *anything*. His calm and cool approach to problem solving and his calm and effective management style just naturally carried over to his troops. He had *been there and done that* and you felt it and were reassured by it. His leadership style was definitely infectious and it rubbed off on all his subordinate officers and sailors in the various air and intelligence units he commanded, and then later it likewise rubbed off on the commanding officers of the various reserve units under him.

He was also very "forehanded," to use a navy term from World War II; he saw issues coming in advance and he either headed them off or when they came he was fully ready with a plan or a solution. Thus, I can recall no leadership or management problems of any significance that surfaced while he was the RIAC. We all admired and respected the obvious deep and solid character of the man. He gave you the impression of being laid back and relaxed, but underneath he really was a no-nonsense leader that would and could get the job done no matter what the situation. As I recall, interestingly, he always looked younger—and acted more energetically—than the age he really was at the time we were working together.

Warner also had a great sense of humor combined with great charm. One example that comes to mind: the RIAC staff occasionally went out in town during our lunch hour on drill weekends, and on one occasion there were some helium balloons in the restaurant where we were having lunch. I had tied a book of matches to the end of the string on one balloon to make it just hang in suspension. However, as it slowly drifted around the room it got caught by a slow-moving ceiling fan and was swinging around in leisurely circles. This caused the matchbook to swing out in a large arc and every time it passed by the bar near our table the book would tap a lady in the back of the head who was sitting with her back to us. Although we were embarrassed about this unexpected situation, we nevertheless were laughing while watching for her to react. Well, she ignored this a couple of times; she didn't know what was hitting her. Warner was trying not to laugh but, embarrassed and feeling that he needed to take control, he got up to put an end to it. Right then she finally turned around and because Warner was the closest and was approaching her, she gave poor "Captain Chaos" what-for. She thought he or we were throwing things at her, though of course we weren't—that said, we clearly weren't entirely innocent! This interplay had now caught the amused attention of everyone in the restaurant. Turning his considerable charm on to maximum, Warner apologized politely and profusely to her for any discomfort she had experienced. About this time the matchbook came around again. He caught the errant missile and made a big show of giving it to her as a formal present from the United States Navy. She laughed, and all was forgiven.

Rear Admiral Bruce A. Black, U.S. Navy, Retired

Formerly Commander, U.S. Naval
Reserve Intelligence Command

Farmington, New Mexico
August, 2021

P.S.: A fourth Pacific War sailor that I knew (and had played with as a little boy and thus remember well) was very special to me. He was my second cousin, Seaman Randolph (Randy) Black, who was killed in action on board the *Essex*-class aircraft carrier USS *Franklin* on 19 March 1945. Two Japanese bombs penetrated the flight deck and killed all but two men stationed on the hangar deck. In total, almost 800 crewmen were killed and 500 wounded. The *Franklin* suffered the most severe damage and highest casualties experienced by any U.S. fleet carrier that survived World War II.

Steve and I first encountered Captain Warner W. Tyler in the early 1980s when we both joined the Naval Reserve Intelligence community in Denver.

As a seasoned Vietnam War combat fighter pilot I assumed that I was the "old salt" in the group, but I soon found out that was not the case. The blue and white ribbon of the Navy Cross, which he wore beneath his gold Naval Aviator wings, was a clue to Warner's early career that Steve and I had yet to discover. The Navy Cross is the second-highest medal the Navy can award for combat—right below the Medal of Honor.

As a newly minted Ensign via the Direct Commission program, Steve was to distinguish himself as the most competent, ambitious, and dedicated junior officer in the area. His years as an enlisted petty officer gave him experience and insight beyond his rank. Our friendship over the years has been a treasure as I watched him develop as an officer and I observed his skills as a storyteller mature. Now, some forty years later, he has set about to tell us the tale of Navy Cross recipient "Captain Chaos" as well as the stories of his World War II cohorts. Steve has delved into many sources, including considerable first-person accounts, to capture the unvarnished exploits of these selfless patriots.

I immediately discovered a new and particular kinship with Warner after reading just a few passages of this book. He and I both were combat aviators from Carrier Air Wing-19, albeit of different times. But air warfare was different back in those days for a "new guy" in 1944. Courage in the face of formidable danger, for then-Ensign Tyler and his comrades, was palpable. Those guys are real heroes in every sense of the word. Without needless embellishment Steve recounts many combat engagements that put you right in the cockpit behind your thundering fourteen-cylinder radial engine. As I read, with clenched teeth, I could envision AAA tracers whiz by the windscreen—and felt the airplane shake from nearby explosions—while on the attack to lay down a 2,000-pound ship-killing torpedo. Fire, smoke, AAA, and multiple aircraft attacking the same ships at the same time in incredible—dare I say—chaos. While there were many targets of opportunity there were also many very real risks of not surviving.

Moreover, the kinship I felt went beyond the realities of "just" being combat aviators on board a U.S. Navy aircraft carrier. What Steve and I, and the rest of the intel types in the Denver reserve community, soon learned was that Warner Tyler's Carrier Air Group Nineteen—justifiably famous for its performance in the great sea battle of Leyte Gulf, actually spent the majority of its tour onboard the USS *Lexington*—about four months—attacking Japanese ground targets. These included places like the Philippine Islands (Mindinao, Cebu, Manila, Luzon) as well as Guam, the Palau Islands, the Bonin Islands, and Formosa. Rather than torpedoes, Warner usually carried bombs (and sometimes even naval mines) in these attacks, which were all heavily defended by ferocious Japanese AAA. This was very similar to my experience in Vietnam, as our carrier aircraft didn't really fight ships but attacked rather heavily defended ground targets. We launched strikes against North Vietnamese and Viet Cong logistics infrastructure, storage areas, bunkers, and various parts of the enemy's lines of communication. Therein lay my other common connection with Mr. Tyler, for even though 25 years had passed and although some things were very different, there were many things that didn't change at all. Combat carrier aviation is a young man's game for valiant warriors able to rise above the fear and danger of near impossible challenges in the name of honor and duty.

Well, fortunately, I survived Vietnam and, fortunately, Warner survived World War II. Lieutenant (junior grade) Tyler returned stateside a few months before the war ended. Then, after the Japanese surrender, he left active duty and came back to the Denver area; there he lived the post-war dream with a beautiful family, a successful business, and continued service to his country in the Naval Reserve—sharing that passion and dedication that sustained him through those battles in 1944. And I can say that Steve and I, as well as many others, were certainly beneficiaries of his unique leadership style and his amazing sense of humor.

Steve knew there was a lot more to Warner's story beyond what we saw as "Captain Chaos's" time in the Reserves during the '70s and '80s. Serious research, insatiable curiosity, and relentless persistence have all paid dividends in writing this fabulous book—a great read about a great man.

Captain Michael L. Waldron, U.S. Navy, Retired

Formerly F-8 *Crusader* pilot, VF-191,
USS *Oriskany*, Vietnam War, and
formerly Commander, Reserve Intelligence
Area Three, New Orleans

San Marcos, California
November, 2021

Introduction

The Battle for Leyte Gulf was the largest naval battle of World War II and, by most criteria, the largest naval battle in history with over 200,000 naval personnel and around 280 ships and 1,800 aircraft engaged. "Largest" is an impressive claim considering the remarkable size of some previous battles—such as Salamis (480 BC), Cape Ecnomus (256 BC), Actium (31 BC), Lepanto (1571), or Trafalgar (1805).

At Leyte 34 ships were sent to the ocean floor—337,000 tons—and 15,000 men were lost. It was fought in waters near the Philippine Islands of Leyte, Samar, and Luzon during 23–26 October 1944, and spanned almost 100,000 square miles of sea—about the area of the State of Colorado. The contestants were combined American and Australian forces against the Imperial Japanese Navy (IJN). This event was part of the Allied invasion of the Philippine Island of Leyte, which was a key step in the strategy aimed at isolating Japan from the countries it had occupied in Southeast Asia—countries which were vital sources of industrial and oil supplies.

By the time of the battle, Japan had fewer operational aircraft carriers and battleships left than the Allied forces had aircraft carriers alone. This underscores the disparity in force strength at this point in the war. Regardless, here the IJN mobilized nearly all of its remaining major naval vessels in a powerful attempt to defeat the Allied invasion.

The overall battle consisted of four major interrelated, but in many ways separate, engagements: the Battle of the Sibuyan Sea (24 October), the Battle of Surigao Strait (25 October), the Battle off Samar (25 October), and the Battle off Cape Engaño (25 October).

Of note, this was the first occasion in which Japanese aircraft carried out organized *kamikaze* suicide attacks, and it was the last naval battle in history where battleships fought against other battleships. The Japanese Navy suffered extremely heavy losses and never sailed in force thereafter, essentially stranded in their bases for lack of fuel for the rest of the war.

At 2126 hours on 25 October 1944, Adm. William F. Halsey, Jr., (the commander of the Third Fleet), summed it up in a message to Adm. Chester W. Nimitz (Commander in Chief, Pacific Ocean Areas): "It can be announced, with assurance, that the Japanese Navy has been beaten, routed, and broken by the U.S. Third and Seventh Fleets."

***

One of the 200,000 sailors engaged in this incredible event was a young 22-year old American naval aviator from Denver, Colorado, named Warner William Tyler. He had come out into the Pacific Theater in April 1944, joining Carrier Air Group Nineteen (CAG-19) and specifically Torpedo Squadron Nineteen (VT-19), which shortly came aboard the large fleet-carrier USS *Lexington* (CV-16). Ensign Tyler saw considerable activity and action on board the *Lexington*, culminating in the Battle for Leyte Gulf. It was there that he and his two enlisted crewmen, flying a Grumman TBM-1C *Avenger* torpedo bomber and facing considerable deadly anti-aircraft fire, dropped their torpedo at the Japanese hybrid battleship/carrier

Ise. Of course, many other torpedo bombers, dive bombers, and fighter aircraft contributed to anti-ship combat this day, with many Japanese ships targeted. The *Ise* did not sink in this engagement, but she sustained damage and subsequently retired from the area. For this action Mr. Tyler received the Navy's second- highest medal, the Navy Cross; his gunner and radioman received the Distinguished Flying Cross.

Warner Tyler fortunately survived the rest of the war, returned to his new bride—Mavis—whom he had married in February 1944, and came back to Denver. He joined the Naval Reserve and had great success in that endeavor, first in aviation units and then in intelligence units. In addition, post-war years saw him operating as a creative and successful businessman and entrepreneur, and as a devoted family man.

Among the many people whom he befriended, charmed, mentored, and led in later years was a young naval reservist, thirty-two years his junior. And now *that* man—no longer young and himself long-retired from the Navy and Naval Reserve—has imagined that you might like to know Warner's story as well as the story of World War II's Carrier Air Group Nineteen. I hope I'm right, and I hope you enjoy it.

Captain Steven E. Maffeo, U.S. Navy, Retired

Formerly Director, Joint Intelligence Center
Pacific Detachment Denver,
and formerly Director, Part-time Programs,
National Defense Intelligence College

Colorado Springs, Colorado
April, 2022

CCNAS-9-22-43-3,000
3270

DEPARTMENT OF THE NAVY

Date 1 December 1943

NAVAL AVIATOR No. C-12282

This Certifies that

Warner W. TYLER

Ensign A-V(N) USNR

born 30 *day of* November 1922 *having fulfilled the conditions prescribed by the United States Navy Department, was appointed a*

NAVAL AVIATOR

on 1 December 1943

C.P. MASON, Rear Admiral
Commandant USN
Chief of Naval Personnel

N. Aer. 4120

14619

U. S. NAVAL AIR STATION
CORPUS CHRISTI, TEXAS
STATION

1 December 1943
DATE ISSUED

This is to certify that

TYLER, Warner William
NAME

Ensign A-V(N) USNR
RANK

has passed the test in INSTRUMENT FLYING prescribed for pilots of

THE UNITED STATES NAVY

and is qualified to proceed on Instruments in

Single Engine
TYPE OF PLANE

TYPE OF PLANE

James E. Baker
JAMES E. BAKER
~~Commander, U. S. N.~~
COMMANDING.

Chapter 1

A pre-dawn combat strike launched from an aircraft carrier is a surrealistic experience." So recalled Captain Warner Tyler, from retirement, as he thought back to when he was very young, very skinny, and an Ensign in the U.S. Naval Reserve—but on full Pacific Theater active duty during World War II. This was back in the summer and fall of 1944, when he was a pilot in Torpedo Squadron Nineteen on board the USS *Lexington.*

"Electric klaxon horns and alarm bells explode in the dark and early hours. Pilots and enlisted aircrew come boiling up through the hatches."

Yet, whether there were a scheduled strike or not, "every day in enemy waters began this way," later wrote Lt. Paul Beauchamp, a pilot in Fighting Squadron Nineteen. "The horrendous blaring sound of *'General Quarters'* was broadcast throughout the ship just prior to the first signs of dawn—the time most dangerous for our fleet in terms of possible air and submarine attack. The first sound of the klaxon brought my roommates and me to our feet, and in less than sixty seconds we had slipped into socks, shoes, and flight suits and were on our way to the squadron's Ready Room."

"Within a matter of minutes," continued Mr. Beauchamp, "all water-tight hatches throughout the ship would be made secure and heaven help the poor soul trapped in a water-tight compartment for the duration of the General Quarters, which could last for hours. The penalty for not being at your assigned post during a GQ alert was quite severe—but opening a water-tight hatch during General Quarters was actually a court-martial offense—and so everyone sped with all due haste to whatever position had been assigned to each of the 3,500 men aboard this incredible floating city."

Each flying squadron's ready room "at this hour had an eerie quality since all lighting in this pre-dawn situation was produced by red bulbs. Should there be an emergency scramble," or should they be preparing for a scheduled launch like today, "the eyes of the pilots would be conditioned to the blackness of such a take-off by the red-lighted interior of the ready rooms."

"The next few minutes," Lieutenant Beauchamp continued, "perhaps it was a half-hour, were devoted to obtaining weather information which was projected onto a screen in the manner of a teletype machine. This information—in addition to code letters for the day—was copied on navigation charts which were shortly stowed under the instrument panels of our aircraft. Other information pertinent to the day's strike also came down from the Control Center located high in the 'island' amidships on the carrier."

These *Lexington* pilots were part of a large and formidable U.S. Navy force: the Third Fleet, commanded by Adm. William F. "Bill" Halsey, Jr. Under Halsey (who disliked his media-imposed nickname of "Bull") were several other task forces and task groups. Notably, Task Force 38, the "Fast Carrier Force," was under the command of Vice Adm. Marc A. "Pete" Mitscher, and he with his staff were embarked on board the *Lexington*. The next subdivision in Ensign Tyler's convoluted chain of command was Task Group 38.3, commanded by Rear Adm. Frederick C. "Ted" Sherman, who with *his* staff were embarked on board one of the *Lexington*'s sister ships, the large carrier USS *Essex*. So, interestingly, the commanding officer of the *Lexington*—Capt. Ernest W. "Ernie" Litch, Jr.—took direct orders from Admiral Sherman a few miles away onboard the *Essex*, rather than from Admiral Mitscher (who was Sherman's superior officer) who at any given moment was literally just a few feet from Litch onboard the *Lexington*. In addition to the two fleet carriers, Sherman—leading TG 38.3—had four light carriers, five battleships, four cruisers, and fourteen destroyers. "We were able to put up a strike of six-hundred airplanes consisting of fighters, torpedo planes, and dive bombers."

So, then, the command "Pilots Man Your Planes!" flashed across the ready-room screens (those screens were actually pretty high-tech for 1944) and those spaces were quickly vacated.

"Within a few minutes," continued then-Ensign Tyler, "all pilots and other air crewmen leapt up ladders to the flight deck. We scattered in all directions to man the aircraft to which we'd been assigned. Burdened with flight suits, parachutes, survival equipment, sidearms, and other paraphernalia, we climbed up into our cockpits. Each plane's crew chief was already in place, and they assisted the pilots and crew, securing all into their seats. The 'Start Engines!' command blared through the loudspeakers and within seconds the air was blue with huge quantities of exhaust smoke. We were ready!"

"Each airplane got a short warm-up as the *Lexington* came about and headed directly into the wind. The 36,000-ton, 870-foot long ship sharply heeled over to the outside of the turn and increased her speed to her maximum of 33 knots. The aircraft, which had been pre-spotted on the deck, taxied to the launch position in prescribed sequence."

"One-by-one we saluted the launch officer and pressed back into our bucket seats. As the launch officer's arm swiftly came down, each plane went up to full power and thundered down the flight deck, vaulting from the slightly pitching bow." The first twenty to thirty planes, mostly fighters—positioned close to the ship's bow and thus limited by a very short 'runway'—were hurled aloft by the hydraulic catapults, and then the remainder took off in the normal way. "I doubt," added Lieutenant Beauchamp, "that any Army Air Corps pilot would have considered a 500-foot take-off normal, but to us it was an everyday procedure."

"From the perspective of the deck," Mr. Tyler continued, "the aircraft began to disappear into the Stygian blackness as they slowly spiraled upward. At the prescribed altitude we began to rendezvous in sections, squadrons, and finally the entire deck-load strike. From the *Lexington* our exhaust flames and smoke gradually diminished and ultimately disappeared. In their place they left a deep-throated rumble which itself gradually faded into silence. There is nothing lonelier than an aircraft carrier whose deck-load strike has been launched. Now the waiting began. Each man left on board intently went about his duties, lost within his own thoughts as to what this day would bring. Will the strike be successful? How many strikes will we launch today? How many planes will not return? Will enemy aircraft attack *our* ship?"

"By very early in that morning of 25 October," went on Ensign Tyler, "Vice Admiral Mitscher, on board the *Lexington*, and his subordinate admirals on other ships had made the decision to attack units of the Japanese Fleet for the second day—having already had solid—though limited—success on the 24th. They order full deck-load strikes, again. The ensuing action will be one facet of what most of us and some newspapers will call the 'Second Battle of the Philippine Sea'—though Admiral Nimitz and historians will call it something else. I was in Carrier Air Group Nineteen, and as already mentioned, specifically in Torpedo Squadron Nineteen on board the *Lexington*."

So, the deck was "spotted" with a full complement of airplanes. These were eight torpedo bombers, TBM-1Cs, designed by the

Grumman Aircraft Corporation and manufactured by Grumman and by General Motors. They were called *Avengers*. There were also eight dive bombers, SB2Cs, designed and manufactured by the Curtiss-Wright Corporation. These were called *Helldivers*. Lastly, there were a dozen fighters, F6Fs, also designed and manufactured by Grumman. They were called *Hellcats*.

"At this time U.S. Navy strike doctrine against large ships required sending the fighters in first. Thus, the *Hellcats* were going to strafe everything in sight on the enemy ship with their six 50-caliber machine guns; this was to get the Japanese anti-aircraft gunners to hunker down and shelter—resulting in them not manning their guns. Then the eight torpedo planes, *Avengers* like mine, would split up into two groups, with four planes attacking on either side of the ship. As the torpedo planes maneuver into position, the dive bombers would begin their dives as soon as the *Hellcats* 'cleared' the area."

"We in the *Avengers* (which some people amusingly called *Torpeckers*) would now approach the ship outboard from the stern at 7,000 feet and an angle of about 45 degrees. This spread of aircraft was designed to minimize and/or neutralize any course changes the enemy ship might make. Whichever direction he might turn, we would still have a good angle shot—and that would also, very likely, make more effective any hits from torpedoes already in the water."

"Despite the intense strafing attacks of our *Hellcats*, we nevertheless expected the *flak* (enemy anti-aircraft fire) to be intense."

Chapter 2

Warner William Tyler was born in Denver, Colorado, on 30 November 1922. An only child, he was the son of Warner and Jane Tyler, who had gotten married in January 1922. The senior Warner (1899-1987) had been born at Granite, Colorado. In the early 1920s he was a salesman, and sales manager, for Chevrolet Motor Co.

Warner William Tyler's mother was the former Jane Esther Darrow (1902-1991). Jane was one of 16 children. Her father was a railroad attorney and she had grown up in Glenwood Springs, Colorado.

The name Warner came from the young Tyler's paternal grandmother, whose maiden name was Eva Estelle Warner—and of course from his father. His middle name of William was taken from one of Jane's brothers.

When Warner William was four years old the family moved to Kansas City due to his dad's new job with Sommers Oil Co. During the next several years the family moved several more times due to the elder Warner's change to, and promotions within, the Continental Oil Company (Conoco): back to Denver, then Boulder, and then back to Denver in 1934. Warner senior became a regional manager at Conoco; the company distributed motor oil, gasoline, kerosene, benzene, and other products first in the western United States and then nationally. As it turned out, Warner had a very successful 37-year career with Conoco.

As of 1940 the Warner Tyler family lived at 176 East 14th Avenue (previously they'd been located at 25 East 9th Avenue) and the junior Warner was attending Denver's East High School. East had been one of Denver's original four high schools and it claimed lineage to the very first school established in Denver.

During his senior year Warner was in the Spanish Club and on the "Red and White Day" Committee. Red and White Day (named after the school's colors) was established in 1930. This spring ritual included at least a dozen floats constructed by the various school clubs. These floats would parade around the school's large esplanade and were judged for their creativity and construction. Then a Spring Queen would be elected who presided over many skits performed by each of the classes as well as the faculty. In the afternoon the entire school would be released to attend the all-city track meet.

At East, Warner knew a young lady named Mavis Ann Lorenzen. Mavis was in the same class (1940), but she was a year younger than Warner, having skipped a grade in elementary school. While they knew each other, it doesn't appear that they dated during that time; however, she will certainly appear again in Warner's story.

After high school graduation, Warner began attending the University of Denver, intending to major in business administration. This was a common move for Denver high school kids in those days. DU was and is a private school, but back then (certainly unlike *now*) the tuition was very inexpensive—particularly if you continued to live at home and rode the bus out to the campus in what was then a fairly undeveloped part of southeast Denver. Some folks thus referred to DU as "Tramway Tech." Indeed, in this scenario, it was significantly cheaper than going to the public University of Colorado at Boulder. Warner clearly did this, as did Miss Lorenzen (and as did the author's parents, they having graduated from Denver's North High School in 1943).

So, a couple of years went by, which among other things saw the entry of the United States into World War II after the attack on Pearl Harbor. Warner decided to join the Navy, so he and a friend went down to the recruiting office. He asked if he could be a flier, which was in line with a youthful interest in aviation—he was a serious builder of model airplanes in earlier years, among other things.

On 29 July 1942 Warner completed preliminary examinations for enlisting in Class V-5, U.S. Naval Reserve Aviation Cadet Training, at the U.S. Navy Recruiting Station in Denver. The station was located in the U.S. Customs House downtown, at 721 19th Street. It was, for decades, the home of armed forces recruiting and processing for the area. He then was required to take a ten-day trip to San Francisco to complete his enlistment. Warner was then brought into the Naval Reserve with a "pay entry base date" of 8 August 1942.

At that time, the U.S. Civilian Pilot Training Program (CPTP) was operating as a flight-training system sponsored by the government with the purpose of increasing the number of civilian pilots—though having a clear impact on military preparedness.

The program started in 1939 with two laws passed by Congress; the government paid for a 72-hour ground-school course followed by 35 to 50 hours of flight instruction at facilities located near eleven colleges and universities. It greatly expanded the nation's civilian pilot population by training thousands of college students to fly. By the program's peak, 1,132 educational institutions and 1,460 flight schools were participating in the CPTP.

For the Navy, this program was conducted by contractors and was designed to teach basics before the Navy actually picked up the prospective pilots. Thus, between September 1942 and January 1943, Warner Tyler did "ground school" at the University of Colorado at

Boulder, and his air work was done at the Municipal Airport in Boulder, flying a *Piper J3 Cub.*

In fact, the *Piper J3 Cub* became the primary trainer aircraft of the CPTP and played an integral role in its success, achieving almost legendary status. About 75% of all new pilots in the CPTP (from a total of 435,165 graduates) were trained in *Cubs.* By the war's end, 80% of all United States naval and military pilots had received their initial flight training in *Piper Cubs.*

From May through July 1943, young Mr. Tyler accomplished further training at the U.S. Naval Air Station Hutchinson, Kansas. Then, from August through November 1943, he trained at NAS Corpus Christi, Texas.

At Corpus Christi, Warner was commissioned as an Ensign, USNR, A-V(N) on 16 November 1943, and he then graduated from flying training on 1 December 1943. (Future U.S. president George H. W. Bush had similarly graduated at Corpus Christi in June 1943). USNR A-V(N) was the abbreviation for "naval reserve aviation flight officers detailed to active duty in the aeronautic organization of the Navy immediately following their completion of training and designation as naval aviators." Thus, Ensign Tyler was duly designated a "naval aviator," assigned the Naval Aviator Number C-12282, and certified as qualified to fly single-engine aircraft in general and on "instruments."

Warner then completed a course in operational training at Fort Lauderdale, Florida, finishing there on 5 February 1944.

A quick trip moved Mr. Tyler to Chicago and Lake Michigan. There he undertook advanced carrier-landing qualifications on board the converted side-wheel lake-steamer *Wolverine.* The *Wolverine* and her sister, the *Sable,* had been converted to replicate aircraft carriers, and operated from what will come to be called Chicago's "Navy Pier," assigned to the 9th Naval District Carrier Qualification Training Unit. Working in conjunction with nearby

Naval Air Station Glenview, the two paddle-wheeled unarmored carriers afforded critical training in basic carrier operations to thousands of pilots and also to smaller numbers of Landing Signal Officers (LSOs). The *Wolverine* and *Sable* enabled pilots and LSOs to learn to handle take-offs and landings on a real flight deck in open water. By the time the war ended, around 17,000 personnel had been trained on board the two ships.

Warner flew three times on 9 February 1944, successfully completing eight carrier landings in a TBF *Avenger* torpedo plane. At this point, since the beginning of his training, he had logged 374 hours in the air as a pilot.

It's not clear why Mr. Tyler was early-on slotted for torpedo planes, or even whether it was his idea or the Navy's. Very likely it was the Navy's, which was constantly assessing its overages and shortfalls regarding pilot manning. The TBF (or TBM) *Avenger* was the biggest carrier aircraft of the war. By all accounts it was remarkably easy to fly. It was extremely versatile; very effective in torpedo attacks, level bombing, glide bombing, antisubmarine warfare, and scouting.

Tyler was then temporarily attached to VRF-2 at Floyd Bennett Field for a ferrying trip to San Diego. While Naval Air Station New York—located in Brooklyn—was the facility's official name, it was universally and informally known as Bennett Field. "VRF" is the World War II naval air squadron designation for a ferry squadron, which transported newly manufactured and tested airplanes all around the country to various embarkation points.

Warner undertook a ferry trip from New York to San Diego, stopping for a few days in Dallas, Texas. There he connected with that previously mentioned classmate from East High School in Denver—Miss Mavis Lorenzen. As discussed earlier, Mavis and Warner knew each other at East and both had graduated in 1940.

Born on July 16, 1923 in Marshalltown, Iowa, Mavis was the only child of Florence A. Zeisneiss Lorenzen (1902-1976) and John

Henry Lorenzen (1897-1977). Florence had been born in Iowa; John (actually Johannes) had been born in Germany. The family moved to Denver in 1935 when Mavis was twelve years old. She was raised in the Methodist and then the Lutheran faith. As she was growing up and got old enough to participate, Mavis helped her mother in the drapery business the family had obtained. As of 1940 they were living at 1658 Garfield Street.

Mavis was very active in high school. She earned Gold "D," Large "D," and Small "D" athletic letters, apparently in swimming and basketball. In those days the "D" stood for Denver Public Schools rather than, say, "E" for East High or "N" for North High. Actually, Mavis was athletic in many areas; she also took dance lessons, played tennis, was a member of bowling leagues, and golfed. She was a Junior Escort. She was in the Clio Club, which in the Denver high schools was a literary club that also did philanthropic work; it was originally called the "Young Ladies Club of Denver." She was also in the Commercial (business) Club as well as the German Club.

For all three years of high school, Mavis was a "White Jacket." This group, formed in 1930, was made up of a large number of girls who were the "spirit" leaders of the school. Dressed in their white jackets, red skirts, red-and-white beanies, and black-and-white saddle shoes, these girls functioned as the school's pep club. (Not to be outdone, a boys' Red Jackets organization was created in 1935. These boys were also spirit leaders and along with the White Jackets would organize pep assemblies in the auditorium.)

Mavis was also a Seraph Sister in her senior year. This group was created in 1938 and only girls with high grade-point averages and "high standards" could belong. For decades these girls were indispensable to East High with their pledge to assist in various aspects of the everyday running of the school. Quite a few Seraph Sisters were assigned to individual teachers as assistants.

Many years later Mavis told her children that she thoroughly enjoyed and was interested in all her high-school activities, but she also didn't mind that they kept her at school a little longer during the day—keeping her from rushing home after class to the drapery business.

In March 1944 Warner and Mavis were no longer merely acquaintances or classmates. They had become close right after high school, meeting up and dating as they both started taking classes at the University of Denver. Mavis completed two years at DU, majoring in Business, and was a member of the Sigma Kappa Sorority.

She did not complete her studies at DU; interestingly, she obtained a job with Braniff Airlines as a ground Morse-code operator. She likely trained for six weeks at the Midland Radio Operator Specialist School in Kansas City—like her colleague Jeanette Kiefer from Stockton, Illinois—and was then stationed in Dallas. Like Jeanette, Mavis' job was relaying weather reports via Morse code to Braniff air crews in flight. Pretty adventurous; this young lady left working in her family's drapery business and quickly obtained a very technical and professional job. Moving to Kansas City, and then to Dallas, was her first time away from home.

However, there and then—whether executing a pre-arranged plan or taking a spur of the moment plunge—Mavis and Warner married in Dallas on 29 February 1944. Apparently it was decided ahead of time. It came as a complete surprise to both of their sets of parents, who were informed with phone calls from Texas. Unfortunately for the newlyweds, the inexplicable and sudden aircraft "radio problem," which caused Warner to detour from his flight plan and land in Dallas, was soon fixed. He was therefore required to complete his aircraft ferrying mission to San Diego.

Warner's and Mavis's daughter, Linda, says that "I remember Dad was pretty proud of himself for figuring out the 'detour' to Dallas with bogus radio problems in order to get married, so indeed it seems like the plan was decided ahead of February 29th, but perhaps not by much."

Upon arriving at San Diego, newly married Ens. Warner Tyler—possibly with his same airplane from Floyd Bennett Field, or perhaps with another—reported on board the small *Casablanca*-class escort carrier *Nehenta Bay* (CVE-74). Departing 1 April 1944, carrying a load of replacement aircraft and military personnel, the ship arrived at Pearl Harbor, on the island of O'ahu in the Territory of Hawai'i, on 8 April.

On the 9th of April, Warner catapulted from the ship—which was at anchor—on a half-hour ferrying assignment. This short trip, with no other aircrew with him, was to NAS Barbers Point at the southwestern shore of O'ahu, where he then reported to VT-100.

There is some documentation which shows that Mr. Tyler appeared on the *Nehenta Bay*'s muster roll as late as 12 April, and that he then was going to transfer to another CVE, the *Barnes*, for temporary duty and further assignment. However, this does not appear to be what actually happened.

So, training squadron VT-100 flew various models of the Grumman TBF *Avenger* aircraft. The squadron's mission was to provide trained torpedo-plane pilots and aircrew for assignment as replacements to squadrons already operating in the Pacific.

NAS Barbers Point had been commissioned on 15 April 1942. Operations initially centered on working-up carrier air groups and squadrons for carrier deployment in combat areas further west. Not long after opening, the station could already accommodate four carrier air groups at the same time and actually became one of the busiest air bases in the world. Barbers Point also became the center of the Navy's aircraft maintenance operations. While Naval Station Pearl Harbor was the Navy's wartime hub for everything pertaining to ships of the Fleet, the corresponding hub for all things related to naval aviation was Barbers Point.

Chapter 3

The U.S. Navy's Carrier Air Group Nineteen was established on 15 August 1943 at Naval Air Station Los Alamitos, California. Lt. Cmdr. T. Hugh Winters was the senior squadron commander present and read the orders to the assembled personnel. This was because Cmdr. Karl Jung—appointed to be Nineteen's "Commander Air Group"—was still *en route* to Los Alamitos. Mr. Winters was the commanding officer of Fighting Squadron-19 (VF-19). Lt. Cmdr. Richard McGowan, an Annapolis classmate and friend of Winters, was the commanding officer of Bombing Squadron-19 (VB-19) and was present. Lt. Cmdr. Albert "Scoofer" Coffin, the new commander of Torpedo Squadron-19 (VT-19), was also *en route* from Guadalcanal.

This was a typical makeup for a U.S. Navy World War II air group—fighters, dive bombers, and torpedo bombers. The primary mission of the fighters was to escort the VB and VT aircraft to and from the target, go in first to destroy or pin-down the enemy's anti-aircraft gunners during the attack, and lastly protect their own ship from enemy attack. At the time that Air Group Nineteen would go out into the war eleven months from its establishment, VF-19 will have fifty pilots, VB-19 fifty-five, and VT-19 thirty.

The group began a rigorous training schedule and, by the first of November 1943, all three squadrons were reasonably proficient with a good number of experienced pilots and a well-trained, streamlined ground crew sent up from San Diego.

"Prior to the war," wrote Lieutenant Commander Winters, "naval aviation squadrons had around 150 enlisted men permanently attached—moving lock, stock, and barrel with the squadrons out to the carriers and back, and from station-to-station with all the required gear. But now the squadron complement was reduced to a key group of about twenty men, mostly chief petty officers and first-class petty officers—yeomen, aviation mechanics, ordnancemen, radiomen, metalsmiths, and electricians. The rest of the crews were removed from the flying squadrons and formed into FASRON (Fleet Air Service Squadrons) and were permanently attached to the various aircraft carriers and air stations."

This made logistical and financial sense. Prior to the war, and for the first year of the war, air groups were essentially permanently assigned to individual carriers. But post-1942, groups rather frequently moved from carrier to carrier, so to move less men and material each time helped with costs and other efficiencies.

During this period, for some reason which is now obscure to us, the famous musical comedian Robin "Bob" Burns gave a two-month-old female lion cub, named Cleo, to Torpedo-19's Lt. Cmdr. Albert Coffin. Cleo became the squadron mascot for a while, entrusted to Ens. Ed Schulke as her caretaker. Mr. Burns, who appeared on radio and in movies from 1930 to 1947, often played a novelty musical instrument of his own invention, made of brass tubing, which he called a "bazooka." Later, during World War II, the American M1A1 shoulder-fired anti-tank rocket launcher was nicknamed the "bazooka" by soldiers and Marines for its resemblance to Burns's instrument. Thus, the squadron's insignia and flight-jacket patch soon featured Cleo riding an airplane armed with Burns's bazooka [see a photo of the patch in the *Illustrations* section of this book, as well as a photo of little Cleo].

Between Christmas 1943 and New Year's Day 1944, the small escort carrier *Altamaha* was found to be travelling up the coast. Rear Adm. Murr Arnold, Director of Personnel and Training on the staff of Commander Fleet Air, West Coast, essentially "flagged her down to spend a few days off Long Beach to carrier-qualify Air Group 19." Lieutenant Commander Winters wrote that the admiral knew "we were getting bored bouncing on the airfield day and night, and had been ready to go aboard a ship for some time—so we canceled the big New Year's Eve party we had planned."

When Mr. Winters wrote "bouncing on the airfield" he was referring to "field carrier landing practice" which was defined as that phase of required flight training that precedes actual carrier landings. "It should simulate, as nearly as practicable, the conditions encountered during carrier landing operations. FCLP training provides naval aviators this critical and required training at a properly configured ashore airfield that simulates conditions for day and night flight operations aboard a moving aircraft carrier." Of course, like Warner Tyler, all of the Group 19 pilots had previously qualified on carrier landings prior to being sent out to a squadron in the Pacific. At this point this requirement was an additional one, to ensure everyone was truly ready to go on board a big carrier and go into combat.

"So," continued Lieutenant Commander Winters, "We flew out December 25th and back January 3rd. All hands qualified with maybe a flat tire or two, which can happen to any of us—and does. But when a virgin air group qualifies on a small "jeep" carrier without at least a minor 'crunch,' that's something great." Right in the middle of all this excitement, Torpedo-19 had a quick change of command: on 31 December Lt. Cmdr. Albert "Scoofer" Coffin was relieved by Lt. Cmdr. David Dressendorfer.

Fighter pilot Ens. Bill Davis remembered the *Altamaha* event from a different point of view. He was the fighter squadron's mess treasurer, and was responsible for the huge party that apparently was not going to happen. "There was no wind, so we couldn't operate." The small 'Jeep carriers' needed at least a fifteen-knot wind blowing, to launch or land airplanes, because they were somewhat slow. "We steamed up and down the Santa Barbara Channel in a dead calm for three days. Then, the forecast was for winds the next day. 'Good, we'll be back for the party,' we said. But the winds that came presented themselves as gales. Not only could we not operate, we couldn't even go up on deck. These severe winds continued for three days, bringing us to the morning of New Years Eve."

"The winds abated slightly," continued Mr. Davis, "so the staff decided to test if qualifications could be done with three volunteers." Davis and two other young ensigns successfully took off, but after multiple unsuccessful attempts at landing were ordered back to shore. "We few therefore attended one of the most memorable New Year's Eve parties of all time," with over a thousand dollars of food and drink, and around thirty young ladies as dates. "Of course, we three had to go into hiding when the rest of VF-19 and the group finally returned two days later. And, we had to go back out to the carrier and complete our qualifications."

Thus, Carrier Air Group Nineteen was now ready to go aboard any carrier ready to fly and fight, wrote Lieutenant Commander Winters, but right then "no carrier was ready for us."

Chapter 4

Air Group Nineteen departed California on 24 February 1944, catching a ride on—but not assigned to—the USS *Lexington.* They arrived at Pearl Harbor on 28 February. The next day the group was transferred to Naval Air Station Kahului on the island of Maui. Torpedo-19's mascot, little Cleo the lioness, had been transferred to the Griffith Park Zoo (the old Los Angeles Zoo) prior to the group leaving California—for her own safety as well as everyone else's.

The presence of U.S. naval aviation on Maui dated back to before the outbreak of the war. In 1940, Utility Squadron VJ-3 arrived at the existing Puʻunene Field. Puʻunene Field was subsequently redesignated and commissioned as Naval Air Station Maui in 1942. However, since the attack on Pearl Harbor in December 1941, and the subsequent enormous buildup that the Pacific War required, it quickly became clear that NAS Maui at this location did not have the capacity to handle those huge, growing requirements, nor did the naval air stations on Oahʻu—at Barbers Point and Kāneʻohe—with their other substantial commitments.

So, on 15 March 1943, the Navy commissioned Naval Air Station Kahului at a different site, on land leased from the Hawaiian Commercial & Sugar Company. It was intended to have the capacity to handle all of the transiting squadrons that needed further aviation training, air group workups, and final combat training prior to leaving for the war zones. Two asphalt runways of 5,000 and 7,000 feet, plus aircraft parking for two carrier air groups, were constructed in a little over a year. Of course, small portions of the runways were used for mock carrier landing practice.

Many carrier air groups and over forty different squadrons trained at Kahului during the war. Nearby Kaho'olawe, the smallest of the eight main volcanic islands in the Hawai'ian Islands, was heavily used for strafing, bombing, and torpedo runs.

Ultimately, over 900 officers and 5,000 enlisted personnel were based at Kahului during the course of the war. In 1946 the Navy decommissioned NAS Kahului and it remained dormant until, in mid-1952, the Territory of Hawai'i moved commercial airline operations from Pu'unene to Kahului. Thus, the wartime NAS became the site of the future Kahului International Airport.

"I really didn't get to know the rest of the air group very well until we went to Maui," wrote Lt. Max Gregg, one of Warner Tyler's VT-19 squadron mates. "On Maui we really joined the air group at last, and it seemed we of the torpedo squadron were drawn to the fighters much more than to the bombers."

"The fighters gave us—the torpedoes—a feeling of security, and that's because we knew they cared. We knew early-on that they would go in with us all the way. I was with two other air groups before joining Nineteen, and in none of their squadrons was there the faith and trust accorded to their fighters that there was by our torpedoes and bombers to VF-19. I have to say how much I loved and appreciated those guys in VF-19."

In April 1944, Bombing-19 received several *SB2C-1 Helldivers* for transition training, and then the next month received a full complement of *SB2C-3s*. The *-3* model had a larger engine which substantially solved the chronic lack of power that had plagued earlier versions—making them unpopular with air crews.

During this period, Air Group Nineteen kept busy participating in operations *off* Maui—along with substantial periods of "off duty" time *on* Maui. June saw further carrier-landing training on board the USS *Franklin* (CV-13), another one of the *Essex*-class carriers.

Chapter 5

On 12 June 1944, Ens. Warner W. Tyler, Ens. Alton W. Hallowell, and Ens. Robert K. McAdams transferred to NAS Kahului, officially joining Carrier Air Group Nineteen and Torpedo Squadron Nineteen.

The timing was good for Mr. Tyler and his cohorts Hallowell and McAdams because just a few days later, on 23 June, Air Group-19 departed Maui embarked (as passengers) on board the USS *Intrepid* (CV-11). Their destination was Eniwetok, which is a large coral atoll of forty islands, part of the Marshall Islands. The trip took only a week, passing quickly with card games, old Western movies, and skeet-shooting off the fantail. The *Intrepid* arrived at Eniwetok on 30 June.

"As the *Intrepid* anchored in the lagoon," wrote Lieutenant Commander Winters, "she swung into a 28-knot wind and we were catapulted off—much to the amazement of some of the many ships at anchor around us. After a practice in-air rendezvous, and a circle around the atoll, we broke up and landed on the airstrip from which the Japanese had just recently departed."

After a few days of liberty the group moved, in stages, to the carrier USS *Bunker Hill* (CV-17), and then their time was occupied with more 'refresher' carrier landings.

During this training, Ensign Tyler flew once in a TBM-1C, with no aircrew with him, from the *Intrepid* to the *Bunker Hill.* These were catapult launches, since the ships were at anchor with no forward motion to create wind over the deck and help provide lift. Warner always highlighted catapult shots in his flight log because for him (and most others) they were infrequent—and exciting. In the next few days Warner flew and landed four more times, always in different airplanes, but now with aircrew with him.

Then, on Sunday, 9 July 1944, Air Group Nineteen catapulted from the *Bunker Hill,* at anchor in the lagoon, to fly out to the large carrier *Lexington* which was at sea approaching Eniwetok.

The night before, Lieutenant Commander Winters had called a meeting of VF-19. According to fighter pilot Ens. Bill Davis, Winters said, "Tomorrow we're going aboard the USS *Lexington* for an 'extended stay.' This ship has a long and distinguished record, as did the air group that has preceded us onboard that carrier (Carrier Air Group Sixteen). They're going to be a tough act to follow. We want to make the best first impression possible....I want everyone sharp. We're not only going to be appraised by the ship's crew, but also Vice Adm. Marc Mitscher and his staff. This is the admiral's flagship, and he's in charge of all air operations for the fleet. Give it your best. Admiral Mitscher is 'Naval Aviator Number 33' and in some ways the 'father' of carrier warfare. It'll be a tough audience."

Ensign Davis further commented that "the following morning dawned bright and clear, with little wind. Once again we packed everything we owned into the fuselages of our planes and prepared for takeoff. There was one problem: we were at anchor. We were going to be catapulted off the deck, one at a time, while the ship was motionless in the water, with almost no wind over the deck. Until just recently, I hadn't even been aware that this could be done. I hadn't known a catapult was that powerful."

"We started engines and taxied up to one of the two catapults and waited our turn." Unlike some of the other pilots including Ens. Warner Tyler (who had done one a few days before—as well as one back in April) Davis wrote that he had never made a catapult shot before. (Writing almost seventy years after the fact, Davis was likely confusing 9 July with the Air Group's catapult evolution of 30 June). Whichever was his first time, "I was more than a little nervous. A mechanic hooked the sling up to my plane. The launch officer made a small circular motion with his hand, and I ran the engine up to full power. I tightened the friction knob on the throttle and pressed my fist against it so that I wouldn't pull power off when I was hit with the 'G' forces. I braced my right elbow into my stomach so that I wouldn't pull back on the stick, and waited. The launch officer dropped his hand."

"The force pinned me back against the seat. I had no control whatsoever over the airplane until it left the end of the deck....I was barely five knots above stalling speed and literally staggering into the air. It seemed nip-and-tuck for a moment until the wheels came up and I gained speed. I was going to make it!"

"The entire air group slowly joined up, and we flew out a hundred miles to the carrier. We were in as tight a formation as possible to try to impress our new hosts."

On the way out, "we passed Air Group Sixteen in the air," wrote Mr. Winters, "who were coming off the *Lexington* being relieved by us, and they wished us luck. Their planes looked a little beat-up, even from a distance, and ours looked so new..." Be that as it may, Nineteen was now officially attached to the *Lexington* until further notice, to fly and fight.

"The fighters are always the first to land," said Davis, "so we broke off and dropped to 300 feet. The formation was perfect. We dropped our tail hooks and started to break up for our approach to the ship. The skipper made the first approach and got a 'cut,' followed by the rest of the squadron." But one of the fighter pilots was having trouble, making poor passes, coming in too fast, and being repeatedly "waved off." The entire dive-bombing squadron landed, and then the torpedo bombers, but not Lieutenant Hutto. Out of patience, Lieutenant Commander Winters borrowed the ship's Air Officer's microphone and went on the air. "John, if you don't slow her down in the groove I'm coming up there and shoot you down myself." So, next pass, the Landing Signal Officer gave him a cut and he slammed his plane to the deck, bursting all three tires. Winters was not amused, nor was the commander of the Air Group, Cmdr. Karl Jung. "Well, we *indeed* made a hell of a first impression."

Moreover, according to Winters, "we all thought the *Lexington* would welcome us with open arms—a fresh new air group full of derring-do, ready to clear the Western Pacific of enemy aircraft and ships, sights set high, nobody tired or beat-up. But it didn't turn out exactly that way."

"For one thing, the *Lex* had just gone through the famous First Battle of the Philippine Sea in late June; her original Air Group-16 had really punished the Japanese fleet, and it had covered itself with glory at the 'Marianas Turkey Shoot.'" In that action, looking at air statistics alone, the Japanese had lost 600 airplanes versus 123 American. "So, the ship had had a bellyful of glory, and now *their* air group was going home to Pearl Harbor, to bedroom and bar, and Tommy Dorsey's live music while, with no break, the tired *Lexington* now had to be garage and housemother to this *new* batch of conceited flyboys. Who the hell do they think *they* are? The *Lex* and her crew didn't even get to go back to Pearl for a little rest—rather, they got *us*."

"Of course, Cmdr. 'Andy' Ahroon, the ship's air officer, with Cmdr. L. B. 'Sheik' Southerland, the executive officer, and Capt. Ernie Litch, the CO, greeted us with *Welcome Aboard* in the official manner of senior officers, but the true warmth of a carrier for its own air group just was not there. Our enlisted boys felt it even more down below."

One of Ensign Tyler's squadron mates in VT-19, rear-seat gunner Petty Officer Tom Kelley, later wrote that "when we first boarded the *Lexington* the ship's company really gave us a hard time, beating up on guys, etcetera. Air Group-16 had had a pretty good record, and I guess the ship thought they'd at least get to go back to Pearl for a brief rest. Well, they didn't lay off us until our fighters in VF-19 later started to score. Then we gave it to them: '*My* fighters did this. What a day *our* fighters had. Hey, did you hear about *our* fighters? What a helluva outfit we got!'"

Winters knew, prior to Air Group-19 coming aboard the *Lexington*, that his fighter pilots had already developed many close friends in VB-19 and VT-19. However, he wasn't totally sure—particularly with the Navy's all-time top-scoring ace "next door" on board the *Essex* (Cmdr. David McCampbell)—that some of his boys might not be tempted to leave their primary mission and fly for "Glory." So after things had settled down in the first couple of days he summoned them to their ready room. He discussed escort missions against the enemy, and then really laid it on them.

"Now that you know *why*," he said, "I will say here and now if any one of you *ever* leaves the dive bombers or 'torpeckers' (torpedo bombers) you are escorting in order to go after an enemy plane that is not currently attacking you or yours, not only will you not fly again in this squadron—you will be grounded and your flight status re-evaluated. But don't worry; at other times there will be plenty of fighter sweeps and combat air patrols (CAPs) for going after enemy planes."

At this time, Vice Admiral Mitscher commanded the huge Task Force 58. Mitscher reported to Adm. Raymond A. Spruance, the commander of the huge Central Pacific Force, which had recently been redesignated as the U.S. Fifth Fleet. Admiral Mitscher was using the *Lexington* as his flagship. But the *Lexington* herself—and her Air Group—was specifically assigned to Task Group 58.3, which was commanded by Rear Adm. Frederick C. Sherman, using the *Essex* as his flagship. So, aside from the *Lexington*, TG 58.3 consisted of a lot of ships, including the large carrier *Essex* and the light carriers *Princeton* and *Langley*. These four carriers alone could put hundreds of planes in the air.

So, after getting her new air group on board—slowly, but without major mishap—the *Lexington* entered Eniwetok from where the air group had just come. Winters wrote that the ship was "low on bombs, ammo, fuel, and food—and also needed two or three nights for movies, relaxation, and comfortable sleep for the ship's crew, uninterrupted by sea watches and predawn battle stations." If the ship's company couldn't have Hawai'i, they at least could have that.

Lt.j.g. Don Engen, in Bombing-19, later wrote that "Many ensigns from the three squadrons of Air Group Nineteen lived in the Junior Officers Bunk Room, commonly referred to as 'Boys Town.' It was *togetherness at its best* and thus caused us to spend most of our time in one of the three squadron ready rooms on the ship. The squadron ready rooms were the only spaces on board the *Lexington* that were air conditioned." It's likely that Ens. Warner Tyler, fairly junior at this time, was accommodated in "Boys Town."

According to Lieutenant Commander Winters, these three days at anchor were also very valuable to the air group's personnel. Everyone needed to know their way around the big ship—particularly in the dark—as well as a myriad of other things. There were many briefings. The pilots—especially the fighter pilots—"spent a lot of time in the Combat Information Center, where the people who would be directing them out to intercept incoming enemy planes worked the radars and ship-to-air voice communications."

Intelligence officers gave them all the information they had on what they would find at the Japanese stronghold at Guam, which would be their first target. The job was to give the U.S. Marines there close support.

Chapter 6

One of 24 large *Essex*-class "fast aircraft carriers," the USS *Lexington* (CV-16) was the fifth U.S. Navy ship to be named after the 1775 Battle of Lexington—the first battle of the American Revolutionary War. She was originally laid down as the USS *Cabot,* in July 1941, by Bethlehem Steel Co. at Quincy, Massachusetts. Her namesake at that point was John Cabot (actually Giovanni Caboto), the Venetian navigator who in 1497 explored coastal North America under a commission from the English King Henry VII.

However, while being built, her name was changed to *Lexington* in honor of the fourth *Lexington* (CV-2) which was, of course, an aircraft carrier sunk at the Battle of the Coral Sea in May 1942. CV-16 was launched in September 1942 and was commissioned in February 1943 with Capt. Felix B. Stump in command. Carrier Air Group Sixteen, which had been established in November 1942, came on board with four squadrons of aircraft.

After a Caribbean Sea shakedown cruise and further yard work at Boston, the *Lexington* sailed for Pacific War action via the Panama Canal, arriving at Pearl Harbor, Hawai'i in August 1943. She subsequently raided Tarawa in late September and Wake in October, and then returned to Pearl Harbor to prepare for the Gilbert Islands operation. In late November she made searches and flew sorties in the Marshalls, and covered the landings in the Gilberts. Her aviators downed 29 enemy aircraft during 23-24 November.

In December 1943 the *Lexington* sailed to raid Kwajalein. Her first strike on 4 December destroyed a cargo ship, damaged two cruisers, and accounted for 30 enemy aircraft. Her gunners downed two of the enemy torpedo planes that attacked the ship, and opened fire again later that night when a major air attack began. At 2322 hours, parachute flares silhouetted the carrier, and ten minutes later she was hit by a torpedo to starboard, knocking out her steering gear. Settling five feet by the stern, the carrier began circling to port amidst dense clouds of smoke pouring from ruptured tanks aft. A make-shift hand-operated steering unit was quickly devised, and the *Lexington* made for Pearl Harbor to undergo emergency work, arriving on 9 December. She reached Bremerton, Washington on 22 December for full repairs, which were completed on 20 February 1944.

The *Lexington* then sailed, via Alameda, California and Pearl Harbor, for the large anchorage at Majuro Atoll in the Marshall Islands. There, on 8 March, Rear Admiral—later in the month becoming Vice Admiral—Marc A. "Pete" Mitscher, commanding Task Force 58, broke his flag in her. After a "warmup" strike against Mille Island in the Marshalls, TF 58 operated against some major centers of resistance in Japan's outer empire, supporting the Army's landing at Hollandia on 13 April, and hitting the supposedly invulnerable base at Truk on 28 April. A heavy counterattack left the *Lexington* untouched—her planes splashing 17 enemy fighters—but, for the second time, Japanese propaganda announced her as being sunk.

A surprise fighter strike at Saipan on 11 June virtually eliminated all air opposition over the island, which was then battered from the air for the next five days. On 15 June the *Lexington* fought off a fierce attack by Japanese torpedo planes based on Guam, once again to emerge unhurt, but "sunk" a third time by Japanese propaganda pronouncements. Japanese opposition to the Marianas operation provoked the major Battle of the Philippine Sea on 19 and 20 June—known by U.S. pilots as "the Great Marianas Turkey Shoot." The *Lexington*, and Carrier Air Group Sixteen, certainly played a major role in TF 58's great victory. With hundreds of enemy aircraft destroyed the first day, and a carrier, a tanker, and a destroyer sunk the second day, American aviators virtually knocked Japanese naval aviation out of the war; moreover, with those destroyed planes went a huge number of trained and experienced pilots—without whom Japan could not effectively continue air warfare at sea.

Chapter 7

Thus, after replenishing and rearming at Eniwetok—with Carrier Air Group Nineteen newly installed on board—and in company with other ships of Task Group 58.3, the *Lexington* went back to war. Mr. Tyler was able to get in one more takeoff and landing as they sailed towards Guam, logged as "tactical training."

"So," wrote Lieutenant Commander Winters, "instead of a shakedown cruise at our leisure...we had three days' steady steaming towards Guam to perfect air operations with the ship. Every time we were launched or recovered, the ship had to turn back into the wind, and the longer it took to get us off or on, the harder it was for her to keep position in the task group. Sometimes it was late at night before the *Lexington* was able to catch back up." That said, the ship's crew—*fairly* soon—was *reasonably* patient with the newcomers who were trying hard to act like a seasoned air group.

Bombing-19's Petty Officer Minor H. Nickens later wrote that, "When Air Group-19 first went aboard the *Lady Lex*, the torpedo squadron was short some aircrew men, so the bombing squadron agreed to loan them a few men temporarily. I was one of those 'lucky few,' along with Dwight Woolhouse and L. H. Brown. My job in the torpedo plane was to operate the radio gear and man the single 30-millimeter gun under the tail. This was really just a 'peashooter.'

I was on six or eight strikes in TBMs—not the most enjoyable time of my life."

"As our mini-shakedown cruise blended into a combat deployment," wrote Winters, "our three squadrons took it in stride." But when it came time for the strike they were told, by the American naval surface forces already there, that the aircraft must stay above 1,500 feet because the surface ships were not going to cease their shore bombardment—and it would be bad if any American planes were hit by "friendly" fire. Winters thought it was stupid to attack from that high altitude, but "orders are orders."

So, from 18 July to the 21st, the Task Group engaged in several combat strikes against Guam—which is an island in Micronesia, in the Western Pacific. These were the first combat missions for Carrier Air Group-19. For four days its aircraft—along with aircraft from other ships—bombed and strafed target areas behind the beaches, helping to prepare for the forthcoming amphibious landing.

Ensign Warner Tyler flew all four days (flying twice on the 20th), dropping high-explosive conventional bombs—rather than torpedoes—from five different TBM-1C *Avengers* in the squadron.

It's worth noting that very few pilots had aircraft permanently assigned to them; on any given flight "planes were assigned to pilots down in the ready room by the squadron flight officer—and even then the ship's flight-deck officer would make changes regarding aircraft which had just been declared "up" or "down."

It was easy for torpedo planes to carry bombs in their torpedo-bays, and this was often done when the planned targets were land installations and not ships.

Ensign Tyler's crewmen for these five flights, and for his next eight combat flights, were Aviation Machinist's Mate Orie G. Haddox as gunner and Aviation Radioman Lynn H. Brown as radioman. As mentioned earlier Brown, along with two other ARs, had been temporarily "borrowed" from VB-19 because VT-19 was momentarily short some air crewmen.

Another of those men, Petty Officer Minor H. Nickens—from whom we've already heard—shared an anecdote from those first combat days. "One day when we came back from a strike the pilot landed as usual, taxied to the forward end of the flight deck on the port side next to the catwalk, parked, opened the bomb-bay doors, and a 500-pound bomb fell to the deck with a loud 'clunk.' There were a number of sailors in the catwalk alongside, and I have never seen such scurrying as they did to get away. But one of them, probably an ordnanceman, ran over and quickly unscrewed the fuse from the errant bomb. They all reacted quickly, but their concern was unnecessary, as the bomb was not armed. Before making a bombing run, it was the responsibility of the pilot to make sure the bomb-bay doors were open, and it was my responsibility to remind the pilot to arm the bomb. In this particular instance the pilot forgot to open the bomb-bay doors, and we would have brought back a live bomb, with disastrous results, had I not forgotten to remind him to arm the bomb. My mistake canceled out his mistake, or I would not be here today. Surely, there must have been a guardian angel watching over us that day! The pilot was invited to come up and discuss the incident with the Skipper and I expected to be called also, but I never was. I don't know if the pilot was disciplined."

Writing in his official—but fairly brief—*History of Torpedo Squadron Nineteen,* squadron leader Lt. Cmdr. Frank Perry commented that along with the rest of Air Group-19, "Torpedo-19 started to play 'marbles for keeps' from 18 to 21 July 1944, when pre-invasion strikes were launched from our Task Group against the Island of Guam. The tenseness which prevailed in our ready room, 'Ready Two,' soon gave way to a businesslike routine when the first returning strikes reported no Japanese fighter interception and only meager and inaccurate AAA. Our previous air support work with target coordinators and commanders' support aircraft paid dividends as strikes reported on station, carried out their missions successfully, and returned to base without loss. Eight-plane divisions of torpedo bombers carried 100-pound general purpose and fragmentation bombs in to the targets, unloading over AAA positions, pillboxes, trenches, and personnel shelters—all with good results." During this period Air Group-19 flew 131 sorties.

Tyler's squadron-mate Lt.j.g. Morris Goebel, flying *Mohawk 88* in the second strike of the day—0930-1300—made this note in his flight log: "18 July 44: First combat. Guam—four 500-lb. bombs on each attack." His crewmen were ARM^2 Clair Mitchart and AOM^2 Eliot Campbell.

Ensign Tyler flew in the fourth strike on 18 July, 1545-1800, along with seven other *Avengers* led by Lieutenant Commander Perry. Tyler was in *Mohawk 94*, and Perry in *Mohawk 95*. As with so many others in Air Group-19, this was Warner Tyler's first taste of combat.

Fighter pilot Ens. Bill Davis wrote, "Three a.m. came suddenly on 18 July. The VF-19 ready room was unusually silent. I glanced around the room and noted a strained look on everyone's face. I suspect this is the moment of truth, when you face all of your worst fears and hidden doubts. Your thoughts mean nothing. It was simple: you were going, and that's all there was to it."

"Leaving the ready room," continued Davis, "I was plunged into total darkness. It's *really* black at sea at night. My crew chief caught my arm and led me to my airplane. I could make out the 500-pound bomb as well as the 1,000-pound drop tank. In addition, there was the unseen *ton* of .50-caliber ammunition in the wings for my six machine guns. Routine for the *Hellcats*, my plane was spotted *far* forward, so my takeoff had to be a catapult shot. A catapult shot! My heart sank. I might never even make it into combat." As noted earlier, Mr. Davis was absolutely no fan of the catapult.

"My turn came on the starboard catapult. I set the trim tabs in the dark and hoped I'd set them right. The launch officer circled his hand, and I went to full throttle. He listened for a moment and then dropped his hand. I was pinned against the back of the seat and went off into the darkness, struggling to keep the aircraft in the air. I used everything I knew about flying to keep the plane between those two boundaries: the water 80 feet below, or a stall if I pulled up too sharply. Once the wheels came up and I started to accelerate I felt more comfortable. I looked for the 'turtleback' light of the plane ahead of me and joined up. Once at a safe altitude we spread slightly, took our guns off safety, and fired a few rounds to be sure they were working properly. We slid back into tight formation. Climbing steadily we flew toward Guam, concentrating on the flying rather than what was coming. Guam rose unseen out of the dark sea as we timed our approach to arrive over the target exactly at dawn."

Lt.j.g. Jack Scott, in Bombing-19, wrote that "July 18th was our first strike. We bombed Orote Peninsula on Guam. We particularly hit coastal defense guns, and Intelligence later reported target achievement."

Petty Officer Arno Droske, also in Bombing-19, wrote that the next day, "July 19, 1944, saw us attack Guam four times. As my plane, piloted by Lt. Price Stradley, began the pull-out after dropping our bomb, there was an explosion and pieces flew everywhere. We glided into the water and came to an abrupt stop, to say the least. The plane started going down—engine first, of course, due to the weight. I inflated the raft, pulled the strings on my 'Mae West' inflatable life jacket, and pushed away from the elevator as the plane sank down from under us. The water was warm and the waves were small. We were safe and alive but a little bloody with minor head injuries. It was only a short time before a boat from the destroyer USS *Guest* picked us up. The next day we were taken to the battleship

USS *Colorado*. The *Colorado* then proceeded to shell Guam. Then on the 22nd of July we were taken to Isley Field, Saipan. Later that same day a torpedo bomber picked us up and returned us to the *Lexington*." This TBM was piloted by Lt. Max Gregg, accompanied by radioman/gunner ARM2 Harold Haas.

Torpedo pilot Lieutenant j.g. Goebel tersely noted in his flight log: "19 July 1944. Guam—four 500-lb. bombs," and then on 20 July: "Guam—twelve 100-lb. bombs." On the 19th Goebel flew *Mohawk-86*, and on the 20th he flew *Mohawk-98*.

Ensign Tyler flew on the third strike of the 19th, 1130-1345. Along with Petty Officers Haddox and Brown in *Mohawk-92*, this was an eight-plane formation led by Mr. Perry, carrying high-explosive bombs.

On the group's third day in combat, 20 July 1944, Lieutenant Commander Winters lost one of his favorite fighter pilots—Ens. Dan "Duke" de Luca, Jr.—who was roommates with Ens. Bill Davis.

"The moment we crossed the coastline the antiaircraft started," wrote Mr. Davis. "It was both accurate and plentiful. The air around us filled with black clouds from exploding shells. I couldn't hear them because of the roar of my engine, but the noise must have been horrendous....The four of us [fighters] headed for our assigned target, an 8-inch coastal-defense gun. We took violent evasive action." Going in for the attack, "Duke and I increased the interval between us so we could dive without fear of a mid-air collision. We started our dives and immediately the antiaircraft fire increased. They were throwing everything they had at us. I glanced over at Duke—one moment he was there, the next there was a tremendous explosion, then nothing. There weren't even any pieces. He had caught a big shell, probably a 5-inch, and there was nothing left. I tore my gaze away and concentrated on the target and dropped my 500-pound bomb. We all took evasive action after the dive."

Flying back to the *Lexington*, going over it in his mind, "all I could see was that explosion." Duke de Luca had "gone through all the trials and tribulations of growing up. He'd made it through college and two years of training, only to be killed in his first twenty seconds of combat."

Bombing Nineteen's Lt.j.g. Wallace "Wally" Griffin added, "This was my first combat strike against the Japanese, bombing a large airport on Guam. Needless to say, it was quite a thrill. That is, until I saw one of our fighter pilots in an F6F get blown up into a huge ball of fire, off to my left, as I pulled out of my dive. Then the real impact came to me when I returned to the ship and found out who it was—a handsome ensign with whom I had played poker the night before."

The second day of this attack at Guam saw a dive bomber lost to AAA but, fortunately, the pilot and gunner were picked up. However, "on the third day," recalled Mr. Davis, "a dive bomber spun in the sea on takeoff, and both crew members were lost."

"The takeoffs and landings," Davis continued, "were becoming routine—but of course they were *not* routine. Every single one took total concentration and expert flying. Sometimes it was hard to stay at that level, with the added hazard of combat that drained energy from you and left you less sharp. I'm sure that most of the pilots, like me, relaxed some when we departed the combat area and thus were not fully at our best when approaching the ship to make our landings. That contributed to losses around the carrier."

In between the air strikes, the American battleships were "raking the beaches and fortifications with 16-inch gun barrages," wrote Davis. "Life for those Japanese on the island must have been a living hell."

"We were getting used to calling our ship *Mohawk*—which was her radio call-sign in the combat zone—and she was beginning to feel we were her chickens," wrote Lieutenant Commander Winters.

"The chickens started with *Mohawk-1*, my call as the fighter-squadron commander, and went on up to about *Mohawk-36*. The dive bombers started about 40 and went up to about 60, and then the torpedoes took it on up to about 90. The air group commander was always *Mohawk-99*, and of course the *Lexington* herself was just plain *Mohawk*. These were inspiring warlike calls and we were proud to bear them."

On 20 July, Mr. Tyler flew in the first of four strikes—in *Mohawk-89* along with POs Haddox and Brown. Torpedo Squadron Nineteen put up 45 airplanes that day—obviously some pilots and planes flew more than once. In fact, Tyler was one of those, flying again in the third strike, in *Mohawk-84* with the same crew.

That same day Bombing-19 suffered two non-combat losses. Petty Officer Paul Dulong said that "I was watching from the port-side catwalk when Ens. Paul Gevelinger and ARM[3] Louis Nitchman went into the sea on takeoff. I was able to see the plane from about fifty feet away. As the ship passed close by, the plane was sinking. The pilot was slumped forward in the cockpit. Louis, in the rear, was struggling to get out. He appeared to have a large aerial camera on his lap and was trying to disentangle himself when the plane went under."

It was Torpedo-19 that was hard-hit the next day, the 21st. On the fourth day of TG 58.3's strikes against Guam, the squadron put 22 planes in the air. Lt.j.g. Joe Hebert, in *Mohawk-96*, and Lt. Cmdr. David Dressendorfer, in *Mohawk-85*, had to return early to the ship due to mechanical problems. And, Lt. Joe Black came back with *Mohawk-83* pretty well shot up.

Then it got worse. Lieutenant Commander Perry had to write that "Squadron casualties, which occurred on 21 July 1944, involved the loss of three pilots, five enlisted air crewmen, and three airplanes. These were our first casualties—operational or combat—since the commissioning of the squadron on 15 August 1943."

Warner Tyler's squadron mates that were confirmed killed or forever missing in action, on that terrible day, were Lt.j.g. Bob Sinclair, Lt.j.g. Chuck Wendt, Ens. Al Hallowell, AOM^2 LaMark Dees, ARM^2 Bernard Murphy, ARM^2 Orville Jasper, AOM^2 Jack Mitchell, and ARM^3 Phil Largo. In the official Torpedo-19 "radio logbook," Chief Aviation Radioman W. Ernest Powers closed the page for 21 July with "**BAD DAY !!**" in extra-large letters. Al Hallowell had been one of the three replacement pilots—including Warner Tyler—who just five weeks earlier had joined Group-19 and VT-19 at Maui.

These losses were due to very heavy anti-aircraft artillery. "This was our first taste of Japanese AAA," wrote Lieutenant Commander Winters. "Do you want to know what it looked like to run through AAA coming up at you while you are diving down on a target? Well, they usually loaded one tracer to three or four rounds in the belting, but the rate of fire was high such that it appeared to be a steady stream—like water out of a strong hose. The tracers are tiny orange balls, growing in size to that of tennis balls as they come up straight at you; then *just* as they get almost to you they bend quickly under your plane as if controlled by some powerful magnetic field, or by a giant magic hand. And if they *don't* bend down under you at the last moment, then you've 'bought it' as Duke did—and all the experience in the world wouldn't have helped you. When you have to go in against heavy AAA it's like rolling the dice, and we hated it. The fact that Lt. Joe Paskoski later went in and destroyed the gun emplacement that hit Duke didn't really help our feelings that much—but, oh, you may be sure Joe didn't do *that* at 1,500 feet!"

After four days of this softening up, "D-Day" had arrived. Fighting-19 flew several close-support strikes for the landing craft as they went in. "I felt for those men in those boats," wrote Ensign Davis, "as they bobbed up and down on the rough sea. Most of them were probably very seasick before they hit the beach, but they were going to have to fight regardless." Fortunately, "by nightfall the Marines had a strong foothold on the beach."

"Fourteen days of naval shelling and coordinated air strikes had preceded the Guam landing," wrote Rear Adm. Frederick C. Sherman, commander of Task Group 58.3. "At 0830 on 21 July the troops went ashore on schedule." It then took 20 days of intense fighting to secure the island.

That evening, on board the carriers, the aircrews were briefed that "since there was no air opposition and the Marines were ashore, the light carriers were going to take over ground support. The large carriers were going to hit Palau—an island group to the west, because it might serve as a staging point for Japanese reinforcements for Guam."

As mentioned earlier, Air Group Nineteen had flown 131 sorties against Guam. All told, they had lost six airplanes and ten fliers in this, their first combat action of the war.

Chapter 8

Task Group 58.3 then moved, from July 22nd through July 24th, toward the Palau Islands. While *enroute* Mr. Tyler flew *Mohawk-84* on the 24th, joined by Petty Officers Haddox and Brown, on a four-hour scouting and anti-submarine patrol mission. Three other torpedo bombers were also sent up for the same reason.

In addition, "Daily Combat Air Patrols [CAPs]," wrote Ensign Davis, "kept the fighter squadron sharp during the trip."

Using Eniwetok as her base, the *Lexington* and the Task Group next flew 45 sorties over Guam and against the Palaus and Bonins. From the 25th through the 27th of July the focus was on the Palau Group; Palau is an archipelago of over 500 islands, part of the Micronesia region.

Early on July 26 the *Lexington*'s flight deck was spotted with fully half the air group. This strike was going against Anguar Island in the Palaus.

For VF-19 fighter pilot Bill Davis, the strike started off with a bad omen. "Lt.j.g. Israel H. "Hal" Silvert flew the fourth plane to take off. He came to the end of the deck and seemed to be struggling. He fought it but to no avail; the plane stalled and went into the ocean upside down. We all held our breaths as the trailing destroyer raced to the spot. We, in turn, were moving at 25 knots and were quickly out of sight while the strike launch continued."

It was a pre-dawn launch, so the group was over the target right around sunrise. The AAA over the town was not too bad. The group dove on the dock facilities "and pretty much wiped them out, scoring hits with everything from 500- to 2,000-pound bombs. We all gave a sigh of relief that no one had been shot down" as they all headed back to the ship.

Bill Davis and the other fighters landed first, as usual. After he climbed out of his plane he headed for the catwalk along the side of the flight deck. But then he noticed a Torpedo-19 bomber that was currently making a landing approach. To Davis it didn't look right; perhaps he'd been hit. The LSO gave him a 'cut' and the plane made a slight dive for the deck. "Realizing that he was picking up too much speed, the pilot pulled back on the stick. The plane rose slightly and then floated down the deck and *over* the triple barriers. It now hovered for a moment over a mass of dive bombers closely parked together with their wings folded—but hovered only for a moment. The torpedo plane dropped squarely on top of the packed aircraft. Crash crews raced to the spot because the potential for a disaster was incredible. All of those planes had partially filled gas tanks, and any leak from one of them could start an inferno that might be impossible to put out."

The *Avenger*'s pilot—Lt.j.g. Ed Myers—and his crew were quickly pulled from their aircraft and then the crash crews hastily started pushing the damaged planes over the side. "I stood there amazed as one plane after another splashed into the ocean—nine in all—but it was done so quickly that no fire ignited." The absence of a flight-deck fire with ensuing explosions, and the successful rescue of the *Avenger*'s crew, were fortunate strokes of luck. Moreover, speaking of luck, upon going into the Fighting-19 ready room

Mr. Davis was thankful to learn that "Hal" Silvert had survived his morning takeoff accident.

Torpedo-19's radio log describes this nine-plane accident very briefly: "***Mohawk-92*, Lt.j.g. Edward C. Myers, Jr., ↓ Deck Crash**." Not much there to be proud of; perhaps the less said the better. However, in a few weeks Mr. Myers will have a better day; on 25 October he will earn a Navy Cross. Interestingly, Lieutenant Commander Perry does not mention the accident at all in his squadron history.

Bombing Nineteen almost lost another aircraft that day. Petty Officer Paul Reischman, flying with Lieutenant j.g. Herbert "Walt" Walters, wrote about the incident. "I remember the bomb in the bomb-bay of our SB2C would not release, nevertheless we were allowed to land on the carrier with it still up in its rack. Because of the weight we blew out both tires when we landed, but that bomb still stayed hung up—thank God!"

"We hit the Palau Islands on July 26th," wrote Lieutenant Commander Perry, "with the same feeling as a boxer who has received a black eye in the first round—which is to say a little 'left-hook shy,' but determined to win. The seaplane base at Arakabesan was 'glide-bombed' and three large hangars were destroyed. And, as 500-pound general-purpose bombs became 'unaccountably' mixed with the phosphate, the Anguar Phosphate Company's stock dropped several points on the Tokyo Stock Exchange. Malakal's oil-storage tanks were also hit and, in general, the Palau Islands were heavily damaged by our aircraft. This was another encounter with effective AAA fire, both heavy and light, which was particularly concentrated in the area of Koror Town, Malakal, and Arakabesan."

In this case, the term "glide bombed" did *not* refer to the use of radar-controlled glide bombs with variable flight-control surfaces, but rather a simple style of shallow-angle bombing. The U.S. Navy did have such radar-controlled sophisticated weapons and had deployed some early versions to the Pacific, but they don't appear to have reached Task Force-58 at this time and, in any event, they had considerable trouble distinguishing between targets in a cluttered environment.

Here, Air Group Nineteen pilots with regular bombs were just trying to use shallower dive angles than were used in dive bombing—which did not require a sharp pull-up after dropping the bombs. Of course, this technique did not normally confer anywhere the same level of accuracy as a steep dive from a dedicated aircraft.

Torpedo-19's Lt.j.g. Goebel wrote "26 July: Palau—four 500-lb. bombs at a Japanese merchant ship. Missed with all four. Then strafed patrol boat with .50 caliber gun." His next entry read: "27 July: Palau—2,000-lb. bomb dropped on a ship, possible hit. Strafed a patrol boat. Made photographic runs."

"On these strikes," continued Mr. Perry, "our Torpedo-19 division leaders experienced difficulty in maintaining position with our dive bombers. The dive bombers, with their Curtis SB2C-3 *Helldivers*, had considerable more 'horses' and were maintaining more manifold pressure than our Grumman/General Motors TBM-1C *Avengers* could take without burning out our engines (1,900 hp versus 1,700 hp). We had realized this situation in training, of course, but in actual combat it was a very serious matter."

Torpedo-19 lost another aircraft later on the 26th—that of Mr. Goebel. "***Mohawk-97*, Lt.j.g. Morris R. Goebel, ↓ *over ship's side*,**" but, fortunately, the pilot and crewmen were recovered. Unlucky this day, Mr. Goebel will have a better day coming up on 25 October, earning a Navy Cross.

The torpedo squadron put up 23 aircraft on 26 July, participating in two strikes. Some of the airplanes flew more than once, but none of the pilots did. Ensign Tyler flew in the second one, piloting torpedo-bomber *Mohawk-88*, again dropping high-explosive bombs. His crewmen were Petty Officers Haddox and Brown. Their takeoff, flight, and landing—fortunately—were without particular incident. Lt. Len Mathias, in *Mohawk-86*, had to return early with mechanical problems.

Carrier Air Group Nineteen flew 45 sorties against the Palau Islands during this period, 25-27 July.

"Debriefing after each flight," wrote Ens. Bill Davis, "had become routine. It was similar for all three squadrons, but for Fighting-19 our part-time fighter pilot and mostly full-time Air Combat Information Officer—Lt. Jack Wheeler—sat at a small table at the front of the ready room and each pilot reported to him immediately as he entered the room." For Torpedo-19, the ACIO was Lt.j.g. Bob Thorsen; for Bombing-19 it was Lt.j.g. George Lewis. "Most of the debriefings were carried out in a minute or two," continued Davis. "Jack was interested in what you saw, especially the number of aircraft and the number destroyed. Of course, ships were of great importance, and if you had seen a major ship such as a cruiser or battleship, that report would take precedence over anything else. Once the pilots gave their reports, they took off their flight gear and relaxed in one of the chairs."

Mr. Davis was fascinated by Mr. Wheeler. "We only thought the squadron skipper was old until we got a look at our intelligence officer, Jack Wheeler. His hair was silver-gray and he seemed to have difficulty walking. He was fifty years old and only a senior-grade lieutenant. Was the United States really that hard-pressed for manpower? It turned out Jack owned a seat on the Chicago Stock Exchange." Jack had been in the Army Air Corps during World War I, but had not gotten to fly before the war ended. "He'd gone through his entire life regretting the adventure he'd missed, and he wasn't going to let this one get away. He had enough connections to get ten medical waivers and had gone through the school for intelligence officers."

That night the Task Group headed northeast and three days later arrived at Saipan, anchoring in the strait between Saipan and

Tinian. Tinian had previously been secured by American ground forces, but there remained some enemy holdouts on the southern tip of Saipan. While Air Group Nineteen watched an evening movie, they could hear U.S. Army 155mm shells flying over their heads from Tinian to Saipan.

It's interesting to note that a few weeks earlier—on the 9th of July—after terrible fighting Saipan had been "officially" secured. Several high-ranking Japanese commanders committed suicide, including Vice Adm. Chūichi Nagumo, the commander who led the Japanese carriers at both Pearl Harbor and Midway; he had been in command of the Japanese naval air forces stationed on Saipan. In the end almost the entire garrison of Japanese troops on the island—at least 29,000—died. For the Americans the victory was the most costly, to date, in the Pacific War: out of 71,000 who landed, 2,949 were killed and 10,464 were wounded.

"The fall of Saipan," wrote Rear Admiral Sherman, "produced the resignation of Prime Minister Tojo's cabinet, which had been in power in Japan since before the Pearl Harbor attack. General Hideki Tojo, the one man most responsible for Japan's entry into the war, then stated: 'Japan has come to face an unprecedentedly great national crisis.'"

"Indeed," went on Sherman, "our carrier striking forces roamed the sea wherever they chose, bringing death and destruction to the Japanese. Our submarines, cruising in Empire waters, were continually whittling down the fleet of merchant ships Japan so vitally needed for bringing in the food and oil necessary for her existence. Although a long war was still envisioned in Washington, the Americans in the combat area sensed that the end was approaching. The stage was now nearly set for the return of our forces to the Philippines."

Thus, on August 2nd, Task Group 58.3 finished refueling and rearming, and then set sail "just a little east of due north." After two days they were back in action.

On 4 and 5 August the Task Group flew strikes against the Bonin Islands. The Bonins are an archipelago of over thirty islands approximately 1,000 kilometers south of Tokyo. In addition, they struck the Kazan Islands—or the Volcano Islands—a group of three Japanese islands south of the Bonins. The Volcanos included the island of Iwo Jima. Iwo Jima, of course, will a few months later be the site of some of the war's fiercest and bloodiest ground combat, during February and March of 1945.

The first strike launched at 0953 on the 4th, and consisted of twelve *Hellcats*, eight *Avengers*, and twelve *Helldivers*.

"When we saw our targets," said Fighting-19's CO, Lieutenant Commander Winters, "they were blackish, steep, rocky, and forbidding-looking islands. These were the Bonins and Volcanos, aptly named for there were very few beaches on them."

Warner Tyler flew for four hours on 4 August in *Mohawk-92*, dropping high-explosive bombs, on an unspecified target in the Bonins—but no doubt it was Iwo Jima. His crewmen remained Petty Officers Haddox and Brown. Torpedo-19 put up eighteen aircraft and, fortunately, they all came back. Morris Goebel wrote in his log: "4 August: Iwo Jima in Bonin Group, 700 miles from Japan. Dropped four 500-lb. bombs on a circling ship. Missed. Ack-Ack <u>very</u> heavy." The torpedo squadron had planned to put up 24 planes, but an unusual number were "downed-engine" prior to launch.

"I took the first fighter sweep in ahead of the dive bombers and torpedo planes," wrote Mr. Winters, "to shoot up AAA emplacements and aircraft on the field." He brought his fighters in with two divisions—the other division under Lt. Howard 'Redbird' Burnett. "We swept five or six parked planes into fire, hit gas trucks, hangars, AAA positions, and a few men in brown uniforms running around."

That said, the air attack on Iwo Jima was extremely challenging. In fact, the first strike was the worst that Carrier Air Group Nineteen had seen so far. When they arrived over the target airfield just after dawn the Japanese were awake and ready. Not only did they have fighters already up and at altitude, but the whole side of the mountain next to the airfield—the to-be famous Mount Suribachi—seemed to be alive with AAA. VF-19 pilot Bill Davis recalled that "They were actually firing *down* on us. Fighter pilot 'Redbird' Burnett and his wingman Lt. Herschel 'Rusty' Gray both took hits, with Redbird's *Hellcat* bursting into flames. No sign of any parachutes. We went on and hit every target we could see and then got out of there. Every aircraft was riddled with holes."

Bombing-19 lost two airplanes. Ens. Roy Majors and ARM[2] Edward Albini were killed; Ens. Bill Emerson witnessed it. He wrote that "I saw one of our SB2Cs go in. When I saw him he was at about 1,000 feet and going straight down. There was nothing but a big splash and explosion. Nothing else." Ironically, Mr. Emerson himself, along with Petty Officer Milton Harvey, were shot down just moments later—but they managed a successful water landing and were recovered by a submarine.

Later that day "the second strike was more of the same, but with less disastrous results." This strike launched at 1259, consisting of four *Hellcats*, eight *Avengers*, and twelve *Helldivers*. The *Helldiver* of Lt.j.g. Herbert "Walt" Walters and Petty Officer Paul Reischman was hit, but they managed to get it back to the *Lexington*. Reischman wrote "that day we were 'Tail End Charlie,' the last of Bombing-19 to dive...on some shipping in the bay....Mr. Walters made a high bank to the right and it was at that point that I was hit by antiaircraft fire. I was hit in my head, right shoulder, right leg, thigh, and foot. My right shoe was nearly taken off. My face was burned. This occurred at 1420, and we arrived back at the carrier at 1600. I was in sick bay for three months to remove what metal they could and get a skin graft to cover the badly burned areas."

One of the *Avengers* couldn't make it back to the *Lexington* and had to land on the USS *Bunker Hill*.

When he got back to the *Lexington*, fighter pilot Bill Davis was relieved to learn that Rusty Gray had been able to make a high-G pullout and nurse his damaged fighter back to the ship. However, Ens. Blair 'Bob' Wakefield failed to return; sadly, no one even saw him go in.

On a more cheerful note, Ensigns Doug McLoughlin and Bob Blakeslee jointly shot down a Mitsubishi A6M *Zero* fighter—Fighting-19's first aerial victory, shared by two of the youngest pilots. Just a few minutes later another two fighters, flying cover for the American rescue submarine positioned just offshore—call sign "Goodyear"—encountered a *Zero* taking a dive on the sub. "Our fighters were on him like a rooster on a Junebug," wrote Winters. Lt. John Hutto's guns failed, but Ens. Burras Critcher's did not, and he "burned the *Zero* 200 feet above the water" making the squadron's second aerial victory. Mr. Hutto was the official aerial photographer of Fighting-19 with special training, special modifications to his airplane, and with extraordinary luck over a long period of time.

The following morning, 5 August, the Task Group mounted a strike on Chichi Jima, but the fog and clouds were extremely heavy. Thus, they flew on to the secondary target, Haha Jima. Ens. Bill Davis, flying along with eleven other *Hellcats*, wrote that "As we arrived we saw a wonderful harbor with docks suitable for large ships with several tied up." Without hesitation they dove on the target. "Instantly," he continued, "the air was black with exploding AAA shells—by far the heaviest we had ever seen. The gunners knew where we were headed and laid out a barrage over the docks. I was being violently rocked by the concussion of the exploding shells nearby."

"Two dive bombers right in front of me were suddenly blown out of the air." In one plane were lost Ens. John Cavanaugh and ARM[1] Mike Blazevich. Bombing-19's Lt.j.g. Donald Engen said later that "Cavanaugh's SB2C-3 was hit and either he or Blazevich was seen to bail out—there was only one chute. As the chute came down in the harbor of Chichi Jima, every Japanese AAA gun seemed to concentrate its fire on the chute and the person in it until the chute collapsed and the person fell into the water. Whoever it was, he was dead long before he hit the water. No one was ever recovered."

In the other bomber were Lt. Don Helm and ARM[2] John Snow. Mr. Helm survived and was picked up by a rescue submarine, but Petty Officer Snow—another young man from Denver, Colorado—didn't make it. A third dive bomber, out of Mr. Davis' view, was hit by AAA and went down with a water landing. Fortunately, Lt.j.g. Robert Smith and his gunner P.O. Louis Ortiz were rescued by a destroyer. Mr. Engen said that "they were returned to the *Lexington* by a bos'n's chair the next day. In accordance with the accepted procedure, ten gallons of ice cream were sent back to the destroyer in exchange for the rescued crew."

As Bill Davis released the small bomb from his fighter he saw two of his squadron mates, who had done likewise and were pulling up near him, bracketed by AAA bursts. Taking a hit in the engine, Lt. Joe Kelley's *Hellcat* exploded into flames but he was able to bail out. He successfully hit the water—but in the middle of the harbor. Lt. Elvin "Lin" Lindsay's plane was damaged but he was able to drop his life raft down to Joe and fly cover for him for a while. Eventually, after taking more AAA hits, Lindsay had to depart but was able to reach the rescue submarine, USS *Gato*, fifteen miles out to sea, and make a good water landing. The sub was unable to enter the harbor to attempt a rescue. Mr. Kelley, sadly, was captured, tortured, and killed—and then his body was horribly desecrated. After the war the two Japanese officers found responsible were tried for murder and war crimes and then executed.

"One of the most interesting days of my life in combat," wrote Bombing-19's Petty Officer Reynold Ross, "was when Lt. Bob Parker and I drew *four* flights over Chichi Jima. That was the hottest AAA that I had ever encountered. On the last flight, as we winged-over to go into the dive, we had already armed the bomb and kicked the bomb-bay door open. Right then the Japanese hit us with a shell which jammed the door. After we completed the dive, I told Mr. Parker that I didn't see the bomb drop, so we radioed Lt.j.g. Bob Duncan to fly under us, and he confirmed that we still had the bomb in the bay. It was then we realized we were sitting on a live bomb and had no alternative but to fly back to the carrier. A water landing next to the carrier was proscribed, but the sea was extremely rough, so we begged them to let us land on the ship. Finally after all other airplanes had landed, they cleared all planes to the hangar deck, and then they gave us permission to land *very carefully.* After landing we pulled the guns, radio, and radar from the plane. The *Lexington* was put at full-speed ahead and our plane was shoved backward off the tail of the ship—where it immediately exploded when it hit the water."

Ens. Warner Tyler did not fly on 5 August because his airplane for that day, *Mohawk-82*, was downed for an engine problem. Lt.j.g. Joe Hebert, in *Mohawk-94*, was also downed for a "fuselage" problem, and Lt.j.g. Ed Myers, in *Mohawk-88*, had to return shortly after takeoff. Nevertheless Torpedo-19 certainly participated that day, and they flew in force. They sent out 25 *Avengers*—several of them twice with different crews. They all, fortunately, came back to the *Lexington*, even if some came back with holes in them. All said, the air group flew 43 sorties in these two days.

After this strike, during 6 to 9 August, the Task Group headed toward Eniwetok for rest, refueling, rearming, and re-provisioning. At this point, at least for Air Group-19, there was a great need for replacement pilots and especially replacement aircraft. "Everyone needed to nurse some spiritual wounds," wrote Lieutenant Commander Winters, "and to recover from losing close friends without much to show for it."

The carriers continuously maintained several fighters as a Combat Air Patrol over the ships when they were anywhere near enemy territory. And, Bill Davis wrote, "in addition to the CAP, we kept at least four pilots in 'Condition Eleven.' This meant four pilots, fully dressed in flight gear, were ready to race to the flight deck and take off in one of the ready fighters spotted on deck in case of an attack by a large number of Japanese planes." Davis said that these four-hour watches waiting to fly were mostly occupied by censoring mail. "Every morning a large mail sack was deposited in the ready room, and the Condition Eleven pilots went to work on it. It was required that all mail that left the ship be censored, as you could not reveal the name of the ship, the air group, where we were, losses, and so forth. The funny thing was, all you had to do was go to the ship's post office and buy a 'mail order' for a dollar and send it home. It not only had the name of the ship, but a picture of the *Lexington* as well!" Davis was amazed to see how many letters, to wives and girlfriends, were full of detailed plans of future sexual encounters; he hoped that the men could occasionally put aside such thoughts and concentrate when they were repairing and maintaining the aircraft and associated complex equipment.

In addition to the continual CAP flights there were frequent flights for general scouting. The CAPs were comprised of fighters, while the scouting missions were usually dive-bombers or torpedo bombers. As an example of this, on 9 August, along with some other aircraft Warner Tyler flew a five-hour scouting mission with his crewmen Brown and Haddox.

After sailing for four days the Task Group arrived at Eniwetok. As stated above, the goal was refueling, rearming, re-provisioning, and resting. Most of the pilots "quickly adjusted to a relaxed schedule of reading, basketball, swimming, cookouts, sunbathing, and spearfishing."

Mr. Davis continued, "We stayed at Eniwetok for over two weeks—10 through 29 August—while the Marines prepared for the landings on Peleliu, in the Palau group, and the fleet prepared to cover them. We had been there before, and the one thing you could count on was the fact that the Japanese would have brought in *more* AAA guns. And, CAPs were again the order of the day." The two-week-plus rest "was a good thing," wrote Lt. Cmdr. Hugh Winters, "because on the next trip out the *Lexington* was going to have no rest and recreation for about *eighty days*—a long time to keep the sea watches posted."

Having witnessed so many air group shoot-downs and water landings, Ensign Davis "took advantage of the free time in port and practiced for the two emergencies I might face on any flight—bailing out or making a water landing. I'd find a plane spotted on the flight deck or on the hangar deck and climb in the cockpit in full gear. I'd strap myself in, then assume I was going to bail out as quickly as possible. This meant disconnecting the wire to the earphones and releasing the tube to the oxygen mask, then the seat belt and shoulder harness."

"A water landing," he continued, "required the same actions with the radio and oxygen equipment, but here the seat belt and shoulder harness were pulled up as tight as possible, with the parachute harness loose. I'd jump on the wing, pull the survival pack and life raft out, and prepare to ditch. I took a lot of ribbing from my fellow pilots, but if the time came, I was ready." (His time did come, later on 5 November, making a good water landing in a rough sea and getting into his raft within ten seconds).

On 12 August Ensign Tyler flew a four-hour "ferrying and testing" mission, accompanied by Aviation Machinist's Mate Third Class J. L. Ellis and Aviation Chief Machinist's Mate Allen W. Alexander.

On 26 August 1944 Adm. Bill Halsey relieved Adm. Ray Spruance as commander of the Fifth Fleet. This pattern of alternating command had been previously established; thus, now the fleet was redesignated as the Third Fleet. So, the "Fast Carrier Task Force" was in-turn redesignated as Task Force 38. This "split" command structure was intended to confuse the Japanese, but more importantly it allowed for a higher tempo of operations. While Spruance and his staff were at sea operating against the enemy, Halsey and his staff were ashore planning the next series of operations—and vice versa. This change of command doesn't seem to have impressed the flight-deck aviators or aircrews; it's not mentioned in the first-person accounts the author has examined.

Apparently, more important to Lieutenant Commander Winters was that "We were actually glad to leave that big atoll at the end of August." Admiral Mitscher's staff had been hard at work, and they now had all-new intelligence, "new maps, sketches of AAA positions, the mountains, harbors, vague small airfield locations, a grassy training field or two, a prisoner of war camp, supposedly well-marked." The task group sailed on 30 August, arriving at Palau on 5 September.

"Since we hadn't been in combat for almost three weeks," wrote Ensign Davis, "the brass decided to stage a practice mission using the entire Air Group. We were going to carry out a coordinated attack on a target towed by a destroyer, with live ammunition and bombs—the full works." This was on 31 August.

"The initial eight fighters had to be catapulted because the deck was fully loaded with aircraft," continued Davis. "Lt.j.g. John Morrison's was the fourth plane to be catapulted. He seemed to struggle from the moment he left the deck." Strangely, and unfortunately, he had been assigned an aircraft which had 300 pounds of photo equipment on board, which altered its center of gravity; apparently he was unaware of this and was caught off guard. "The plane staggered and never recovered. He flew for a few moments and got his wheels up, but the fighter never got out of the near stall. Suddenly it spun in. Johnny didn't get out. I sat there in my plane on the deck watching and hoping, but to no avail." Morrison had been a superb saxophone player; 66 years later Davis wrote that he could still hear Morrison's improvised solos running through his mind.

Ensign Tyler participated in this coordinated attack exercise, executing a 3.5 hour "tactical training" flight with Aviation Machinist's Mate First Class Orie Haddox as gunner and Aviation Radioman Third Class Arthur Davis as radioman.

"Upon landing one day on the *Lexington*, maybe September 3rd," wrote Petty Officer Minor Nickens, "the dive bomber in which Lynn H. Brown was the crewman—I don't recall who the pilot was—instead of going straight forward veered off at an angle to the port side of the ship. At the last second, thinking the plane was going over the side, L. H. 'bailed out,' and landed on the teakwood deck on his head. Actually, the plane safely came to rest with one wheel in a 40-mm gun mount. L. H. was out cold, and they hauled him off to the sick bay. A few hours later several of us went down to check on him. He had regained consciousness and was in a jovial mood. He asked 'What happened?' and when somebody told him that he dived out of the plane and landed on his head, he said, 'Well, that was a hell of a thing to do, wasn't it?' and laughed and laughed. About two minutes later he asked the same question, and gave the same response. This was repeated a number of times, and we figured that he was playing it crazy, that he wanted to go home and was angling for a medical discharge. However, a couple of days later he was back to normal—or at least whatever was normal for him."

"One day in the first week of September," wrote Petty Officer Victor Stankevich, "Lt.j.g. Bill Good and I had taken off in our *Helldiver*, from the *Lexington*, for a training hop. We were joining up with the formation when we noticed a miss in the motor. It kept getting worse, and we had to make a decision to jump or ditch. I asked Mr. Good what he was planning and he replied 'ditch.' I replied that anything he wanted to do was OK by me. I got prepared for setting the plane down in the water but what came next was a big surprise.

The plane hit the water and the sun went out. That's the only way I can describe it. I just knew we were on the way to the ocean floor. But just as suddenly it was over. The sun came out again, and the plane was afloat in the ocean. I pulled the raft off its rack, climbed out on the wing, and inflated the raft. By that time Mr. Good was on the wing with me. I asked that he get in the raft but he motioned me aboard, and I was holding the raft line. Of course when I stepped into the raft, still holding the line, the inflated thing took off. There was nothing for Mr. Good to do but dive in and swim to the raft. He climbed into the raft and he and I frantically, with our hands, rowed as far away as we could from the sinking plane. It must have taken three to five minutes for her to go down. About fifteen minutes later we were picked up by the destroyer *Ingersoll*. They gave us dry clothes, and they received ten gallons of ice cream when they turned us over to our carrier. I don't know if it was ten gallons per person or for both of us—at any rate it was a cheap price for a couple of trained fighting men like us!"

Then the Task Group began attacks on Mindanao, the Visayas, the Manila area, and shipping along the west coast of Luzon. This was all in preparation for the forthcoming Allied assault on Leyte.

From 6 to 8 September the *Lexington* executed strikes on Peleliu Island in the Palau Group, totaling 48 sorties.

"At first my division of four fighters," wrote Fighting-19's Bill Davis, "was assigned to act as a CAP over the main airfield in case any Japanese planes showed up from the Philippines. The AAA was relatively light. Three American cruisers appeared and radioed for our help in spotting for their 12-inch guns shooting against the buildings and warehouses." The *Mohawks* had not been trained in this but soon got into the swing of it. The explosions of the shells were devastating. "I felt a surge of raw power flow through me," admitted Davis, "as I realized the power I had under my control. The next hour was pure fun."

The group continued their strikes, trying to soften Peleliu for the forthcoming amphibious landing. "Once again," wrote Bill Davis, "we worked-over the only airfield and then went after the docks. There were a number of small supply ships which we sank. Then we set the oil tanks near the dock on fire."

The AAA fire had now become pretty heavy, and the dive bomber of Lt. William "Whiskey" Cravens was shot down. "However," added Davis, "he managed to glide far enough out to be picked up by the rescue submarine. Boy, did we love having a rescue sub off almost every island we hit!"

Rescue submarines so often being where they were needed was no coincidence. "When planning was in progress for the Gilbert Islands invasion in the fall of 1943," wrote U.S. Naval Academy professor Elmer B. Potter, "Vice Adm. Charles A. Lockwood, commander of the Submarine Force, Pacific Fleet, adopted a suggestion that submarines might well be employed to rescue downed flyers. Thus was born the Lifeguard League, which before the end of the war rescued 504 airmen." Whenever available, according to Potter, "submarines were stationed in appropriate locations and airmen were briefed accordingly. The pilot of a crippled plane would set it down as near a submarine as possible."

In any event, Whiskey Cravens' gunner, ARM[3] Ira Gray, wrote that in their SB2C-3 they'd "left the great ship USS *Lexington*. We led our group of planes over the island of Peleliu. We made our dive but the bomb did not release. We then made our rendezvous with the other planes but then we went back over the island and tried again to drop the bomb. The bomb did release, but the anti-aircraft fire hit our starboard wing and caught it on fire. Mr. Cravens decided to make a water landing because the submarine *Grouper* was there to pick up anyone who got wet. I thought he was going to land on the sub! I threw out the life raft, got on the wing, and Mr. Cravens was tangled up in the antenna wire, but we got in the water as the plane went down. I passed out, and Mr. Cravens saved my life. Mr. Cravens was a very good pilot and a very good man. We got aboard the *Grouper*, and it was reported back to the ship that I was dead. Not so, thank God for my life. I was OK in 24 hours. After the submarine picked up 15 or 20 people, it still carried out its mission. I know it was pretty crowded, as I slept in the night cook's bunk. As we were going through the Formosa Strait, very close to Japan, an airplane spotted us and then ships were over us real soon dropping depth charges. The sub went down as far as it could go, as the water was not real deep. It was a scary situation for several hours. At times everything shook in the sub. They finally gave up, and we continued into the China Sea." Cravens and Gray were returned to the *Lexington* almost a month later.

Warner Tyler flew on the 7th and 8th, dropping the usual high-explosive bombs. His crewmen were AMM^1 Orie Haddox and ARM^3 Arthur Davis; they flew *Mohawk-81* on the 7th and *Mohawk-87* on the 8th.

"On 8 September," wrote VB-19's Petty Officer Paul Dulong, "I was on a bombing mission with my pilot, Ens. Al Adlman, over Peleliu Island. We were directed to hit targets of opportunity since all the 'good stuff' had already been wiped out. The pickings were poor, so Mr. Adlman dove on what appeared to be a large amount of lumber or timber on a large stone pier. Well, that bomb hit resulted in a tremendous explosion—underneath the lumber was an ammo dump."

Fighter pilots Lieutenants John Hutto and Paul Beauchamp were the air group's photo-recce pilots. In particular, and as already mentioned, Hutto was the official aerial photographer of Fighting-19 with special training and special modifications to his airplane. The brass really wanted a lot of good photos of Peleliu. "I got my assignments from the admiral's staff, particularly Lt. Byron 'Whizzer' White." To make a long story short, "Peleliu was especially rough—those bastards were just not going to let me come over at low altitude. Instead of four runs it took me eight. I got worn out. Back on the *Lexington* I shortly heard over the loudspeaker 'Lieutenant Hutto, report to the flag intelligence spaces on the double.' When I opened the door there were all my photos spread all over the deck in rows; a whole bunch of senior officers and Whizzer were down on the floor trying to figure things out. I watched them for a few minutes, scared to death—they all looked confused and angry. Whizzer saw me and came over, shaking his head. 'Hut, we can't figure anything out of this mess.'"

"I replied, Whizzer, I forgot to report that I had to make eight runs instead of four because the Japanese almost got me and all my film—go down and look at the holes in my plane! So Whizzer and some of the big boys picked up a half row of photos and turned them around and fitted them in together, and then matched the new row, and so on. Thank God they fit, with the nice overlap we allowed. They had the whole Palau Island group, and how they carried on! They came over and shook my hand to congratulate me and told me that one flight had done the job the whole task force had been brought down here to do. It made the lousy, onerous, unglamorous, and dangerous job of being a photo pilot worthwhile for once."

The Battle of Peleliu, codenamed "Operation Stalemate II" by the Americans, was fought during the Mariana and Palau Campaign from September to November 1944.

U.S. Marines of the 1st Marine Division, and later soldiers of the U.S. Army's 81st Infantry Division, fought to capture an airstrip on the small coral island of Peleliu. This battle was part of a larger offensive campaign known as "Operation Forager," which ran from June to November 1944.

The commander of the 1st Marines initially predicted the island would be secured within four days. However, after repeated Imperial Army defeats in previous island campaigns, the Japanese had developed new island-defense tactics and well-crafted fortifications that allowed stiff resistance, extending the battle through more than two months. The heavily outnumbered Japanese defenders put up such tough resistance, often fighting to the death in the Emperor's name, that the island became known to the Japanese as the "Emperor's Island."

For the Americans this became a controversial battle because of the island's negligible strategic value and the high casualty rate, which exceeded that of all other amphibious operations during the Pacific War. The National Museum of the Marine Corps calls it "the bitterest battle of the war for the Marines."

"Although the issue was never in doubt," wrote Rear Admiral Sherman, "the capture of Peleliu involved some of the bitterest fighting that took place in the entire Pacific. Direct air support for the landing was furnished by a group of 'escort carriers' which was later augmented first by one, and then by two, fast-carrier groups. Behind smoke-screens laid to hide the reef and black-out enemy information posts on the high ground north of the airfield, and with dive bombers and fighter planes darting in and out, strafing enemy positions, dropping bombs, and launching rockets, the Marines had gone ashore."

The Task Group moved on to fly strikes on Mindanao in the Philippines.

"Those first strikes against Mindanao on 9 and 10 September, were like, well, like nothing we had ever experienced," wrote Torpedo Nineteen's Lieutenant Commander Perry. "Never before in the Pacific Theater had U.S. Navy planes penetrated so deeply over such a large land mass. Sure, Mindanao was an island, but to us it was a small-size continent. Palau, the Bonins, and even Guam were easy compared to this large island, where a 'cut' engine would mean a hazardous crash landing and a trip through some of the roughest terrain in the world."

"So, we left the coast and headed inland. We struck military targets at Valencia Airfield No. 1, Del Monte Airfield No. 7, Surigao Harbor, Cagayan Harbor, and Lianga Bay with great success."

"I think," wrote Mr. Winters, "that the Japanese had already been driven into caves. It was here that we had the experience of dropping our first napalm. They put some chemical gel in our belly tanks and then filled them up with gasoline. We could come in fast and low and release the tanks as we did when getting into a fight. It was great for hard-to-see targets as it tumbled onto the ground and spread a wide ribbon of flame for about a football-field length. Very impressive sight from ground or air. They hadn't put it into bombs yet, and we soon ran short of belly tanks."

"Mindanao," Mr. Perry continued, "wasn't so bad, we thought, after it was all over. There had been only meager AAA fire and we had sustained no losses. Again, our tactics had to be revised; because the terrain was from 2,000 feet to 6,000 feet above sea level, pull-outs and rendezvous were begun at higher altitudes. Pin-point bombing became an absolute necessity—since bombs out of a target area meant that Filipinos might be killed. The Mindanao strikes were the forerunners of a stepped-up campaign against the Japanese in the Philippines. We had found them weak and we intended to hit their Achilles heel with all our might."

"We flew toward the island in the dark after 9 September's pre-dawn launch," wrote Fighting-19's Bill Davis. "Mindanao was nothing like the small islands we'd been hitting. This was quite large, almost 300 by 300 miles at its widest. The island had high mountains completely covered with forests and perhaps a number of newly constructed airfields. The flight headed for Cagayan Harbor, which was filled with sampans. We dove on them and I got one in my sights. One blast with my six .50-caliber machine guns and the little 'ship' burst into flames."

Davis continued, "Bruce 'Lucky' Williams lived up to his name. He chose a sampan in the center of the group. He went into his run and was down to two hundred feet when the sampan exploded—it was an ammunition ship and it blew sky high, literally. 'Lucky' suddenly found himself at 3,000 feet with the wings of his airplane bent upward: he had been blasted straight up 2,800 feet!"

Carrier Air Group Nineteen executed 76 sorties against Mindanao. Warner Tyler flew on the 9th and 10th, once again dropping high explosive bombs, and once again flying with AMM1 Haddox and ARM3 Davis. On the 9th they were in *Mohawk-81*, and on the 10th *Mohawk-82*. A later strike on the 10th was cancelled due to bad weather.

Nevertheless, earlier on the 10th, "we had gone further north," wrote Mr. Davis, "and hit the Del Monte area, striking first at the airfield there. Having hit Mindanao the day before there was little hope for surprise—they were ready for us. We dove on the field and encountered a blistering barrage of AAA."

"Fighting-19's Alfred 'Ruff' Ruffcorn took a direct hit as he flew down the field. He was only twenty-five feet above the ground. Although his plane was engulfed in flames he managed to pull the nose up and was gaining altitude. The fire reached the cockpit and forced Ruff out onto the wing, where he hung on hoping to get high enough to jump. I watched as he tried to stay with the plane, but at 200 feet he had to give up and jumped. His parachute had barely begun to stream out when he hit the runway and bounced up almost a hundred feet."

The rest of the *Mohawks* pressed on with the attack. Finally, leaving the field in ruins, Davis recalled that they circled the countryside but couldn't find more targets. "Landing back on the *Lexington* we found that seven of our planes had sustained hits from the AAA guns."

"The overwhelming resistance that we expected from the Japanese did not materialize," Mr. Davis commented, "so the fleet moved north during the night of 11 September and a strike was scheduled to hit Cebu Island the following day."

"When the weakness of the enemy reaction on Mindanao was discovered," wrote Rear Admiral Sherman, "Admiral Halsey decided to probe farther north. Thus, on September 12th we were back in Philippine waters for what was designated the first Visayas strike. The three task groups of Task Force 38 were each assigned separate areas in the central Philippines."

"My group," continued Sherman, "was given the mission of destroying enemy aircraft, shipping, aircraft facilities, and ground installations on the islands of Cebu, Negros, and Bohol. For three days we sent in hordes of planes. Our first sweep encountered many Japanese planes in the air over Cebu and reported shooting down forty to fifty. It also attacked more than 100 enemy aircraft on the ground. Without air opposition, subsequent attacks concentrated on large ships found in Cebu Harbor and extensive oil tanks on nearby Mactan Island. In these three days of strikes the whole force destroyed over 300 Japanese aircraft and burned 13 large merchant ships, 20 smaller ones, and 35 sampans or barges. We had lost few planes by comparison—my group's losses consisted of ten aircraft—three of them in operational accidents—and ten men."

"On 12 September," agreed Lieutenant Commander Perry in the Torpedo Nineteen history, "we launched strikes against the Visayas with the main objective being to knock out airfields, aircraft, and aircraft installations—and we succeeded. Our torpedo planes, with the confidence gained from the Mindanao raids, shuttled back and forth over the Visayas carrying destruction to the Japanese air force. On the 12th the revetment areas at Lahug Airfield at Cebu felt the weight of our bombs as fourteen planes were destroyed on the ground. Shipping at Cebu was attacked and several merchant ships were heavily damaged. Lt.j.g. Robert Goforth and his crew, ARM^2 William Martin and AOM^2 James Reese, were hit by AAA fire on one of these strikes and their aircraft—*Mohawk-91*—was seen to crash into the bay at Cebu. None of them were recovered."

In addition to Mr. Goforth's aircraft, VT-19 put up fifteen planes in two strikes on the 12th, although two were "downed" for mechanical issues—Lieutenant Commander Perry in *Mohawk-82* and Lt. Don McMillan in *Mohawk-97*.

At Cebu, VT-19's Bill Davis encountered his first Japanese *Zero* fighter aircraft. This famous machine, the *Zero*, or *Zeke*, was the Mitsubishi A6M Navy Type '0' fighter.

"Quickly getting over my surprise, I led the target and fired a burst. I led the target too much, sending tracer rounds tearing past the *Zero*'s nose. The Japanese pilot immediately made a sharp turn to the left which put me right on his tail. I closed until there was no chance of missing and fired. It took only a short burst to blow the plane up. I was aware of someone screaming over the radio; I listened for a moment but it had stopped. Then I realized that the screaming had been me. As I fired my guns I had automatically screamed at the top of my lungs. I suppose that mankind has no doubt been screaming during combat since the beginning of time."

The rest of the fighter squadron had a "field day." They caught a group of Japanese planes taking off to challenge them and shot down 17 in the air and destroyed 35 on the ground. The dive and torpedo bombers sank several large cargo ships—with the loss of Mr. Goforth's plane and crew.

Ensign Davis went for the "daily double," on 13 September, with strikes against Cebu and Negros. At one point he approached a small island in the bay "that was completely covered with an oil refinery." He didn't think he could do any real damage, but made an attempt, hoping to at least rupture some pipes. "I flew low about twenty feet. I opened up and could see my tracers ripping into the equipment. Our ammunition consisted of an alternating mix of general-purpose, tracer, and armor-piercing rounds. Suddenly a fire erupted. As I climbed I could see the entire refinery going up in flames, going up in a gigantic fireball."

"Back on the ship I couldn't wait to tell our intelligence officer, Lt. Jack Wheeler. But I had barely got it out when the squadron executive officer, Lt. Roger 'Smiley' Boles, came over mad as hell. 'You blew up that refinery?' 'Yeah, the whole damn thing.' 'God damn it, Davis, that wasn't on the target list.' 'Sir, it was an enemy refinery, what the hell was I supposed to do?' 'That refinery was the property of the Texaco Oil Company, and I was hoping it would survive the war. I own *stock* in Texaco!'"

On one of these Visayan strikes there was an incident that immensely impacted the Air Group's chain of command. Cmdr. Karl Jung, the commander of Air Group Nineteen, was "right down with us fighters, slugging it out with the AAA as the *Lexington*'s CAGs were wont to do, until he caught one in his oil line." According to Lieutenant Commander Winters, Jung's "loyal Pratt & Whitney engine pulled him back to our Task Group spewing black oil all the way, but then it gave up as he neared the carrier. He made a beautiful water landing—except for a few things. First, he forgot to drop his belly fuel-tank which, being virtually empty, was in its most dangerous condition. Next, he also had forgotten to turn his gun switches off, and this is quite important before landing, anywhere. Well, the plane crushed the belly tank on impact with the sea, spreading considerable explosive gas-air mixture, and the machine guns, all six of them, started firing as he pulled the stick way back in order to "squash" into the sea—unconsciously squeezing the trigger as he did so."

Thus, Winters went on, "Karl immediately found a ring of fire on the water surrounding him and his still-floating F6F. His gun fusillade had, in addition to igniting the gas mixture, also sprayed a nearby destroyer but, fortunately, no-one was hit. I circled low over him and saw him shuck his chute and dive off the wing. He emerged a minute or two later, having swum under the ring of fire, smartly upwind. His wingman, Ens. George McPherson, made a low pass and dropped green dye-marker all over him. When a destroyer brought him back to the *Lexington* his face was a lurid green, and stayed that way 'til the nurses cleaned him up on the hospital ship USS *Solace*. Unfortunately, the fire had burned his hands such that he couldn't fly for a while."

However, actually, that was all right because simultaneously—and *totally* coincidentally—orders came giving Commander Jung a temporary promotion to captain and assigning him as the non-flying "air officer" in the ship's company of another carrier. As a result, on the *Lexington*, Lieutenant Commander Winters left his position as CO of Fighting-19 to become CAG-19, and received a temporary promotion to full commander.

As already mentioned, during the three days of 12 through 14 September, the Task Group delivered strikes on the Visayas. The Visayan Islands are one of the three principal geographical divisions of the Philippines, along with Luzon and Mindanao. And, as mentioned, the air groups also hit Cebu, which is a province located in the Central Visayan region and consists of a main island and 167 surrounding islands and islets.

Lastly, they struck Mactan, which is a densely populated island located a few kilometers from Cebu Island. In these actions Air Group Nineteen flew 73 sorties.

On 12 September, Fighting Nineteen shot down sixteen Japanese planes—and Lt. Bob Parker of *Bombing* Nineteen shot down one.

Petty Officer Reynold Ross wrote that "Lieutenant Parker and I were in a dive when a Japanese plane came up behind us and strafed across our port wing. Mr. Parker shouted, 'Where are those bullets coming from!?' because neither of us could see as we were looking back right into the sun. About that time the enemy plane came underneath us and, as he pulled up, Mr. Parker shot down his first Japanese plane. Then, as we swung south after our dive, we went around the island, and as we had the official camera that day, he requested I aim over the side and take pictures of the shoreline, although it looked like nothing but trees. About an hour later after returning to the ship they called me to the Intel spaces where they had blown up my shoreline pictures, and they disclosed three Japanese cruisers lined up and all camouflaged like trees. Shortly after, needless to say, the group was called to go on another raid to attack those cruisers."

Lt.j.g. Donald Engen commented that "Lieutenant Parker, flying his SB2C *dive bomber*, engaged a *Zero* and shot it down. Thus, he became Bombing-19's instant hero and provided much material with which to rib our sister fighter squadron!"

"On 13 September," wrote Lieutenant Commander Perry, "Mactan Airfield on Mactan Island was bombed and, like Lahug Field, it was loaded with planes which we either destroyed or damaged. Oil storage facilities on Mactan Island were set afire by 2,000-pound bombs. It was during one of these attacks that Lt.j.g. John McDonald was required to make a water landing when his load of fragmentation bombs exploded too-near his plane. Commander Hugh Winters, the new Air Group Commander, mapped the scene of the landing and the next day returned with Vought OS2U *Kingfishers*—which were catapult-launched observation float planes—and fighter cover to locate and rescue Mr. McDonald and his crewmen, AOM^2 Richard Henry and ARM^2 Robert Hessong. Also, one strike of our Torpedo Squadron hit Manapla Airfield on Negros Island, destroying numerous parked aircraft."

Lt.j.g. Jack Scott in Bombing-19 said that, on 14 September, "Our strike hit Fabrica Airfield on Negros Island. We bombed the field and then came back with a low-level strafing run. On the pull-out from the strafing run we spotted a Japanese ship in the middle of the channel. So, five of us went down and sank it with our 20mm guns. I later got hell from the Skipper for not expediting the rendezvous—the real problem was that the rest of the group joined up on me rather than the Skipper."

Lieutenant j.g. Engen, of Bombing-19, said that "it was on a strike to attack Japanese facilities on the Island of Panay, on September 14, that I added full power during the pullout but became aware that my airspeed was decaying rapidly, and the group was going off and leaving me. I advised Lt. Don Banker, and he assigned one of his wingmen, Ens. Bill Good, to come back to stay with me. I found that the maximum airspeed that I could maintain was 95 knots, and I could just barely maintain 400 feet altitude. Good and I were left to navigate through and around—not over—the central Philippine Islands much like Portuguese explorer Ferdinand Magellan did over 400 years ago. We kept vigilant watch, expecting some *Zeros* to come out to get the easy targets, but none showed. Suffice it to say Bill and I made it back to the ship. However, I couldn't stay in the air when I put both flaps and landing gear down. My gunner, Ted Stevenson, and I talked the situation over. Since his life hung in the same balance I wanted to give him a vote in what we would do. He threw his lot in with me and I then convinced the LSO on the VHF radio that I could get the airplane on board *if* he would 'wave me' with my landing gear down and my flaps up. Which he did, and I did."

Torpedo 19's history reads that "Panay Island was hit on 14 September with a long-range strike against the wharf and warehouse area at Iloilo on Guimaras Strait. Aircraft and aircraft installations at Lanog-Lanog (or Alicante), Bocolod, and Manapla Airfields on Negros Island were also attacked with success. On all of these strikes excellent results were obtained against grounded aircraft, and scores of enemy aircraft were destroyed."

Ens. Warner Tyler flew on 12, 13, and 14 September, each time dropping high-explosive bombs. Once again his crewmen were AMM[1] Haddox and ARM[3] Davis. Interestingly, on these three days, they flew *Mohawk-81*, *Mohawk-82*, and *Mohawk-83*.

"The first carrier strikes against the Japanese-occupied Philippines," wrote Rear Admiral Sherman, "were carried out by three out of the four Task Groups of the Fast Carrier Task Force. Intelligence gained in the course of the strikes, and the virtual elimination by our planes of air opposition, gave evidence of the weakness of the Japanese in the Leyte area."

This significantly changed American strategic planning and scheduling. The fleet moved north; now Luzon was going to be seriously addressed. This was the main island of the Philippines, with the capital city of Manila. "The Japanese," wrote fighter pilot Bill Davis, "had to have overwhelming power here, either that or they must be resigned to defeat. So far, we hadn't seen any evidence of the latter." The task force took from 15 to 20 September to reach the new operating area.

"The night before our arrival off Luzon," continued Davis, "we had our briefing for the following day. We were going to hit Nichols Field, the main American air field before the Japanese conquered the islands."

Bombing-19's Lt.j.g. Wally Griffin wrote that "Somewhere off Luzon, just before dawn, Petty Officer Eno 'Hijemo' Leaf [another person from Denver] and I were sitting in our plane on the extreme port side of the flight deck, along with all of the other aircraft assigned to the first strike. We all had full loads of ammo, bombs, and fuel. It was pitch black except for the bow wake streaming under my port wing. Over the bullhorn came the command to 'START ENGINES.' We fired up our engines and within a minute or two we heard 'WE HAVE A BOGIE ON THE SCREEN.' Then we received the command to 'STOP ALL ENGINES.' After the last engine was stopped there was an eerie silence with the soft swish of the wake. No one moved, and after a few more moments I could hear the low distant sound of an aircraft engine coming from my left side."

"There was an enemy aircraft approaching our task force—low and fast! He was bearing down directly on the *Lexington*, and as he got closer I could tell it was an in-line engine, humming like a P-51. We sat there in our cockpits, motionless, hoping he would not see us. As the noise got louder and louder I knew that he was heading right at me and that I was sure he was going to crash into the port side of the ship. Maybe he would crash right into our whole deckload of fully fueled and armed aircraft, sitting like ducks on the flight deck ready to go up in a ball of flame. He zoomed up into a steep climb almost directly over my aircraft—so close, in fact, that I saw the flames coming out of his exhaust and the red "meatball" under his right wing! He must have seen the white bow wave and realized he was going to crash into a large ship, so he pulled up and at the same time released his single bomb which went over the ship and landed on the starboard side in the water where it exploded. They don't come any closer than that! He got away in the darkness. A few moments later we prepared to start engines again and get ready for our assigned strike. On our starboard quarter the USS *Princeton* launched its aircraft. In the dim morning light of sunrise, and as the first aircraft took off, our 20mm gunners on the starboard side aft opened fire on them! Fortunately the *Princeton* was out of range and the shells fell harmlessly into the water. The attack on our ship had made those boys real 'trigger happy.' We found out later they were mostly cooks and stewards and they were going to fire at *anything* that moved. This was long before the *Lexington* had a terrible *Kamikaze* attack on 5 November; at this point we had not even heard of such a thing. Thank the good Lord that this particular pilot this day was not a *Kamikaze* corps member!"

Petty Officer Leaf added that “it was one of the most frightening moments to remember. I don’t know how he missed us with that bomb. I had trouble getting it out of my mind for several nights.” ARM^2 Albert Thorngren wrote, forty years later, “whenever I hear the word ‘bogie’—and that’s not very often since I gave up golf—I sure remember that one.”

“The predawn strike,” according to Mr. Davis, “took off and headed for the docks at Manila Bay.” Interestingly Davis, in his autobiography, doesn’t mention the incident reported above by Griffin and Leaf. “We took off slightly later and flew toward Nichols Field. The flight consisted of torpedo-bombers at 12,000 feet, dive-bombers above them at 15,000, and fighters spread above, below, and around the bombers. As we approached the field we could see Japanese fighters in the air at a distance.”

“Approaching the edge of the field,” continued Davis, “we dove, looking for the flashes of AAA guns. We spotted some and took aim as we closed the range, then opened fire. The more havoc we could create, the better chance our bombers would have. The Japanese fighters had been staying well out of range, but they no doubt had hopes of picking off some bombers as they pulled out. All hell was breaking loose everywhere.”

“Pulling out low over the AAA guns, we headed for the rendezvous point. There was a wild melee of planes at low altitude and high speed, ours trying to close ranks for maximum protection. Our division of fighters that had followed the dive-bombers got the gravy: they shot down six planes without the loss of a single one of ours.”

“Our air coordinators,” it says in the Torpedo-19 history, “had designated good targets—this time over Manila on the island of Luzon.” Thus, on 21 September, VT-19 flew a morning strike against the Manila area—aircraft and aircraft facilities at Nielson Field were the primary targets. (Before the war Nielson Field had been headquarters for the U.S. Army’s Far East Air Force).

Interestingly, naval depth-charges designed for anti-submarine warfare proved to be excellent on-the-ground plane destroyers as the violence of their explosions could be seen in tremendous concussion waves from the air.

"Manila, so quiet at dawn, soon awakened to the fury which was pouring down on her Japanese-held airfields. And, those weren't house lights that soon began to blink sporadically throughout the sleepy city; rather, they were AAA positions firing frantically at our attacking aircraft."

"During those initial assaults on the central Philippines," wrote Bombing-19's Lt.j.g. George Lewis, "when we were bombing Cagayan on the northeastern tip of Luzon, VB-19's skipper—Cmdr. Richard McGowan—took the bomber flight in and pretty well gutted the shipping and harbor facilities, and then another squadron picked out the two most beautiful buildings in the little city, bombed them and brought back some great pictures where they had leveled them almost to the ground. But Admiral Halsey and Vice Admiral Mitscher, when they heard this, were beside themselves because the buildings were the bishop's palace and the Roman Catholic cathedral on a predominately Catholic island—where we had been trying hard to build goodwill for years. However, a few days later the intelligence came through that the Japanese had seized them from the Church and stocked them with tons of ammunition—which helped account for the tremendously large explosions."

"The second strike on the 21st," continued Torpedo Nineteen's history, "found the Japanese wide-awake and throwing up everything at us but the kitchen sink. To help protect ourselves we used 'window,' later called 'chaff'—a cloud of small, thin pieces of aluminum, metallized glass fiber, or plastic—over the target to foul up enemy radar-controlled AAA, which they appeared to be using here. Nielson Field was hit again with 500 pound bombs."

"The third strike hit barracks areas and revetments at Quezon and Zablan Airfields—and then that strike was jumped by eight to ten Japanese fighters. Our own fighters were on their toes, shooting hell out of our attackers and driving them off."

"The fourth strike of this same day found three merchant ships as a part of a north-bound convoy off the west coast of Luzon. This strike was led by Lieutenant Commander Perry, in *Mohawk-82*, and consisted of eight planes minus Ens. Bob McAdams, in *Mohawk-81*, due to a downed engine. Lt.j.g. Edward Myers in *Mohawk-89* sank one ship, and Lt.j.g. Frank Fox, in *Mohawk-86*, damaged another."

Lieutenant Commander Perry also wrote that "on the second day at Manila—22 September—we found that we could stay out of the AAA and still hit our targets. Nielson Field's hangars, revetments, and dispersal areas were again hard-hit. Also, Manila's vital harbor and dock facilities were plastered with 2,000-pound bombs with several direct hits being secured on important targets. The attacks on Manila re-emphasized for us the necessity of quick after-takeoff rendezvous and the importance of staying with the group. Glide-bombing attacks were no longer made in echelon but rather in simultaneous dives of from six to nine planes. It was a healthy feeling to know that you had a lot of company on the way down."

Lt.j.g. George Peck, of Bombing-19, said that 22 September began somewhat unpleasantly. "At 0525 a non-routine 'General Quarters' sounded—bogies were all over the sky. We manned our planes at 0620 and it was dark as hell. As soon as we got in our planes the bastards came in at the *Lexington* from dead astern. All hell broke loose. Every gun aft opened up. A 5-inch gun just to the left of my plane almost deafened me. However, we were able to launch at 0645. We hit Nielson Field at Manila. The AAA was a repeat of the Bonins—thick as hell. A lot of our planes came back with freak holes in them. And then, just one minute after we manned the planes for another flight, we were told to secure—apparently a typhoon was on the way."

"When airborne," wrote Bombing-19's Lt.j.g. Stu Crapser, "it seemed to me that fear was something one could handle because there was plenty to do to control the aircraft and try to accomplish the mission. But back aboard ship, when an attack came, we aircrew couldn't really grab a gun and shoot back when the Japanese had at us. We were east of the Philippines, preparing for a launch, sitting in our aircraft on the *Lexington*, when our Task Group came under attack. We had not yet received the command to 'START ENGINES' when the big 5-inch turret guns began going off. The target was aft of the ship. After a time I discerned the sound of the 40mm quads on the fantail join the firing. Then some seconds later the deck-edge single 20mm began firing aft also. The enemy was getting closer. I made myself as small as possible in front of the armor plate in my cockpit. Suddenly I heard the very rapid fire of ARM[1] James Burns' twin 30-calibers from the rear of our plane. In a few seconds all firing stopped. I stuck my head out of the cockpit and looked aft. There was an aircraft wing-rolling over like a falling leaf with a big red ball on it, just off the *Lexington's* stern. What a relief!"

Lt.j.g. Wally Griffin wrote that he and P. O. Eno Leaf had an even more "hairy" adventure on top of the early morning attack on the ship. "On 22 September we had just finished our attack on Nielson Field. We were strung out heading for Laguna de Báý, a large lake south of Manila—in fact the largest lake in the Philippines—to rendezvous with all other *Lexington* aircraft for the return to the ship. Just as I settled down straight and level at about 500-feet altitude, our plane was peppered by heavy AAA fire and we were being riddled with bullets. I zigzagged like crazy and prayed they wouldn't hit our engine. Lt.j.g. George Peck was flying about 1,000 yards to our left and he told me later that he saw my plane completely enmeshed in tracer fire and thought I was a 'goner' for sure. When we finally reached the rendezvous area we joined some torpedo planes and flew back with them. As I prepared for the landing, I discovered there was no hydraulic pressure, which meant I had no flaps but could drop my landing gear and the tail hook by gravity. After a straight-in landing and stop in the gear, I couldn't taxi forward because both tires were in shreds! As my plane captain came up beside the cockpit to unhook my parachute harness he exclaimed 'My God, sir, look at this!' He held up the harness and we could see where a large-caliber machine-gun bullet had torn a groove completely across the padding and under the riser straps. As the bullet passed across my back—an inch from my spine—it had hit the edge of my open cockpit sliding hatch and knocked out the entire right side of the plexiglass panel."

"Later on I had to take the harness with me to show to Vice Admiral Mitscher up on his flag bridge, and he said with a twinkle in his eye 'Well, son, I'd say you were pretty lucky today, weren't you?' I answered, 'Yes, sir, Admiral, I sure was.' Our maintenance boss, Chief Petty Officer Joe Nance, said my plane was so shot up that they took off the engine, guns, and other good parts and then dumped the whole airplane over the side into the sea."

Petty Officer Leaf added that after their *Helldiver* was hit "I saw the hydraulic fluid, in the right wing, vaporize—looking just like smoke. Mr. Griffin and I couldn't communicate as our intercom was knocked out. We kept going lower and lower, so I turned around and faced forward, watching the front cockpit in case Mr. 'Griff' bailed out. Actually we were too low to bail out. We joined up with some other stragglers and made it back to the formation and the ship. Mr. 'Griff,' with his great pilot skills and knowledge, brought us back in one piece. Of course, as a Catholic, he always went to Mass before any flights, so that might have helped!"

During this period of 21 and 22 September, Carrier Air Group Nineteen struck Manila and other targets on Luzon, flying a total of 49 sorties.

Ens. Warner Tyler flew twice on the 21st, dropping high-explosive bombs. In the morning his aircraft was torpedo-bomber *Mohawk-86*, and then in the afternoon it was *Mohawk-93*. For both flights his crewmen were Petty Officers Haddox and Davis. Torpedo Nineteen flew two strikes on the 22nd, one of nine aircraft at 0630 and the other of seven planes at 0700; both were against Manila. Mr. Tyler and his crew did not fly that day.

Fighter pilot Bill Davis grew whimsical at this time. "I—we—had fallen into a routine, the routine of war. I got up every morning around three, had breakfast, got into a plane, and after the usual hair-raising catapult shot in the dark, commuted to 'work'—usually about a two-hour flight. A commuter back home might read a paper on the train, but I was busy testing my guns and checking on my oxygen."

"Other than that," he continued, "it was flying formation, just like driving on a freeway. Once at 'work,' over some Japanese installation, things changed. Normally, work took only about fifteen minutes and, of course, death was a constant companion, as far away as the next exploding shell from the ever-present AAA guns. Interestingly, the Japanese never seemed to run out of ammunition. Blowing up everything of value we could find, we beat a retreat and headed for home."

"Oh, and at the end of the commute, there was always the thrill of a landing on a moving aircraft carrier—just to keep you on your toes."

During this time, in any given afternoon, Davis might fly another sortie. And then, later, he might fly a four-hour CAP over the fleet. "All told, many days I was flying twelve hours a day. This was followed by a few drinks with friends, and dinner served on white linen tablecloths by smartly dressed stewards, and then either some bridge or classical music." My compatriots seemed to favor Tchaikovsky's Second and Fourth Symphonies. When I listen to either of those pieces today—66 years later—I can still feel the motion of the ship."

On 23 and 24 September the Task Group flew strikes against the Visayan Islands, Cebu, Coron Bay, and Negros Island. Negros is the fourth largest island of the Philippines and is one of the many islands that comprise the Visayans.

"We hit Cebu Island again on 24 September," reads the Torpedo-19 history, "using delayed-action bombs against several small merchant ships. Two ships were sunk and several more were damaged. On the second and third strikes we hit harbor installations, and another medium-size merchant ship was set ablaze." VT-19's first strike launched at 0600 with seven planes; the second strike at 0900 went with four; and the third at 1300 with eleven. Ens. Tyler and his usual crew flew in the second strike, in *Mohawk-98*, led by Lieutenant Commander Perry in *Mohawk-93*.

Petty Officer Arno Droske, of Bombing-19, wrote that "on 24 September, if I remember correctly, we were to hit a convoy in the South China Sea. We had to use auxiliary gas tanks. But, in my airplane we couldn't get suction on our tanks and had to turn back alone. Boy, was that a *big* ocean! In my mind I wondered where the ship was and what kind of reception we would receive when we got near the Task Force flying alone. We climbed until we intercepted the homing beacon, found the ship, and our 'IFF' worked, and we were taken aboard."

IFF, or "Identification, Friend or Foe" was and is an identification system for aircraft. It uses a transponder that listens for an interrogation signal and then sends a response that identifies the broadcaster. Early IFF systems usually used radar frequencies, but other electromagnetic frequencies, radio or infrared, could be used.

All told, Air Group Nineteen flew 23 sorties on 23 and 24 September.

From 25 September to 7 October the *Lexington* and Air Group 19—and of course the other units in Task Group 38.3—moved to rearm and provision. "At the northeast end of the Palau group," wrote Rear Admiral Sherman, "was the excellent anchorage of Kossol Roads, formed by outlying small islands and a coral reef, and large enough to contain several hundred ships. Its disadvantage was that it was in plain sight of the Japanese on Koror, who could observe the goings and comings of any ships using its facilities. I anchored there with my task group several times before Ulithi became available as a fleet anchorage." On the 27th the group did some provisioning and rearming at Kossol.

The day before, in a brief ceremony on 26 September, Lt. Cmdr. Frank Perry assumed command of Torpedo Squadron Nineteen, relieving Lt. Cmdr. David Dressendorfer. Perry was originally from Lincolnville, Maine, and Dressendorfer was from Springfield, Illinois. Mr. Dressendorfer was returned to the U.S. due to medical issues. He had been medically grounded after an anti-submarine patrol on 24 September; the specifics are unclear. Dressendorfer had held the command since 31 December 1943.

Ulithi Atoll is in the western group of the Caroline Islands, 360 miles southwest of Guam. It consists of 40 islets surrounding a lagoon about 19 miles long and up to 13 miles wide—one of the largest in the world. Seized—essentially unopposed—by American forces in September 1944, it became a major staging area for the U.S. Navy in the final year of the war. Task Group 38.3 arrived at Ulithi on 2 October. For the next couple of days the Task Group, including the *Lexington*, worked on completing provisioning and arming.

When the Task Group pulled in to Ulithi, according to fighter pilot Bill Davis, "it appeared to be another typical atoll, the remains of an ancient volcano. The entire navy support fleet of several hundred ships had moved forward to this anchorage. It was rest and rehabilitation time, and we were ready for it."

Not all personnel thought it was wonderful. During this period, according to Bombing-19's Petty Officer Gerald Warnke, "We spent many long and boring days anchored at Ulithi as the ship underwent re-provisioning and waiting for the next assignment. Our Ulithi R&R turned out to be a visit to the 'great' Mogmog Island where we were deposited on a barren beach, handed two cans of lukewarm beer, and instructed to 'have a good time.' Most of us preferred to catch the next boat back to the ship and our air-conditioned ready room. So much for life in the fast lane!"

It's hard to resist commenting that the author's father, a sergeant in the U.S. 32nd Infantry Regiment, had a brief shore leave on Mogmog in the summer of 1945. His impressions of the island are lost now, unfortunately.

Back to October 1944, for Task Group 38.3 there was some excitement of a different nature at Ulithi. Two or more Japanese two-man submarines slipped in past the anti-submarine net one morning. One was accidentally rammed by a destroyer, and another torpedoed an oil tanker. "All hell broke loose" as every destroyer that had steam up then combed the lagoon dropping depth charges.

Ens. Bill Davis wrote that apparently "these small subs had been towed by a large sub to Ulithi and waited just off shore. The plan was to get six subs in the lagoon, line up on six aircraft carriers, and fire their twelve torpedoes simultaneously. Had they been successful they could have crippled six carriers and might have even sunk some. It was a bold plan and might have succeeded except for the accidental ramming by that destroyer. We realized that the war was *always* with us."

"On October 3rd," wrote Lt.j.g. George Peck of Bombing-19, "we moved from the anchorage so as to get out of the path of a typhoon, but it seemed to me that we steamed into the face of it. Plenty of rough sea all night. I got up to keep from being tossed from the bunk to the deck."

Chief Radarman Robert Whitham, of the *Lexington*'s ship's company, added that "Our force left Ulithi this morning as the storm grew worse. We bucked the typhoon all day and night. Two damaged destroyers were forced to return to Ulithi as they were dangerously shipping water. A 50-knot wind was tearing across the flight deck and the waves at times reached 20 feet. Several doughnut life rafts were torn from their moorings under the flight deck which is 50 feet above the waterline. The light carrier *Langley* lost six planes over her side."

Lt.j.g. Peck had more to say about this. "On 4 October, the ship went to 'General Quarters' at 0430. The squadron XO—executive officer—had said to stay out of the sack, so at 'secure' I tried to sleep in the ready room. Then the Bombing-19 skipper (Cmdr. Richard McGowan) came in and told me to stay out of both my sack *and* the RR for the rest of the day. The sea was rough and later in the morning even our huge ship took water over the bow."

Bombing-19's Lt.j.g. Daniel Sadler wrote that "we had four of us in our stateroom aboard the *Lexington*: Lt.j.g. Bill Good, Lt.j.g. Arnie Jancar, Lt.j.g. Jerry Wilton, and me. Our room was on the port side, in the bow, at the water line. Jancar's and Good's bunks were welded to the angled hull. During the typhoon the bow would rise to its peak, shake violently, then come down and smack the water. This occurred on a very regular frequency. Jancar finally put his mattress on the deck but with the roll of the ship he would roll off onto the deck. He spent a whole night God-damning President Roosevelt and Prime Minister Churchill for his discomfort—strangely he never mentioned Chancellor Hitler or Emperor Hirohito!"

Interestingly, Bill Davis was going to hear something similar around Christmas 1944. At that point, back in the states, he made it a point to take a trip from his parents' house in Philadelphia to visit his friend Duke De Luca's parents in Atlantic City. "I was hoping I could lessen the sorrow of Duke's death. I didn't even come close. They were the most bitter people I'd ever met in my life. And they didn't blame the Japanese, but rather the United States government and especially the U.S. Navy. They were absolutely beyond consoling. I've never seen such pain in a family. After a short time, I beat a hasty retreat."

Back to early October 1944, Mr. Davis also wrote about the typhoon. Davis—who about this time was promoted to lieutenant, junior grade (having been an ensign since May 1943)—wrote that "We were looking forward to a week of recreation, but suddenly the fleet was a beehive of activity. With little fanfare we weighed anchor and put out to sea. The barometer was dropping precipitously and it was safer to be out at sea in a bad storm than inside the atoll. The first day out gave little indication of anything unusual. The following day the wind picked up. That night we had our first taste of the typhoon. Starting at sundown the winds increased every hour and by midnight they were over 100 miles per hour. The winds whipped the ocean up until it resembled mountains."

"By the second night," continued Lieutenant j.g. Davis, "the ship was climbing the side of these mountains. At times the propellers would come out of the water at the stern! We started to make bets as to whether this huge carrier would survive, or not. As she burrowed into the big waves the flight deck would go under water as much as twenty feet. She would start to shake from side to side as she tried to pull herself up from the tons of water pressing her down."

"Increasing, the winds reached 150 miles per hour. I wondered if anything almost 900 feet long could continue to withstand nature's fury indefinitely. Would high-tensile steel and man's genius for construction meet their match tonight?"

"At 0200 we found out. The bow of the ship dove into the next wave and a frightening, rending sound of metal-on-metal screamed through the hull. We were all convinced the *Lexington* was breaking up. But the loudspeaker system quickly came alive throughout the ship:

> 'Now hear this, now hear this: We are NOT sinking. The ship is built with expansion joints above the water line so she can flex in extreme conditions. All that's happened is the ship bent so far that a joint went up against its stop, sending a shock through the hull.'

Chief Bob Whitham was also pretty impressed by the storm. "We had to get out of the lagoon in the morning as the typhoon was headed our way. Very heavy seas. Took green water over the flight-deck bow. When we would hit a big wave, the hangar deck (three-inch steel plates) would ripple like a stone dropped on a pond. The expansion joints sure got an awful workout. There were no planes on the hangar deck so you could see that there seemed to be differences of six to eight feet between the fore and aft ends at times. Very eerie sight. I had the 8-12 watch there at night; plenty scared. Sure thought a couple of times that the old gal was going to come apart at the seams. Had to use my bunk straps to stay in bed at night."

"On the 4th," he continued, "we anchored again about noon. On the 6th we were underway at 1730. Got no food stores as the transports hadn't arrived."

"The following morning the storm started to subside," fighter pilot Davis added, "and we received word that we were on our way to strike Okinawa. We were also advised that our navigators were using Commodore Matthew C. Perry's ninety-year old charts, because they were the most recent ones the navy had for this area."

These charts dated back from when Perry headed the American expedition that essentially forced Japan—in 1854—to enter into trade and diplomatic relations with the West after more than two centuries of isolation.

Mr. Davis also added a poignant note to his story of the typhoon. As he had mentioned, "the first day had given little indication of anything unusual. I ran into Glen Seagrave, the aerological officer on the ship's staff. 'How's it look?' I asked. 'We can't really tell yet, but I don't think it's going to be too bad,' he replied. 'It looks as it it'll pass to the west of us.'"

"I had talked to Glen a number of times, but we'd never introduced ourselves. 'By the way,' I started, 'my name is....' He held up his hand. 'Oh, don't introduce yourself!' Immediately he looked embarrassed. 'I don't want to seem unfriendly, but I got to know a couple of pilots in the previous air group, and it tore me to pieces when I'd see their names on the list of pilots lost the previous day. I enjoy talking to you, but I don't want to know your name.'"

This exchange hit Davis particularly hard, as just a few days before—14 September—he had been saddened by a related incident. During a strike, and "Finding Japanese planes on the runway, I dove through the usual AAA and set two twin-engine bombers on fire. A number of us were hit, and one fighter went down. The pilot had just joined the squadron as a replacement, and no one knew him. What a sad fate to be the new man in the group, whom no one had time to get to know, and then be lost on one of your first flights—if not your *first*. Who would write the letter home?" It's not totally clear, but this new man may have been Lt. Warren H. Abercrombie. Commander Winters knew him as much as anyone, having exchanged fishing stories, and it was Winters who wrote the letter home—though he stated it appeared to be engine failure close to the ship rather than AAA.

The word then came down from Admiral Halsey, informally, that the previous Philippine raids had been really only a prelude to more daring things which he had in mind. This of course sparked considerable interest among the crews. From 7 to 9 October the ships moved towards Okinawa. Moreover, as the ships approached the Nansei-shotō—Ryukyu Islands—part of Japan's inner defense ring, the mornings became noticeably cooler and the water became a deeper gray-blue.

"Moving in behind the typhoon," wrote Rear Admiral Sherman, "which grounded enemy reconnaissance planes, we arrived off Okinawa at daylight on October 10th. Our mighty armada of carriers launched their planes to strike enemy targets along a 300-mile arc from Amami Ōshima on the north to Myako-Jima on the south. Again, the Japanese were seemingly caught napping. No airborne opposition was encountered, but as usual our planes had a great deal of AAA to penetrate. Nevertheless, once more they wrought havoc and destruction."

So, the Task Force blasted Okinawa-Jima on Tuesday, 10 October. This is the largest of the Okinawa Islands. The plan was to destroy bases from which opposition to the Allied Philippines campaign might be launched. Strikes were also flown against the Nansei-Shotō islands in the Kyushu region. These islands are a chain of Japanese islands that stretch southwest from Kyushu to Formosa. (Months later, Okinawa will see the bloodiest ground battle of the Pacific War, with combat operations ranging from 1 April to 22 June 1945).

"The morning of October 10, 1944," wrote VF-19 fighter pilot Lt. Paul Beauchamp, "began in the usual fashion of an attack day. The blaring loudspeakers throughout the ship carried the bugle call of 'Flight Quarters,' followed by the 'General Quarters' and a klaxon horn guaranteed to rouse even the deepest sleeper. Jumping into flight clothes, Lt. Barney Garbow and I headed to the VF-19 ready room."

"We had been briefed," continued Beauchamp, "in the previous two days concerning today's action. The war in the Pacific was proceeding far more rapidly than projected. So we were now briefed about a group of islands called the Nansei-Shotō, and the particular island in this group called Okinawa-Jima. It's hard to realize that this now-familiar name was strange and meaningless to us before the briefing. Air Intelligence believed that the main Japanese Air Force might be located on this island, so the plan was to approach the target at sea level to avoid the possibility of radar detection. It's ironic, in view of Japan's position in electronics in today's world, that in 1944 their radio and radar equipment was somewhat primitive and unreliable."

"It was a strangely oppressive morning," Beauchamp went on, "much too warm for October, with a solid cloud cover at around 2,000 feet. The first planes to be catapulted were shot into an almost completely black void. As the light increased, the greyness of the world was even more apparent. Grey ships on grey water beneath a grey sky. The sea was rolling in an oily way—no whitecaps for relief to the monotone world."

"It was to be a one-day strike—a hit-and-run stab to the islands that lay but 200 miles south of Japan. The early morning strike was rather unusual for me. I was to fly wingman on Commander Winters, who was designated the target coordinator for the morning strike. At his option he could direct action against specific targets as the need arose. This morning flight was to last three hours, and I was scheduled for an afternoon photo mission, also of three hours duration."

"The launch proceeded without incident. Commander Winters took off; immediately upon becoming airborne I spotted Commander Winters circling ahead and joined up on him. The entire strike force of some 600 planes—from several carriers—was soon rendezvousing and holding at an altitude of 1,000 feet. When the last planes were launched, Commander Winters took a heading for the target and the strike force formed behind us. Somehow at this low altitude the 600 planes seemed even more impressive than when rendezvousing at normal altitudes, and since the target was relatively small the force was grouped more tightly than usual."

The first strike on the 10th was against Yontan-San Airfield No. 2 on Okinawa-Jima. The group hit grounded aircraft and aircraft installations with 100-pound bombs which resulted in several fires and the destruction of numerous airplanes. The second wave attacked a large merchant ship northwest of the island, scoring several hits.

"We found many targets," wrote Lieutenant Beauchamp, "sitting ducks for our bombs and strafing runs—ships, airfields, planes on the ground, oil storage tanks, etc. Everything proceeded smoothly and Commander Winters as target coordinator actually had little to do except observe."

"Within three hours I was back over the scene on my photo mission, attempting to make a systematic photographic record of the considerable destruction below. I covered as much of Okinawa as possible to obtain a good record. But the story has a very disappointing ending. Our good photographic crew let me down. They had neglected to put film in my cameras, and so for a full hour I put my fighter through all kinds of maneuvers for nothing!"

Ens. Warner Tyler, in *Mohawk-82,* flew from 0745 to 1100 with the second strike of the 10th. Overall, on this day, VT-19 put up 33 torpedo bombers with one downed for hydraulic issues and another with a serious oil leak. Tyler flew with a division of nine aircraft, led by Lt. Len Prater in *Mohawk-85*; they dropped high-explosive bombs on unspecified Nansei-Shotō targets. Tyler's crewmen now were Aviation Ordnanceman 2nd Class Wilmer Mark Dewees as gunner, and Aviation Radioman 3rd Class Arthur Davis as radioman. Dewees was from Ontario, California, and Davis was from Belle Mead, New Jersey.

"It was on this second strike," reads the Torpedo-19 history, "that a couple of our turret gunners got a chance to show their mettle. A *Val*—a Japanese Aichi D3A Type 99 carrier-borne dive bomber—made a high-side pass on our torpedo-bomber formation, but he was immediate shot down by the accurate fire of AOM[2] Elmo Hockman (flying with Lt. Richard Greer in *Mohawk-90*) and AOM[2] Virgil English (flying with Lt. Luther Prater in *Mohawk-85*)."

The history goes on to say that "The third strike of nine *Avengers* was led by Lieutenant Commander Perry in *Mohawk-98*; it hit Yontan-San Airfield No. 1, lining its runways with five-hundred pounders." This attack also hit the disabled merchant ship which had been previously damaged, sinking it with accurate glide bombing. The fourth and last strike, of six *Avengers*, was led by Lt. Fred Doll in *Mohawk-91*.

Fighting-19's Ens. George McPherson—who actually hailed from Zamboanga City, Philippine Islands—wrote that "on our first visit to Okinawa, Lt. Luther 'Del' Prater's plane was shot up, and beyond that he had to wait for landing until everyone else had come back aboard. The problem was that while he pumped the flaps and gear down by hand, the tail-hook would just not come down. So, Del was given the option of landing in the water or on board by hitting the crash barrier. He elected the latter. His first pass looked good, but the Landing Signal Officer waved him off, and called up to the bridge that he thought Prater could land safely with no hook *if* he had five knots more wind over the deck." So the *Lexington*'s commanding officer, Captain Litch, sent word to the engine room for more turns. "Del continued around," according to McPherson "and made a perfect approach and landed after the 'cut,' with his brakes locked. The plane slowed rapidly, and each time *just* before nosing over and hitting the prop, Del released the brakes and as the tail came down, he hit the brakes again. The deck crew on the barriers dropped the first barrier just before he reached it, and likewise the second (and last) just as the *Hellcat* came to a stop. I was on the carrier's island, and I happened to look over at Vice Admiral Mitscher who had been watching the whole operation from his chair on the flag bridge. He got up with a smile and departed for his sea cabin with the comment, 'Nice job.'"

Fighter pilot Lt.j.g. Bill Davis wrote about an interesting experience, that he and seven of his squadron-mates had, just prior to returning to the *Lexington*. They spotted a lone Japanese destroyer some distance from shore. Although they were out of small bombs, they couldn't let "this juicy target go unmolested." So they dove on the ship and let go with long machine-gun bursts at her waterline.

"All eight of us completed two runs with our combined 48 machine guns. Preparing for a third run, I noticed the destroyer was riding lower in the water." They circled the ship for a few minutes. "I estimated that there might be as many as 2,000 half-inch .50-caliber holes drilled through the light skin of the destroyer, many below the waterline. As we watched, the ship sank. We'd sunk a destroyer with machine guns! It makes you realize how absurd movies are today, with machine-gun fights where no one and nothing gets hurt."

Not through with excitement on this day, Davis went on to report that "I landed back on the carrier and I then watched as they pushed one of our planes over the side. It was so shot up it wasn't worth saving. Thankfully the pilot was uninjured."

"I was making my way off the flight deck when a dive-bomber taxied by," continued Davis. "The pilot opened his bomb bay doors so that the plane could be rearmed. I stared in horror as the 2,000-pound bomb he had been carrying dropped out. It seemed to fall in slow motion. If that bomb is armed, it is all over. Several of the deck crew also saw it and raced towards the plane. The bomb hit the deck but didn't explode. The deck hands immediately rolled it toward the side of the ship and pushed it over. We still held our breaths—but it surprisingly didn't go off when it hit the water."

"The pilot had opened his bomb bay doors when he dove on a cruiser. He pushed the release and pulled out, blacking out for a short time as often happens. He, of course, assumed he'd dropped the bomb and didn't realize he still had it aboard. We were all lucky—twice lucky!"

Carrier Air Group-19 had made a total of 32 sorties against Okinawa-Jima. "Task Group 38.3," wrote Rear Admiral Sherman, "destroyed 93 enemy planes and sank 87 vessels. Ammunition and fuel storage at the city of Naha on Okinawa was left blazing and exploding, and numerous air facilities were demolished. None of our ships were damaged."

"On 11 October," Admiral Sherman continued in his narrative, "we fueled from tankers within range of Luzon and at the same time sent fighter sweeps against bases on that island. Upon their completion, we headed in for a raid on the Japanese-occupied island of Formosa, off the China coast."

Thus, on 11 October, the Task Group moved towards Formosa where, from the 12th to the 14th, it flew strikes against Formosa and the Pescadores Islands. The Pescadores are an archipelago of ninety islands and islets in the Formosa Strait. During this movement the air group put up several flights; VT-19's assignment was one five-plane flight of a "Snooper Anti-Submarine Patrol" led by Lt.j.g. Ray Stacy in *Mohawk-91*.

Lt.j.g. George Peck, in Bombing-19, wrote that on the evening of 11 October "at 'General Quarters' we each were issued an American flag, a "pointy-talky" sheet for English and Chinese, and 162 yen in cash."

Chapter 9

"From October 12th to October 16th," wrote Rear Adm. "Ted" Sherman, "there occurred the greatest battle of the war—up to that date—between ships and shore-based aircraft. This would be known as the 'Battle off Formosa' or the 'Formosa Air Battle.' The Japanese on Formosa had been alerted by the Nansei-shotō attacks and were ready for us. They made the mistake, however, of initially using their planes defensively over their air bases instead of striking at our more vulnerable aircraft carriers."

"When our pilots arrived over Formosa they found many enemy planes in the air waiting to engage them in combat. The Japanese had rushed air reinforcements from the homeland to the threatened area on a lavish scale, and had even sent in partial carrier air groups in the hope of striking a crushing blow. Our planes engaged aggressively and the sky was full of aerial dogfights. The incursion into one of their strongest areas had provoked the Japanese into fighting back with all they had."

"Our plan of attack," continued Sherman, "had contemplated continuing the action for only two days, but at dusk on the second day the heavy cruiser USS *Canberra* was torpedoed by enemy planes and left dead in the water....The *Wichita*, another heavy cruiser, maneuvered alongside in the darkness and took the *Canberra* in tow. The enemy attacks continued and at 2100 the heavy cruiser *Houston* was also torpedoed."

"Japanese torpedo planes and bombers," Sherman went on, "continued to attack our ships during the next two days with many of them being shot down. The *Houston* was hit by another torpedo but remained afloat. But, from the air, the attacking planes had clearly seen the great number of American carriers and surface ships. Their fleet, which had emerged from Japan's Inland Sea, thought better of its mission and discreetly returned to safer waters."

On 12 October the Japanese flew 101 sorties against the American task force, and first reports to their headquarters indicated notable results. As a result, the Japanese ordered the entire operational air strength of their Carrier Air Divisions Three and Four to attack. Thus, according to Harvard historian Dr. James Fields, 13 October saw 32 sorties, the 14th had 419, then 199 on the 15th, and 62 on the 16th. Astounding reports of success, from many aviators, came back to the Japanese admirals.

However, wrote Rear Admiral Sherman, the Americans saw it differently. "In the four to five days of the Formosa Air Battle, we destroyed over 680 Japanese planes, sunk 140 vessels, and damaged 248 others. Our losses were 95 planes and two cruisers damaged. Significantly, many of *our* downed flyers had been recovered."

"But Japan's terrible plane and pilot losses, and huge consumption of scarce aviation gasoline, were to play an important part in Japan's inability to repel our landings at Leyte—which occurred a few days later—and in the forthcoming great naval Battle for Leyte Gulf."

Admiral Sherman wrote that "About 1700 on 14 October, my task group—TG 38.3—had recovered its planes and we were heading eastward to refuel. Suddenly the radar picked up a large group of approaching bogeys and the CAP was vectored out to engage them. Although many of the attacking planes were shot down, our visual lookouts sighted 12 to 15 hostile aircraft closing our formation at high speed, and at such low altitude that they had successfully avoided radar detection. Amidst the furious barking of our AAA guns they made runs upon our carriers and heavy ships. Making radical evasive turns, and with the sky black with flak, the ships narrowly avoided several torpedo hits. In this *melee*, most of the enemy planes were destroyed by ships' gunfire and by our CAP."

The Japanese, or at least Japanese propaganda, took a different view. "The extravagant claims," wrote naval historian Rear Adm. Samuel Eliot Morison, "broadcast by the Japanese through every known means of radio communication, and of which the *only* grain of truth was the torpedoing of the *Houston* and *Canberra*, reached American crews through the popular 'Tokyo Rose' transmissions." Admiral Halsey's subsequent message to Admiral Nimitz at Pearl Harbor, addressing the Japanese claim that the American forces had been practically annihilated and the surviving ships had retired in disarray, signaled his boss that his sunken and damaged ships "had been salvaged and are retiring at high speed toward the enemy."

Fighter pilot Davis listened to one of Tokyo Rose's broadcasts. The melodious Japanese voice—in perfect English—came in loud and clear.

"You sorrowful Americans on your sinking ships," she began, "you should have stayed cozy and warm at home, taking your Sunday drives in your oversized automobiles. But no, you had to make war on us, and now your precious Third Fleet has been sunk." Davis looked at his friend Skip Hensen. "What's she talking about?" Hensen was a Japanese linguist—he'd been raised by American missionaries in the Orient—and was a radio intelligence officer on the admiral's staff.

"She's putting out the story that their planes have sunk our entire fleet."

"Two minor hits on cruisers?" asked Davis.

"Not only that, but we've been intercepting 'official' reports all day from their headquarters. They think they've done major damage."

"Skip, do you think their pilots got confused, or outright lied about their hits?"

"Well, pilots do *sometimes* exaggerate," replied Hensen.

Davis, in mock horror, replied, "Oh, Skip, pilots *never* do anything like that!"

Tokyo Rose went on to list the ships the Japanese claimed to have sunk, including the *Lexington*. Davis wondered if their high command actually believed any of it. He was sent up the next day on a CAP to cover the damaged cruisers, but saw no Japanese planes.

"Tokyo Rose," wrote Cmdr. Hugh Winters, "actually did a great deal for us on the *Lexington*—believe it or not. Her titillating news comments, beamed to our radio frequencies, gave us in particular a tremendous boost in spirits and morale. For example, she would interrupt a new Tommy Dorsey swing tune with a news flash. In a throaty, sexy voice, she would announce in very *English* English, '... and a hero's welcome to all you gallant men of the *Blue Ghost* [her nickname for the *Lexington*] as you enter Paradise. Aircraft of the Imperial Air Fleet have just torpedoed and sunk Admiral Mitscher's flagship with all on board.' Our intrepid and gallant *Lexington* crewmen got a real bang out of that one—they had heard it before on several occasions, in fact after each big fight the ship got into! This was the *fourth* time Rose had reported us as 'sunk.' We all liked her, and when some do-gooder upstarts wanted to get her hanged after the war for war crimes, most of us who were out there thought they were crazy."

Admiral Toyoda, in Tokyo, apparently took all these positive reports at face value. Beyond the Tokyo Rose broadcasts, wrote Professor Potter, "Radio Tokyo announced to the world that the American carrier fleet had been just about wiped out and that

Japanese ships and aircraft were *enroute* to annihilate the remnant, which was in disorderly flight." It was this that caused Halsey to message Nimitz that his sunken and damaged ships "had been salvaged and are retiring at high speed toward the enemy."

Regarding this "Formosa Air Battle" reporting, one Japanese officer, at least, had little confidence in these reports. Vice Adm. Takeo Kurita, commanding the Japanese Second Fleet, looked at the claims made by pilots which indicated that "a dozen or more enemy carriers and many others of his ships have been sunk or damaged." According to Dr. Fields, Admiral Kurita "followed his usual custom and added up the reports and divided by two, thus obtaining a figure which, for lack of anything better, he somewhat skeptically accepted. It was still, of course, grossly exaggerated."

Interestingly, the men in Carrier Air Group Nineteen on board the *Lexington* apparently weren't heavily involved, nor even—at the time—very knowledgeable, regarding this significant "Formosa Air Battle."

Ens. Warner Tyler gives no hint of anything amazing in his flight log; Cmdr. Hugh Winters and Lt.j.g. Bill Davis likewise in their autobiographies; there's nothing particularly exciting in the Torpedo-19 history. The only hint, among the many contributors to Bombing-19's history compiled in the 1980s, is Lt.j.g. George Peck. He wrote about the night of 13 October, "GQ all night. More bogies tonight. The cruiser *Canberra* hit." Concerning 14 October he wrote "Bogies all night. The *Dōmei* News Agency [the official news agency of the Japanese Empire] reports three American carriers sunk."

In many ways it seemed to be business as usual, although business as usual for Air Group Nineteen was often plenty busy. "On 12 October 1944," reads the Torpedo-19 history, "the bleak Formosan mountain ranges were seen to rise above the now-familiar cold front that paralleled the entire Formosan coast—beginning low over the water and extending up to 2,000 feet. After sweating it out on instruments, our torpedo planes broke out of the weather and lashed out against the largest merchant ships we had attacked to date—two large ships, both over 7,500 tons—which were anchored in Mako-Ko Harbor in the Pescadores Islands."

"Our *first* actual *torpedo attack*—since coming on board the *Lexington*—was led by Lieutenant Commander Perry, flying *Mohawk-90*. This nine-plane formation operated from 0630 to 1100. Lt.j.g. Robert Durian (flying *Mohawk-98*), Lt.j.g. Ray Stacy (in *Mohawk-89*), and Lt. Morris Goebel (in *Mohawk-85*) scored hits on one of the large ships, sinking it instantly. Lt. Len Mathias (in *Mohawk-94*) and Lt. Gordon Whelpley (in *Mohawk-81*) appeared to have hit the other large ship with their torpedoes, putting its decks awash. It streamed oil over a large area of Mako-Ko before it sank."

"All the pilots who got hits had used new high-speed ranges and speeds, and were 'tickled pink' to see the new *Torpex* torpedoes run in this, our first success with torpedoes since we came aboard the *Lexington*." *Torpex* was 50% more powerful than TNT.

On following strikes shipping was hit at Boko-Ko in the Pescadores Islands.

For Ensign Tyler there were no torpedoes in his airplane on this day. Led by Lt. Len Prater in *Mohawk-96*, Mr. Tyler flew with eight other torpedo bombers on a second strike against Formosa, 0815-1230, once again dropping high-explosive bombs. Tyler's crewmen, on board *Mohawk-97*, were AOM[2] Dewees and ARM[3] Davis.

"Then," wrote Mr. Perry in the squadron history, "on the third strike from 1215 to 1615, Lt. Fred Doll, flying *Mohawk-82*, led his division of eight torpedo bombers up the west coast of Formosa to hit Taichū Airfield. They started fires and considerable damage was done to aircraft and aircraft installations." Shortly after takeoff, Lt.j.g. Joe Hebert, in *Mohawk-83*, had to turn back due to a significant engine oil leak. VT-19's last strike of the day flew from 1400 to 1730; it was just two planes, under Lt.j.g. Jim Langrall in *Mohawk-96*.

Lieutenant Commander Perry's plane—*Mohawk-88*—was downed with engine problems.

Bombing-19's Petty Officer Eno Leaf said that "on a strike against Formosa, 12 October, we made a dive on an airfield. As we pulled out a Japanese *Tony* fighter (a Kawasaki Ki-61 *Hien*) got on our tail. I gave him a few bursts with my two 7.6mm Browning machine guns, and he pulled away as then some of *our* fighter pilots had spotted him. All that while my pilot, Lt.j.g. Wally Griffin, was hollering at me about the 'S.O.B. *Tony*,' but when you have your hands on the guns you can't use the mike. Next time we will have throat mikes so I can keep the pilot informed."

According to the Fighting-19 battle report, "The sweep on 12 October, launched at 0530, found rough going over the largest target the fighter squadron had yet attacked. Outnumbered at times as much as six to one, our pilots considered themselves fortunate in emerging with 27 enemy planes shot down. The action, which was centered somewhere between Kagi and Taichu on Formosa, found six of our planes attacked—for several long minutes—by an enemy fighter force of over 30 planes. The dogfight was fierce in all respects and scarcely a plane engaged emerged from it without bullet penetrations." Lt. Barney Garbow's plane returned with 48 holes in its fuselage, all aft of the cockpit. Commander Winters' plane had acquired 47 holes and was deemed unsalvageable, so after removing some key components it was pushed overboard. However, by early afternoon Winters' "plane captain," Petty Officer John Uhoch, had another *Mohawk-99* ready for him, complete with the name *Hangar Lily* and a little French lily painted on the side. (Unlike the majority of the pilots, the same plane, 99, was always ready and reserved for Winters as air group commander, and he had named her "Hangar Lily." An F6F *Hellcat* fighter, she had been modified with special radio, photo, and other equipment).

"Lt. Joe Paskoski," the report continues, "took top honors by destroying four planes, while Lieutenants Bill Masoner, Barney Garbow, and Ens. Paul O'Mara each shot down three." Paskoski was forced to land in the water as he approached the task group. "Strikes during the remainder of the day garnered a few planes, but at no time were the *Zero* attacks persistent or hard-pressed. Air fields and shipping near the Pescadores Islands were our chief targets."

Fighting Nineteen lost their new squadron commander that day. He was Lt. Cmdr. Franklin "Toby" Cook, who only a few weeks before had replaced Hugh Winters when Winters was promoted to be the new air group commander. Cook and most of the squadron dove to strafe the large airfield at Taipei. For some reason he did not pull out of his dive and flew straight into the ground. No one was able to determine what had gone wrong; in fact, there had been very light AAA during their attack.

Unfortunately, Fighting Nineteen also lost their operations officer, Lt. Donald K. "Doc" Tripp. He was last seen chasing two *Tony* fighters alone.

On 13 October, according to the Torpedo-19 history, "one of our 'arson squads' loaded up incendiaries—rather than high explosives—and took to the air to burn Ansan Naval Base in the Pescadores. Once again the weather was overcast, extending over the target and its base at a thousand feet. Making individual passes in the face of intense AAA fire, the strike sowed its incendiaries—but with little success. We then sent our aircraft into central-western Formosa to destroy an alcohol plant and a sugar-refining plant. After strikes against the power plants and dams at Lake Jitsugetsutan (Lake of the Sun and Moon), we departed from Formosa."

"During these two days," it says in the battle report, "our fighters strafed many enemy ships of varying sizes in the Pescadores and near Okinawa. Much effort was expended by air photographic pilots in obtaining coverage of Lake Jitsugetsutan, generally believed to be the center of power at Formosa. Commander Winters and Lieutenant Beauchamp made many strafing runs which allowed them to point out the vital areas of the sprawling target to the dive-bombers and torpedo-bombers. This all was accomplished through intense AAA fire and very poor cloud visibility."

Three Torpedo-19 strikes flew on the 13th, totaling 25 aircraft but with three "downed" for engine, hydraulics, and wing-folding problems. Warner Tyler was in the first strike, 0820-1200, comprised of eight aircraft under the command of Lt. Len Prater flying *Mohawk-92*. Tyler flew in *Mohawk-83*, with AOM^2 Dewees and ARM^3 Davis, dropping high-explosive bombs.

There were several priority targets on the 13th including a large hydro-electric plant in the mountains of eastern Formosa. Bombing Nineteen was assigned to strike this plant, so the third strike of the day consisted of six dive-bombers and twelve fighters.

Lt.j.g. Bill Davis was, of course, in that fighter division. "The flight into Formosa was uneventful. The weather was clear and it gave me a chance to study the eastern coastline of the island. There were sheer cliffs that appeared to rise out of the ocean to a height of over ten thousand feet. Numerous waterfalls tumbled over these cliffs to the sea below."

"We continued into the mountains," Davis added, "and easily found the power plant. The dive-bombers went into their dives and every plane scored a hit. The place was demolished. The bombers rendezvoused with no signs of enemy fighters."

Lt.j.g. Alvin Emig, of Bombing-19, recalled that the Japanese were the least of his problems that day. His assigned target was, of course, that power plant. "I was next to last in the dive. Everything was normal until just a few seconds prior to my intended release altitude when a moving object caught my attention. I looked up and there was a free-falling bomb right on top of me and on the same flight path. It was so close that I felt I could reach out and touch it. The bomb was overtaking me, so I decided my only alternative was to maintain my dive and release my bomb after the free-falling bomb had passed me up. Then, I proceeded to the rendezvous point and, as I neared my section leader, a plane appeared from underneath the left side of my bomber. I could see it edging up toward me over the leading edge of my wing and fuselage. In fact, it appeared that its propeller was just about to strike the bottom of my fuselage! I instinctively and abruptly pulled back on the control stick, and as I did I could feel the other plane strike my tail-wheel assembly. When I felt I was clear, I banked to see what was happening to the other plane. The pilot evidently had taken evasive action as he was flying off in a different direction. So, not only was the pilot of that plane unsuccessful in hitting me with his bomb, but he also failed in getting me with a mid-air collision. I joined my section leader and returned to the carrier. The other plane arrived later and was able to land aboard—with its vertical stabilizer damaged and about one-half of its rudder missing."

After the last strike—1345-1745—and upon Air Group Nineteen's retirement from the area, "the Japanese sent out some torpedo planes to follow us." Torpedo-19's history reports that, "In this daring raid they re-proved to us the importance of tactics. At dusk twelve *Jills*—Nakajima B6N 'Tenzan' torpedo bombers—tried to hit our task group, flying low, 25-feet above the water. But they were unlucky or stupid enough to fly up-wind and parallel with our course: gunfire from the ships knocked down all but two of these raiders and, fortunately, none of our ships were hit."

Mr. Davis added that "With our planes in the air showing up on the fleet's radar screens, the low-flying Japanese were invisible. We landed right at dusk, and the CAP followed us in. There was nothing on radar. After quick debriefings we took off our flight gear and headed to the wardroom for dinner. But just then all hell broke loose! Every AAA gun in the fleet had opened fire. Looking out from the hangar deck I saw Japanese planes everywhere." In his diary Davis recalled that these aircraft were *Bettys*—the Mitsubishi G4M "Hamaki" twin-engine land-based medium bomber/torpedo bomber—rather than *Jill* torpedo bombers.

"Twelve of them," continued Mr. Davis, "were flying between our ships making torpedo runs. We had no fighters up, but our AAA blackened the sky. I previously had no conception of the incredible noise this would create."

"One *Betty* took a direct hit only a hundred yards from the *Lexington* and blew up—then a second, and a third. The hits seemed to rattle the other pilots, as their runs now became erratic. They had had a perfect setup: the fleet was steaming in a straight line and we were caught completely by surprise. The Japanese should have gotten twelve hits, which might have crippled the fleet. Instead they made wild runs and lost their advantage. They flew blindly between our ships and risked midair collisions, forcing them to abort their runs. Meantime, our AAA kept knocking them down. The surviving planes dropped their torpedoes and got out of there. Amazingly, they failed to get a single hit."

"The air had been filled with incredible violence only moments before, but now I was just standing there, admiring a beautiful sunset."

"Then one of my squadron mates walked up and said, 'Ready for dinner?' 'Sure,' I answered. Moments ago we might well have been sunk or abandoning a wrecked ship. Instead, we were going to dinner where it would be served on white linen tablecloths by crisply attired stewards. What an incredibly strange way to fight a war."

"The next day" wrote Commander Winters, "our fighters and bombers flew over Formosa. Then, later, Toyohara Field in Okinawa bore the brunt of our attacks which saw 32 enemy planes destroyed or heavily damaged on the ground."

Meanwhile, "a sixteen-plane CAP was put over the task group. Bogeys were continually on the screen, and the CAP had a busy time from 1600 until dusk as the enemy made his first concentrated attack on our force in these waters. Ens. Bill Garlic got three low-flying torpedo-bombers—*Jills*—and Lt.j.g. Luther Prater shot down two fighters."

Lt.j.g. Bill Davis was in the CAP and suddenly heard fighter pilot Lt.j.g. Bob Blakeslee come up on the radio. Blakeslee was on a low-level sweep fifty miles out in front of the task group. He said he had "six and more enemy planes approaching at 25 feet; twin-engine *Betties*. Splash One!" Davis and the CAP flew out at full power to help. "Splash Two," they heard, then "Splash Three and Four." But when Davis got to the area there was wreckage in the water but nothing in the air. "Such Japanese bombers had a twin 20-mm turret on top of the fuselage, and we could only assume that they had shot Bob down as he got the last of them." "Bob," added Commander Winters, "radioed us that 'I am going to make a water landing,' but despite a thorough search, he is still listed as Missing in Action."

From 12 to 14 October, Carrier Air Group Nineteen had flown 49 sorties, the majority against Formosa.

On October 18th a major Denver newspaper, *The Rocky Mountain News*, published a short article in its *Colorado Men in the War* series. Written by Frank Ricketson, it was entitled *Denver Flier 'Left His Card' on Japan's Ryukyu Islands*, and described action from a few weeks earlier.

> "Surprise paid off for the bold airmen of the Third Fleet, including Ensign Warner W. Tyler of 1345 Madison Street, Denver, when they sank 77 ships and sank or damaged more than 50 small craft in an attack against Japan's Ryukyu Islands, southwest of the Japanese homeland."

"Ensign Tyler's ship sailed a stormy coast on the fringe of a typhoon to reach a position for the strike. Sometimes the waves reached the height of the flight deck of his carrier. As the seas calmed, Ensign Tyler and his squadron mates set off in torpedo planes for the island of Okinawa."

"'As we approached the target I saw an oil tanker burning, together with wreckage and men in the area where a cargo ship was sunk,' Tyler told an Associated Press correspondent. 'As we reached the strait between Okinawa and a nearby small island called Sesoko Shima, the anti-aircraft fire was very thick. It was coming from both sides of the strait. We went down and left our 'calling cards' and headed for home.'"

Chapter 10

From 15 to 19 October, Task Group 38.3 ceased combat operations and moved away from the Formosa area.

On 15 October Warner Tyler flew, with a catapult shot, on "ferrying duty." It's unclear what he was ferrying, but after a flight of 1.5 hours he returned to the *Lexington* for a night landing. His crewmen were AOM[2] Dewees and ARM[3] Davis, in *Mohawk-82.* Later that same day another four of VT-19's torpedo planes went out on an anti-submarine patrol.

Lt.j.g. George Peck, of Bombing-19, wrote that on 15 October, "I attended a sea-burial service for two sailors who drank some aviation water-injection 'alcohol.' They died last night." Petty Officer Minor H. Nickens added that he remembered "a young crewman, I think named Hank, on the *Lexington* who was a mess steward. He was a happy-go-lucky person and was well liked by everybody. Some of the petty officers going on beach liberty at Ulithi would smuggle back on board a bottle of beer strapped to their leg for Hank. Unfortunately, his taste for alcohol was not restricted to beer. He began stealing and drinking 'torpedo juice,' which was powerful stuff, but not deadly." Torpedo juice was typically pineapple juice mixed with some 180-proof grain-alcohol fuel, which was used in torpedo motors. "But, not being satisfied with this, he and another steward drank some water-injection fluid, which was both powerful *and* deadly. Before they died, they became stark-raving mad. An autopsy on their brains revealed that they had been eaten up by this water-injection fluid—which contained considerable antifreeze. Needless to say, this resulted in a bunch of other men reconsidering their drinking habits."

Chief Radarman Bob Whitham wrote that he heard 20 men drank some of this water-injection fluid, with three dying and one permanently blinded.

The Air Group Commander, Hugh Winters, clearly remembered this tragedy 41 years later. He recalled the mess stewards' names as Tom and Leroy, rather than Hank. "They tended to our feeding like they were our mothers. They died under the wing of *Mohawk-99*, my personal airplane, in its corner on the hangar deck."

"How could I," continued Winters, "even in my exalted new rank of commander, have become so insulated from these two fine enlisted men as to fail to be aware of their well-deserved needs—not to get totally drunk or anything, but just to have a good drink with somebody? If nothing else, any of us officers would have gladly shared our liquor ration. I don't remember my exact prayer that night, but it no doubt was another complaint to the Lord about me not having been granted sufficient sensitivity or sufficient wisdom. Prayers aren't supposed to be complaints but it was, none the less, a prayer of sorts." There is a photo of Leroy in Winters' autobiography.

On 18 October it was Warner Tyler's turn for an anti-submarine patrol, flying for three hours from 1500-1800. Onboard *Mohawk-86*, his crewmen were again AOM[2] Dewees and ARM[3] Davis. Other pilots involved in this patrol were Lt. Joe Black in *Mohawk-91*, Lt. Max Gregg in *Mohawk-89*, and Ens. Mercer Jackson in *Mohawk-96*. Mr. Gregg was forced to make a barrier landing when they returned to the ship.

"The afternoon of the 18th," noted Chief Robert Whitham in his diary, "a plane captain on the flight deck was hit by a spinning propeller. The blade severed his right arm just below the elbow. Stunned, the man fell to the deck in a dazed condition only to raise himself to be hit a second time. This second blow tore a large section of his skull, and tore clean through the right shoulder down to his breast. He was immediately rushed to the surgery where he was worked on for eight hours." Incredibly, Whitham further noted that "He will pull through okay, but it will take time."

October 19th saw VT-19 produce another ASP. This involved four aircraft which flew 1200-1500. Similarly, on 20 October, the torpedo squadron flew two 4-plane ASPs, one from 0555-0905 and the second 1515-1830.

Historian Samuel Morison wrote that "Instead of making the scheduled strikes on Luzon and the Visayas on 18-19 October, in the hope of tempting the Japanese to tangle with what had been designated as 'BaitDiv1,' Admiral Halsey held the bulk of the fast carrier forces northeast of Luzon through the 19th." Halsey thought that there was a possibility that the Japanese might sortie a surface force to finish off the two wounded cruisers, which became known as 'CripDiv1' (Cripple Division 1) and 'BaitDiv1' (Bait Division 1). If that should happen then the enemy could be ambushed by American forces. As it turned out, however, the Japanese did not take this bait. "Thus, for three days, October 18-20, the main responsibility for neutralizing enemy airfields in the Visayas and Mindanao fell upon several smaller escort carriers."

The American fast carrier groups, after retiring from the Formosa area, resumed the assault on Luzon. Dr. James Fields wrote that the "Japanese now believed that the Americans were moving slowly southward to the east of the Philippines."

At this time, Fields continued, "all Japanese forces involved in their desperate enterprise" to thwart the perceived American invasion of the Philippines "were underway, and from the far corners of their shrinking empire the entire remaining combatant strength of the Imperial Japanese Navy converged on Leyte Gulf." The Japanese felt that "the fate of the Empire was in the balance; everything they had was being thrown onto the scales."

The Torpedo-19 history summed up this period, regarding themselves and the *Lexington*, like this: "We ultimately had one of those big *rest* periods at Ulithi. We *rested* riding out a typhoon with the ship bobbing like a cork and the waves pouring over the hangar deck. Then, when it subsided, we made a dash into the lagoon to load—for 48 hours straight—ammunition and supplies."

"*Well rested*," continued the VT-19 history with more sarcasm than one might expect in an official document, "we again headed out to the Philippines" on 21 October. The strikes were going to be against Coron and Luzon Islands.

Ens. Warner Tyler flew against airfields in southeastern Luzon, dropping high explosive bombs. Flying in *Mohawk-94*, his crewmen were AOM^2 Dewees and ARM^3 Davis. Led by Lieutenant Commander Perry in *Mohawk-91*, this 15-plane strike flew from 0930-1200. Lt. Joe Black in *Mohawk-97* had to return to the ship with a major oil leak, and Ens. Mercer Jackson, in *Mohawk-92*, had to return with an engine malfunction.

Lieutenant j.g. Bill Davis wrote that "once again we hit the airfields of southern Luzon. There was no air opposition, but the AAA was heavier than ever." The targets were mostly parked aircraft and then sampans on nearby docks.

At that point, according to the Torpedo-19 history, "we just sat around, flew more ASPs, and perked up our ears regarding rumors about the Japanese Fleet."

Torpedo-19 flew another ASP on 22 October, 1215-1500. This four-plane patrol was led by Lt.j.g. John Middleton in *Mohawk-81*.

That ASP was followed by one more on 23 October, launching at 0900 and returning at 1210. This four-plane patrol was led by Lt. Fred Doll in *Mohawk-93*.

"At noon on 23 October," wrote Samuel Eliot Morison, "Rear Admiral Bogan's Task Group 38.2, Rear Admiral Sherman's Group 38.3, and Rear Admiral Davison's Group 38.4 were operating about 260 miles northwest of Samar. With Admiral Halsey's permission, Vice Adm. John 'Slew' McCain's Task Group 38.1 was on its way toward Ulithi to replenish. During the night of 23-24 October all groups but McCain's were pulled in toward the coast in order to launch dawn searches. Sherman took position east of the Polillo Islands to cover the west coast of Luzon. Bogan moved in close to San Bernardino Strait. Davison operated to the southward near Leyte Gulf."

"Tuesday, the 24th," continued Rear Admiral Morison, "dawned fair and favorable for strikes and searches. At break of day the three fast-carrier groups launched search teams of *Hellcats* and *Helldivers* to comb the west coast of Luzon and the Sibuyan, Sulu, and Mindanao Seas for Japanese ships. Admiral Kurita's flagship, the huge battleship *Yamato*, sighted a plane from the USS *Intrepid* at 0812." Of course, the *Intrepid*'s aircraft in turn sighted the *Yamato*, and "the aircraft contact report reached Admiral Halsey ten minutes later."

"At 0827 on October 24th, Halsey acted. He sent orders directly to the task group commanders, bypassing Vice Admiral Mitscher who, throughout 24 October, was little more than a passenger in his own Task Force. By noon, on October 24th, three fast-carrier groups were deployed on a broad front: Sherman (Group 38.3) to the northward, Bogan (Group 38.2) off San Bernardino Strait, and Davison (Group 38.4) about 60 miles off southern Samar."

"The stage was set for a great air-surface engagement: the Battle of the Sibuyan Sea, first of the four major engagements that would constitute the Battle for Leyte Gulf."

Chapter 11

October 24, 1944 brought forth what later would be called the "Battle of the Sibuyan Sea"—as mentioned earlier a subset of the huge "Battle for Leyte Gulf." For the most part the Sibuyan Sea action was against the Japanese Second Fleet (the Center Force) under Vice Adm. Takeo Kurita. That said, the combat actions of Halsey's Third Fleet on that day were widespread, complex, confusing, and overlapping to the extreme.

At this point, and for several weeks earlier, American intentions and options had been relatively apparent to the Imperial Japanese Navy. Working at his headquarters in Tokyo, the chief of the Combined Fleet, Adm. Soemu Toyoda, had prepared four "victory" plans. *Shō-Gō* 1 would be a major naval operation in the Philippines. *Shō-Gō* 2, *Shō-Gō* 3, and *Shō-Gō* 4 would be responses to any attacks on Formosa, the Ryukyu Islands, and the Kurile Islands, respectively. The plans were for complex offensive operations committing nearly all available forces to a decisive battle, despite the fact that they would substantially deplete Japan's slender reserves of fuel oil. As Admiral Toyoda stated after the war:

> If the worst should happen there was a chance that we would lose the entire fleet; but I felt that the chance had to

> be taken .... Should we lose in the Philippines operations, even though the fleet should be left, the shipping lane to the south would be completely cut off so that the fleet, if it should come back to Japanese waters, could not obtain [a] fuel supply. If [the fleet] should remain in southern waters, it could not receive supplies of ammunition and arms. [Thus] there would be no sense in saving the fleet at the expense of the loss of the Philippines.

Following the American invasion of the Philippines at Leyte Island (which actually had begun on 20 October with four divisions of the U.S. Sixth Army) the Japanese brought into play *Shō-Gō* 1. This plan called for Vice Adm. Jisaburō Ozawa's ships—known as the "Northern Force"—to lure the main American covering forces away from Leyte. The Northern Force would be built around several aircraft carriers, but these would basically have very few aircraft or trained aircrew. These carriers would serve as a decoy or as "bait" for the Americans. As the U.S. covering forces were lured away, two other surface forces would advance on Leyte from the west. The "Southern Force" under Vice Admirals Shōji Nishimura and Kiyohide Shima would strike at the landing area via the Surigao Strait. The "Center Force" under Vice Admiral Kurita—the most powerful of the attacking forces—would pass through the San Bernardino Strait into the Philippine Sea, turn southwards, and then also attack the landing area.

"In ordering *Shō-Gō* 1," wrote Prof. E. B. Potter, "Admiral Toyoda put into motion forces that triggered the enormous naval Battle for Leyte Gulf, actually four separate engagements that involved more tonnage and covered a greater area than any other naval battle in history. The forces involved did much radio reporting and communicating; thus, directly or by relay, most of the radio communications were heard—virtually in *real time*—in Leyte Gulf, Pearl Harbor, Washington D.C., and Tokyo."

"The dramatic moment had now arrived for the Japanese to commit their entire fleet to the defense of the Philippines," wrote Rear Adm. Ted Sherman, who of course was the commander of Task Group 38.3 flying his flag in the large carrier *Essex*. As mentioned earlier, TG 38.3 included the carriers *Essex*, *Lexington*, *Princeton*, and *Langley*. "Although not fully ready, the Japanese navy *had* to be committed to action now if it were to be used at all. Its entrance precipitated one of the greatest naval engagements of all time."

"This last great naval battle of the Pacific war," continued Sherman, "was fought on October 24 and 25, 1944, and was originally called—by its participants—the *Second Battle of the Philippine Sea*. Later, Adm. Chester Nimitz (Commander in Chief, Pacific Ocean Areas) designated it as the *Battle for Leyte Gulf* and directed the use of this name in all official correspondence."

"In my view, the change was unfortunate," Sherman wrote. "The original name much better describes the battle and more fully indicates its broad consequences. The battle area extended 600 miles from north to south and several hundred miles from east to west. The principal actions took place in the Philippine Sea, *far* outside Leyte Gulf. They virtually eliminated the Imperial Japanese Navy as a factor in the war. This result," continued Admiral Sherman, "was more important than the immediate effect on the ground fighting around Leyte Gulf or elsewhere in the Philippines, since it opened the door for a possible invasion of Japan itself."

On 22 October, Admiral Halsey had detached two of his carrier groups to the fleet base at Ulithi to provision and rearm. But at 0116 on 23 October, the surfaced submarine USS *Darter* detected by radar Vice Adm. Kurita's formation on the move. The *Darter* made three enemy contact reports. After sending the reports, the *Darter* and another submarine, the *Dace*, worked into position and attacked the enemy. As Professor Potter later wrote, "Torpedoes from the *Darter* sank one heavy cruiser and put one out of action. Those from the *Dace* sank another heavy cruiser. Thus was drawn the first blood in the great Battle for Leyte Gulf."

When he received the report Admiral Halsey recalled Rear Adm. Ralph Davison's group, but allowed Vice Adm. "Slew" McCain, with the strongest of Task Force 38's carrier groups, to continue towards Ulithi to provision and re-arm. Halsey finally recalled McCain on 24 October—but the delay meant the most powerful of the American carrier groups played little part in the coming battle. Thus, the U.S. Third Fleet was effectively deprived of nearly 40% of its air strength for most of the engagement. On the morning of 24 October only three groups were available to strike Kurita's force, and the one best positioned to do so—Rear Adm. Gerald Bogan's Task Group 38.2—was, as fate would have it, the weakest of the groups, containing only one large carrier, the *Intrepid*, and two light carriers.

Meanwhile, Vice Adm. Takijirō Ōnishi directed three waves of aircraft from the Japanese First Air Fleet, based on Luzon, against the carriers of Rear Admiral Sherman's TG 38.3 (whose aircraft, the reader already knows, were being used to strike airfields in Luzon to prevent Japanese land-based air attacks on Allied shipping in Leyte Gulf). Each of Ōnishi's strike waves consisted of 50 to 60 planes.

However, most of the attacking Japanese planes were intercepted, shot down, or driven off by the *Hellcat* fighters in Admiral Sherman's CAP—most notably one wave by two fighter sections from the *Essex* led by Cmdr. David McCampbell.

Commander McCampbell—the commander of Air Group-15 on board the *Essex*—became the only American airman to achieve "ace in a day" status twice. McCampbell and a division of seven *Hellcats* boldly attacked a Japanese force of 60 land-based aircraft which were approaching Task Group 38.3. McCampbell, one of the world's great aces and an incredible aerial marksman, personally shot down nine—seven *Zeros* and two *Oscars*—setting a U.S. single-mission aerial combat record. During this same action his wingman downed another six Japanese warplanes and his other pilots accounted for nine more. In so doing they disorganized the enemy group to the extent that the remainder abandoned the attack before a single enemy aircraft could reach the fleet. Admiral Sherman wrote that "The Japanese fighters seemed more concerned with defending themselves than with protecting the bombers and torpedo planes which they were supposed to guard." When McCampbell, *in extremis*, finally landed his *Hellcat* aboard the USS *Langley* (the flight deck of the *Essex* not being clear), his six machine guns had just two rounds remaining, and his airplane had to be manually released from the arrestor wire due to complete fuel exhaustion. Commander McCampbell received the Medal of Honor for this action as well as the "Marianas Turkey Shoot" back on 19 June (when he shot down seven aircraft in one day), becoming the only Fast Carrier Task Force pilot to be so honored.

Regarding McCampbell's incredible action of the 24th, "the enemy aircraft," wrote historian Thomas Cutler, "were approaching at about 18,000 feet, so the Americans began a rapid climb as they conformed to the intercept vector provided by the *Essex*'s fighter-direction officer (a young lieutenant by the name of John Connally, who would one day become Secretary of the Navy, Governor of Texas, and Secretary of the Treasury) in the *Essex*'s Combat Information Center." The reader will recall that, when serving as Texas governor, Mr. Connally would be wounded when President John F. Kennedy was assassinated, in Dallas, in November 1963.

On 24 October, mid-morning, Task Group 38.3 was found by enemy planes from Clark and Nichols Fields, precipitating a disaster. At 0938, the *Independence*-class light aircraft carrier *Princeton* was attacked by a lone Yokosuka D4Y Suisei dive bomber; for simplification, the Allies called the Suisei the *Judy*. Surprisingly, this single aircraft slipped through the American defenses and dropped a single 550-pound armor-piercing bomb which struck the carrier between the elevators, punching through the wooden flight deck and hangar before exploding. Although structural damage was minor, a severe fire broke out and quickly spread owing to burning gasoline, causing further explosions. Adding to the problem was the failure of the ship's emergency sprinkler system to operate properly.

Rear Adm. Ted Sherman wrote that "a USS *Langley* fighter shot down the *Judy* as it tried to get away. At first the hit caused me no great immediate concern as I felt that the *Princeton* was much too tough a ship for one hit to cause any very serious damage."

According to Lt.j.g. Jack Scott, in Bombing-19, "As our division was awaiting launch a single Japanese plane came out of the low ceiling overcast and hit the carrier *Princeton*, which was on our port quarter. The *Princeton* had just recovered a number of aircraft when it was hit."

"While the *Princeton* had been trying to extinguish her fires," wrote Admiral Sherman, "we maneuvered in her general vicinity to give her what protection we could."

The fire was gradually brought under control, but at 1523 there was an enormous explosion (the carrier's bomb stowage aft), causing more casualties aboard the *Princeton* and, incredibly, a huge number of casualties—233 dead and 426 wounded, including the captain—aboard the light cruiser *Birmingham* which was alongside to assist with the firefighting. The *Birmingham* was so badly damaged she was forced to retire. Another light cruiser and two destroyers were also damaged.

"The *Princeton* was now a blazing hulk," wrote Sherman, "that would handicap us in our prospective engagement the next morning with the enemy carriers to the north. Vice Admiral Mitscher directed me, after all personnel were removed, to have her sunk.

Much as I hated to give up this gallant ship, it was the wisest thing to do. She was sent to the bottom just after dark by torpedoes from the cruiser *Reno*."

Of the *Princeton*'s crew, 108 men were killed, while 1,361 survivors were rescued by nearby ships. (Of course, one of these survivors was the friend of Rear Adm. Bruce Black, torpedo-plane pilot "Doc" Manget, mentioned in Admiral Black's foreword to this book.) The *Princeton* was the largest American ship lost during the battles around Leyte Gulf.

Vice Admiral Ozawa's force ("the Main Body" or Northern Force) came into the area from the north, with the large aircraft carrier *Zuikaku* as his flagship. He had sortied on 20 October from the Inland Sea of Japan. His four carriers (*Zuikaku* and the light carriers *Zuihō*, *Chitose*, and *Chiyoda*) had only 116 aircraft on board—only half of their normal complement. The hybrid battleships *Hyūga* and *Ise* (sister ships modified with flight decks on their sterns) had no aircraft on board. The Japanese carriers had lost most of their planes in the first Battle of the Philippine Sea in June 1944 and, according to Professor E. B. Potter, "any Japanese fleet aviators who had attained proficiency after that time had been sacrificed in trying to protect the Formosan bases from American carrier attacks."

At this point in the war the *Zuikaku* (which in English means *Auspicious Crane*) was the last remaining carrier of the six which had attacked Pearl Harbor on 7 December 1941.

Chapter 12

"The day of 24 October began innocently enough," wrote Lt. Jack Wheeler, Fighting-19's combat-intelligence officer, "with a number of searches being scheduled, all of which were to the west and beyond the inner shore of Luzon. So began what would develop as Fighting-19's biggest combat day." In each of these searches, one fighter division accompanied four bombers.

"For me," wrote Cmdr. Hugh Winters, "the Second Battle of the Philippine Sea started early with a rare flap between the *Lexington*'s Air Officer, Cmdr. 'Andy' Ahroon, and me over the arming of the torpedo bombers and the dive bombers." As previously mentioned, Winters had been the commanding officer of Fighting Squadron-19 on board the *Lexington*, but "fleeted up" in September to take over command of the entire Carrier Air Group-19 upon the promotion and departure of Cmdr. Karl Jung. "I was feeling my oats in the new job. Also, I was learning that the more senior the job, the more peoples' interests you have to look out for—and sometimes fight for." As Winters described it, the flap was this:

"During the night of 23 October, the rumors of the main Japanese fleet coming to us began to change into specific contact reports from U.S. submarines, giving actual positions and courses—all now in our direction. Therefore, since the 0400 'Flight Quarters' early on the 24th we had been waiting for a mission on something big—hopefully enemy carriers. Well, their surface force kept coming on, so very early on the 24th Vice Admiral Mitscher ordered us on a strike against a battleship-cruiser force, far to our southwest. We were delighted, although the weather *enroute* and the weather-over-target was stinking and the distance was marginal for gasoline consumption."

"But the real trouble was that, for weeks, we had been dumping general-purpose high explosive (not armor-piercing) bombs on many different Japanese airfields and shooting up their planes. Well, our aircraft were still loaded that way that morning—for airfields, hangars, and buildings. But today, going against large ships, we wanted *torpedoes* in our *Avenger* torpedo planes—we (or at least I) amusingly called them 'torpeckers'—rather than H.E. bombs. And we wanted *armor-piercing* bombs in our dive-bombers, rather than H.E. With battleships and cruisers, unless you get a lucky hit, it takes torpedoes or armor-piercing bombs to properly sink such 'heavies'—that is, so you can actually watch them sink before you nearly run out of gas and have to leave the scene, bringing back only the usual vague report."

"In combat days," Winters went on, "tempers can be short, so this argument went up to the *Lexington*'s captain, Ernie Litch. He backed his air officer and made the 'difficult' decision to *not* open up the ship's magazines and change out the ordnance loads. He was concerned about the chance of a possible Japanese air attack at any time or a *Kamakazi* threat against the ship while doing so. To be fair, some enemy aircraft *had* already been seen. I could have gone to the admirals [Sherman or Mitscher], but time was running out and Andy knew it. Win a few; lose a few."

"So we took off before lunch, 'lightly' loaded, but in high spirits. I figured we could at least knock out lots of their ships' AAA on their topsides, and generally scare hell out of them. And, there was always the chance of laying an H.E. bomb down the smokestack of a 'heavy.'"

"That day was truly memorable," added fighter pilot Lt.j.g. Bill Davis. "Weather was building to the west, which was where we were going. Shortly after takeoff, we ran into a front that seemed to slope down to the sea. We couldn't get underneath it, so we had to climb through it. Flying formation in clouds isn't recommended for a long life. You could go one of two ways: the first was to fly very tight formation so that you could see your leader; one very competent person had to be on instruments or the whole flight would go in. The other choice was to spread out, but now you couldn't see any other plane, and *everyone* had to fly instruments, and there was certainly the chance of mid-air collisions. I elected to stay tight and was flying blind a few feet from the next plane."

"We continued to climb," Davis went on, "for what seemed an eternity and we were still in thick clouds. Suddenly, at 15,000 feet, we broke out right in the middle of a flight of Japanese planes rendezvousing for an attack on our fleet. In some cases our planes were within two feet of an enemy! I didn't have to aim; I just pressed the trigger and shot down a twin-engine bomber only 25 feet away. We were all so stunned that it took a few moments to comprehend the situation. There were bogeys everywhere. I shot down a number of aircraft but I had to break off before I could actually see them blow up. The sky was filled with columns of smoke as one Japanese plane after another bit the dust. Having cleared the air, we proceeded to Lingayen Gulf and bombed the shipping in the bay."

"The early searches," added Lt. Jack Wheeler, "took our fighter divisions over the area from Manila north to Lingayen Gulf. Lt. Bill Masoner brought back gun-camera film to substantiate his claim for six twin-engined enemy bombers. Our fighters, returning from their first scouting sojourn into the China Sea, intercepted a large group of enemy bombers presumably on their way to the Clark Field

Area. Lt. "Lin" Lindsay's division handled heavy fighter opposition over Clark Field by shooting down ten single-engined aircraft."

"Meanwhile," continued Mr. Wheeler, "at about 0800, the remaining fighters on board were scrambled and vectored west to intercept many bogeys approaching Task Group 38.3. Lt. Henry Bonzagni emerged top man from this scramble by leading his division into a fighter-protected formation of nine *Vals* (Aichi D3A Type-99 dive bombers)—personally shooting down three. Twelve single-engined planes were also shot down during the scramble."

"Then," Wheeler went on, "at 1050, under the leadership of Air Group-19's commanding officer, Cmdr. T. Hugh Winters as the 'target coordinator,' several squadrons from the *Lexington* and the *Essex* departed to attack heavy units of the Japanese fleet which were steaming east through the Sibuyan Sea. Despite terrible weather conditions, the American aircraft sighted the main force north of Sibuyan Island and inflicted some damage on the battleships and cruisers. In such a scenario the prime fighter-plane duty was low-level strafing to disrupt the heavy AAA fire and thus permit coordinated dive-bomber and torpedo-bomber attacks. Air opposition was practically absent, but two American planes were shot down by AAA during the strike."

"As mentioned earlier," wrote Commander Winters, "the *Lexington's* battle call was MOHAWK. So each of her planes had a numbered MOHAWK call, and mine was *Mohawk-99*, with '99' clearly painted on it for rendezvous and identification. "So, all I had that day were eight MOHAWK fighters with some small 500-pound bombs strapped on; five dive-bombers with those damn general-purpose H.E.—versus armor-piercing—bombs; and eleven torpeckers with H.E. bombs rather than torpedoes. A similar contingent joined us from the USS *Essex*, 'next door' from the *Lexington*, which actually made a very respectable strike force and was quite enough to try to keep together in the lousy weather we were heading for. Oh—the

Essex's dive bombers did have some AP bombs, and their torpedo planes were actually carrying a few torpedoes."

"About an hour out," Winters continued, "in between storms, Cmdr. Richard McGowan—who was skipper of Bombing-19 and one of my good friends from before the war—pulled up beside me and indicated engine trouble. He didn't break radio silence to talk; and as much as I hated to reduce our number of aircraft, I visually signaled him to go and take his wingman 'home' with him. The *Helldivers* only had one engine, so Dick's chances of getting home to the *Lexington* alone were not good. Well, I would never see him again. He actually did make it back to the ship, but he water-landed in the wake behind the ship and then, despite being a good swimmer, he sank with his plane. Fortunately his gunner, Eugene E. Brown, was able to be saved."

"Well," continued Commander Winters, "the weather got worse. We passed over where the submarines had reported the enemy ships to be but without 'making game.' The strike was holding together better than I had expected. I was really proud of the way the *Essex* fighters stuck with us, and I told their Air Group Commander, Dave McCampbell, about it later. Dive bombers and torpeckers would always stick tight for their very survival, but fighter pilots sometimes could be damned independent. There were so many excuses and diversions they could use. But they were really needed to keep close in these coordinated attacks in order to early saturate the AAA defenses—to keep the bombers and torpeckers from being slaughtered."

"We did a cross-leg at the end of our endurance range, came around a small thunderhead, and there was the Japanese battle fleet, or a big chunk of it—minus carriers. They were heading easterly under intermittent batches of high scud-cumulus stuff. The scud cloud was thin enough to see through and seemed to ceiling at about 7,000 feet, which couldn't have been better for us, and we used it. I radioed the *Essex* and *Lexington* torpedo and dive-bomber leaders to pick the 'heavies' on their side of the formation, and to go in through the thin cloud groups rather than around them."

"With only about 40 planes there were no waves or breaks with so many ships in formation. There were about eight 'heavy' ships. The fighters started their dives with the others, and their speed naturally put them out in front enough to be out of the way of the 'load carriers.' We got some pictures of the strike with small fires here and there, but no ship was blazing like it should—and as we so much wanted."

"We climbed back up through the clouds and headed for home, rejoining on the way. I went back down through the clouds for another look and to get specific information for a final report; this curiosity cost me a few holes in *Hangar Lily*, but nothing serious. One cruiser was stopped in a lake of oil, and the biggest battleship was slowing to about five knots (partly due to *Essex* AP bombs and torpedoes.) The whole force was reversing course to the westerly. It looked like nobody was sinking or significantly burning, but we certainly shook them up a bit."

"Flying west," added Fighting-19's Bill Davis, "we found the Japanese fleet headed through the Sibuyan Sea. There were no aircraft carriers but there were a number of battleships and cruisers, as well as escorting destroyers. The moment we came into view they started to turn and throw up intense AAA fire. We carried out a coordinated attack on the battleships and cruisers, and both Group-19 bomber squadrons scored a number of hits, but since the bombs were just general-purpose high-explosive, all they did was burn the paint off the ships."

At 0910 Task Group 38.2, under Rear Adm. Gerald Bogan, launched 21 fighters, 12 dive bombers, and 12 torpedo bombers from the carriers *Intrepid* (Air Group-18) and *Cabot* (Air Group-29). A second equally-sized strike launched at 1045 from the *Intrepid*, the

Lexington (Air Group-19), and the *Essex* (Air Group-15). Then a third strike launched at 1350—consisting of 16 fighters, 12 dive bombers, and 3 torpedo bombers. Finally, another strike flew out from Rear Adm. Ralph Davison's TG 38.4, with carriers *Franklin* (Air Group-13) and *Enterprise* (Air Group-20), contributing 26 *Hellcats*, 21 *Helldivers*, and 18 *Avengers*. All told, some 200 American aircraft attacked the targets.

"Hits were scored upon the battleships *Nagato*, *Yamato*, and *Musashi* as well as the heavy cruiser *Myōkō*," wrote Rear Admiral Morison. "As the *Musashi* tried to withdraw, listing to port, the third wave from the *Enterprise* and the *Franklin* hit her with an additional eleven bombs and eight torpedoes. After being struck with a total of at least 17 bombs and 19 torpedoes, the *Musashi* finally capsized and sank, later in the evening, about 1935 hours."

"Our remaining carriers sent off a strike against the Japanese Central Force in the Sibuyan Sea about 1100," added Rear Admiral Sherman. "The largest attack of the day in that area, it was executed by 32 torpedo planes, 16 fighters, and 20 dive bombers. They reached their targets at 1330 and through a hell of AAA fire they drove home their attack. The fliers estimated that they had scored three torpedo hits on one *Yamato*-class battleship [it was actually the *Musashi*, the *Yamato*'s sister], one or more bomb hits on another, four torpedo hits on a *Nagato*-class battleship [it was indeed the *Nagato*], and additional hits on five cruisers and several destroyers. The intensity of the flak prevented our pilots from determining the precise damage caused by these hits."

"While my Task Group was launching a second strike to the Sibuyan Sea," continued Sherman, "radar contact was made at 1245 with a new group of enemy planes bearing down on us from the northeast at 105 miles distance. This contact at last indicated the whereabouts of the enemy carriers whose location had been a matter of such concern. We had been preparing for a search to the north and northeast, but with a heavy attack coming in, we could not now spare the fighters required for that job. While the enemy planes were still some distance away we got off the strike to the westward, but we had to scramble all the remaining fighters to ward off this new threat."

Lt.j.g. Jack Scott, of Bombing-19, wrote that "of the 61 planes downed by Air Group-19 on 24 October, 20 were gotten by a search and scouting team of four dive-bomber and four fighter aircraft led by Lt. Bob Niemeyer."

"As Niemeyer's eight planes," added Commander Winters, "cruised at low altitude along the length of Luzon, enemy fighters scrambled in formidable numbers to challenge this arrogant incursion." There were several similar American searches in the air, but Niemeyer's attracted more attention than others.

"Over Lingayen Gulf," commented Mr. Niemeyer, "Japanese planes of every description were coming our way in droves. Those of us in the *bombers* saw this as the greatest opportunity we probably would ever have to shoot down some enemy planes. Thus, the eight of us shot down 20 planes—seven by us bombers—and in doing it we were going in every direction. After some time we got back together and finished the scouting mission. Of course, we found no Japanese ships; they weren't in our sector. I was very proud of what we'd done, but later the admiral saw it differently and chewed me out for dogfighting rather than staying focused on our vital scouting mission."

"The absence of carriers," wrote Professor Potter, "from the Southern and Central Forces created the suspicion that there must be another Japanese force somewhere in the vicinity. Admiral Halsey ordered a special search to be made to the north, and on the afternoon of the 24th Vice Admiral Ozawa's Northern Force was sighted, standing to the southward."

"In the north," continued Professor Potter, "Vice Admiral Ozawa was doing his best to decoy Admiral Halsey—breaking radio silence, making smoke. But Rear Admiral Sherman, in the closest American group, was for considerable time too busy launching and warding off air attacks and trying to save the USS *Princeton* to send scout planes northward. At last in the late afternoon he did so, and the scouts found the Japanese carrier force only 190 miles away."

"I was leading," wrote Commander Winters, "a strike of *Lexington* and *Essex* planes against the surface force of Vice Adm. Takeo Kurita in the Sibuyan Sea. At the same time, our bombers (without fighters because all available were needed for Combat Air Patrol) went out to search the northern approaches and find the Japanese carriers."

Bombing-19's Lt. Norman "Bud" Thurmon wrote that "during the early afternoon our Task Group had been under continual air attack by carrier-type planes. The admiral's staff was sure that the Japanese carrier fleet was fairly close and most probably north of us. My three-plane section was assigned to fly single-plane searches to the north. I took the sector 355° to 005°, I assigned Lt.j.g. Stuart Crapser to 005° to 015°, and Lt.j.g. Herbert Walters the sector 345° to 355°."

"We were on the deck lined up for takeoff when we were strafed by a single Japanese fighter. I thank God that the Japanese did not 'boresight' their guns to converge or I might not be writing this. I had the engine started for takeoff when the strafing plane hit, and I got a big hole in each wing straddling the cockpit. I came out of there head first, rolled to the deck, and hit the catwalk. So then my radioman-gunner and I took a spare plane and were last off on the assigned search."

"But the incident that next happened is the one I think about most and that is most interesting to me," continued Lieutenant Thurmon. "I was scheduled to go on a single-plane search due north.

I took off and confirmed that upon take-off I was headed due north. I settled back to endure the four-hour flight. But then I noticed that the sun was right in my eyes, and that gave me pause for thought. I was supposedly going *north* in the late afternoon—however the sun was directly ahead! I checked my 'standby' compass, and, sure enough, I was really going due *west*. I called Petty Officer Frank Stamm in the rear seat and told him we were off course and that I was going to take a heading that would intercept our intended track. So, I started a turn to the right when Stamm said 'Mr. Thurmon, look down there at 2 o'clock!' I looked and saw enough green dye to color the entire ocean, and at the head of the green streak was a yellow raft with two persons in it. So we flew back to the *Lexington* and dropped a note onto the deck (we were in 'radio silence'), telling them of the raft bearing 270^0 at 20 miles. The drop bag we used was like a heavy bean bag. So they dispatched a destroyer to the spot and it picked up Lt. Earl Newman and his gunner, P.O. Robert Stanley. They had been shot down when returning from a flight to try and hit battleships going down the 'gut' west of the Philippine Islands. I am convinced that the Lord had a lot to do with this; the instrument-panel compass stuck on due north was no accident." If that had not happened, *no one* would have overflown and spotted those two men, and they would never have been found."

"In my Navy combat flying," added that same Lieutenant Newman, "coming close to 100 flights, I only once drew a plane that couldn't stay in the air. Of all times it happened when we went to bomb big naval vessels. On returning to the fleet, getting shot down by a Japanese fighter just outside our Task Group was a real downer. But the best thing was being pulled out of the sea by a destroyer—both my gunner Bob Stanley and myself—with only minor injuries." We will have to take his word for the injuries being minor, but Mr. Newman carried some shrapnel in both feet for the rest of his days. "We were returned to the *Lexington* on 27 October."

"On the afternoon of 24 October," wrote VB-19's Lt.j.g. Stuart Crapser, "I was assigned to fly a sector search from the *Lexington* in a SB2C *Helldiver*. My assigned sector was slightly east of due north of the Task Group and the distance outbound was approximately 300 nautical miles. The aircraft was equipped with two wing tanks, and because it had been prepared for a bombing mission earlier, it had a 1,000-lb. armor-piercing bomb in the bomb bay. ARM[1] James Burns, my regularly assigned crewman, was aboard. We left the ship and the task group *without* fighter escort because none were available. The outbound and cross-legs of the flight were uneventful. They were flown in fine weather at an altitude of 1,500 to 2,000 feet. Twenty minutes into the return leg, Burns made a radar contact with ships bearing 45^0 from the plane at a distance of seven miles. Shortly thereafter I saw what appeared to be a large and a smaller escorting ship. I plotted the geographic position of the contact, saw more ships, and it appeared that there were aircraft carriers, at least one cruiser, and several destroyers in the group. I started to climb into a circle outside of anti-aircraft range, and composed a contact message."

"Petty Officer Burns copied the text of the message and sent it out three times over the Medium High Frequency radio and twice over the Very High Frequency. At this point I thought that it was too late in the day for Vice Admiral Mitscher to send out a strike and recover it before dark, so I figured that I should probably try and use my armor-piercing bomb to damage one of the carriers. I dropped my empty wing tanks and positioned the bomb/gun sight. Our climb was made to 14,000 feet during which time some AAA shells were sent in our direction. When this happened, Burns threw out some of the aluminum strips called 'window' which was supposed to confuse gunfire radar. I observed one carrier head into the wind and launch some aircraft and we subsequently saw them climb up. But by this time I was positioned for a dive 'out of the sun.' I pushed over at a 60° angle and dove without flaps. My helmet fell off in the dive because I hadn't fastened the chin strap, which meant I wasn't going to hear anything from my gunner. I 'pickled off' the bomb and then felt the aircraft knocked into a spin to the right. I contemplated bailing out but was able to stop the spin, pull out of the dive, and head for some clouds. The AAA was heavy and I saw tracers pass us from above. I reached the clouds, leveled off in them, and flew for some time southward in and out of them. I noted that the metal upper surface of the wings was wrinkled and both ailerons were pointing up. Burns was able to communicate with *me* by writing notes which he put in a message carrier on a clothesline reel-type unit. I could talk back to *him* by using the microphone on intercom. He reported our plane to be 'shot up,' that some *Zekes* [*Zeros*] had made runs on us, that he had a slight nick over one eye, that the enemy was two probable *Shōkaku*–class carriers, one light carrier, and one light cruiser in the group of ships which we had dove on, and that he had shot down one *Zeke*. We were not pursued (apparently) once we flew into the clouds. At about 35 miles from the Task Group, Burns picked up the *Lexington* and gave me direction to it. We approached from the stern and were given the 'Charlie,' by blinker, for immediate landing. I let down and did a dog leg to pick up the Landing Signal Officer. Despite poor aileron control we landed uneventfully, and I was ordered to report to the Flag Bridge as I stepped from the aircraft. Once the confirmation of the contact location and its composition was given to the admiral, I went to my squadron's ready-room where I learned from Squadron Maintenance that there was a large hole in the underside of the left wing of my airplane (from the anti-aircraft burst which had put us into the spin), and that *my bomb had never left the plane!* It was still in the bomb bay."

Petty Officer Burns added some details. "My pilot, Lieutenant j.g. Crapser, and I were ordered out on a search hop. But the

Lexington was attacked by Japanese aircraft as we manned our planes. Every gun on the ship was firing. I even opened up on them with my plane's rear-seat machine guns, as we sat on the flight deck, when they got too damn close. So when it was clear we took off, and searching our assigned area we discovered—nothing. On the return leg I picked up an indication on my radar screen and reported it to my pilot. We immediately changed course to investigate and through a hole in the clouds we discovered a medium-size Japanese carrier. A bit farther-on we found two larger carriers and quite a few cruisers and destroyers—my God was I scared! My pilot gave me the location and, breaking radio silence, I made a 'contact report' to the *Lexington.* I didn't hear any receipt for our message, so I repeated it over and over. We climbed like bats out of hell to gain altitude and my pilot said he saw some enemy fighters hiding in the clouds—now I felt twice as scared. The whole enemy task force opened up a full barrage of AAA and it appeared to be a sky of solid flak—a ghastly sight. We got into position and nosed over. We were hit by some AAA, jarring the whole plane and putting us into an uncontrollable spin. I was hit by some of the stuff above my right eye. We were out of control and I felt sure we were 'going in.' My pilot, by using all his strength, pulled the plane out in what felt like a ten 'G' pullout—though of course it couldn't have been that much. But it wrinkled the metal of the wings and tail and the ailerons were warped out of gear. The AAA was terrible and it's a miracle that we came out of that alive. Six *Zekes* jumped us when we cleared the formation and made individual runs on us. I called my pilot and yelled that there were fighters on our tail. As each plane came in I opened fire. I set one of them on fire but didn't see him crash—however I officially got credit anyway for downing a plane. My pilot had lost his helmet in that crazy dive and he didn't hear me telling him about the fighters—thank God. I can safely say that this was the most exciting experience I've ever had. Oh, on the actual strike they found four carriers—one was obscured by a cloud when we went over the group."

Petty Officer Raymond Schoener added that "On the return of Mr. Crapser and P.O. Jim Burns, after locating part of the Japanese fleet and making an amazing one-plane attack, Jim came into the ready-room. He was still pumped up and full of excitement after the experience. The first words I heard him say were, "The bastards almost killed us!" I think that's the only time I ever heard Jim use an 'off-color' word."

Lieutenant Thurmon, in VB-19, wrote that "Stu Crapser was the pilot who located Admiral Ozawa's carrier force, in a *single-plane unescorted* search with his gunner-radioman James Burns." Dive bomber Lt.j.g. Don Engen added that "The sighting by Lt.j.g. Crapser and his gunner, Burns, led to Admiral Halsey making the choice to send his carriers north to pursue the attacking Japanese carrier force."

"The procedure for searching for the Japanese Fleet was quite simple," commented fighter pilot Bill Davis, "we went out in two-plane sections made up of one dive-bomber and one fighter. The dive bomber, being a two-man plane, was better equipped to do the navigation, and it had a larger radio that could cover the distance we were going. The fighter was for protection."

"For my part, at one point in the day," Davis continued, "I took off only to be advised that the dive-bomber I was to escort had engine trouble, and I was to go on alone. I headed north for 375 miles, which took me within 60 miles of the southernmost island of Japan! I expected to run into the entire Japanese air force, but as luck would have it, I saw nothing but blue sea. At the end of that leg I headed east for 75 miles, then south and hopefully back to the *Lexington*."

"Returning from the longest flight I had ever made from the ship," Mr. Davis went on, "I arrived at the rendezvous point only to realize the absolute worst fear of a carrier pilot: *the ship wasn't there!* I later learned that this was because one of the search planes had spotted another Japanese fleet west of the Philippines, and our Task Group had already turned west to close with it. Fortunately, I didn't have to search long, and landed aboard. I caught a wire and let the plane roll backwards so the crew could disconnect the hook from the wire. Once my plane was free the signalman gave me the sign for power. I opened the throttle—and the engine quit. I was completely out of gas! Crewmen had to push me past the barrier and into position."

"On 24 October," wrote Lt. Cmdr. Frank Perry in the Torpedo-19 history, "a division of six of our planes took off, led by Lt. Fred Doll, each one with one wing tank and four 500-pound bombs. This was to attack a Japanese task force of battleships, cruisers, and destroyers—*no* aircraft carriers here—steaming into the Sibuyan Sea."

This enemy task force was threatening the landings of four divisions of the U.S. Sixth Army on the western coast of Leyte Island. Those troops had come ashore on 20 October, led by General Douglas MacArthur.

"Once again," continued the VT-19 history, "the weather was undesirable—a huge front blocked our way. Our planes didn't 'spare the horses' and as a result we were spread all over the sky—going through, around, and over clouds until we reached the Sibuyan Sea from the northeast. There most of us actually got our first real look at the Japanese Imperial Navy. This was a big force, to say the least. Many of us had thought, at this point in the war, that the Japanese Navy might be no more than mythical—but here it was out ahead of us, and it was looking as nasty as hell."

"With merely our 500-pound bomb load (H.E. *bombs*, not torpedoes), the cruisers were about the biggest targets we could tackle. There was a six-thousand-foot overcast and Lieutenant Doll, in *Mohawk-92*, used it to advantage to initiate our attacks. Since most of our dive bombers had left us, the remaining few dove down a hole in the overcast heading for the 'battlewagons'; the whole fleet began to spin in evasive action when they sighted us."

"It was about this time that our aircraft split to attack, hitting both sides of the screen simultaneously. Dives began at 6,000 feet and in most cases were short and steep."

"Lt. Fred Doll (*Mohawk-92*) and Lt.j.g. Ed Schulke (*Mohawk-98*) got hits on one heavy cruiser; Lt. Max Gregg (*Mohawk-96*) and Lt.j.g. Bill Garrett (*Mohawk-93*) hit another heavy cruiser; while Lt. Joe Black (*Mohawk-83*) got a hit on a light cruiser. Ens. Mercer Jackson (*Mohawk-97*) got a near miss on another heavy cruiser, while Lt.j.g. Irv Kramer (*Mohawk-94*) attacked a light cruiser with unobserved results."

"Ens. Bob McAdams (*Mohawk-82*) was shot down but succeeded in making a water landing, and when planes flew low over him he and his crewmen gave the 'thumbs-up' signal. (They are now safe in friendly hands in the Philippines). The AAA was intense and colorful—red, yellow, green, blue, white, and black. The sky looked as though large handfuls of confetti had been heaved skyward—just like a party, only different."

"This was the first time that VT-19 had used wing tanks with a 2,000-pound bomb load and so the routine job of 'sweating' a heavy TBM taking off of a flight deck was increased two-fold. Then *enroute* to the target most of the pilots in the flight encountered trouble while trying to cut in their wing tanks."

"On the 24th, Task Force 38—after engaging the Japanese Battle Fleet in the Sibuyan Sea—received contact reports that the Japanese Carrier Fleet was proceeding to the northeast of Luzon on a southeasterly course ostensibly to close with Task Force 38. TF 38 closed with the Japanese carriers in turn during the late afternoon and into the night."

Around 1145 on the 24th, Vice Admiral Ozawa launched a strike on Task Group 38.3. As the reader knows, TG 38.3 included, among many other ships, the aircraft carriers *Essex*, *Lexington*, *Langley*, and the fatally wounded *Princeton*. These 76 Japanese aircraft essentially accomplished nothing with 15 to 20 of them shot down. A few got through, and six to eight *Judys* dove ineffectually on the *Lexington*, *Essex*, and *Langley*. Only 29 returned to their ships—with the remainder flying to friendly fields in Luzon.

That day there were at least five waves of Japanese planes that approached TG 38.3 over a six-hour period. The Americans, with fighter aircraft and intense AAA, downed over 160 of these attackers.

"By the time the day ended," wrote Fighting-19's air intelligence officer, Lt. Jack Wheeler, "54 enemy aircraft had been shot down by VF-19 in several areas, and our fighter squadron had made its first contact with sizeable ships of the Japanese Fleet."

"The most conspicuous lesson learned from the Sibuyan Sea," later wrote Adm. Bill Halsey, commander of the Third Fleet, "is the practical difficulty of crippling, by air strikes alone, a task force of heavy ships which is at sea and free to maneuver."

Halsey subsequently reported to Admiral Nimitz (and General MacArthur) that:

> Searches by my carrier planes revealed the presence of the Japanese Northern carrier force on the afternoon of 24 October, which completed the picture of all enemy naval forces. As it seemed childish to me to statically guard San Bernardino Strait, I concentrated TF 38 during the night and steamed north to attack the Northern Force at dawn. I believed that the Center Force had been so heavily damaged in the Sibuyan Sea that it could no longer be considered a serious menace.

So, on 24 October, five fleet carriers and one light carrier of Admiral Halsey's Third Fleet flew 259 sorties—with bombs carried by *Helldivers*, *Hellcats*, and *Avengers* and torpedoes launched by other *Avengers*—all against the Japanese Center Force. "However," wrote Rear Admiral Morison, "this weight of attack was not nearly sufficient to neutralize the threat from Vice Admiral Kurita. The largest effort of the Sibuyan Sea attack was directed against just one battleship, the *Musashi*, which was eventually sunk; the cruiser *Myōkō* was also crippled by an aerial torpedo. "Nevertheless, every other ship in Kurita's force remained essentially battle-worthy and able to advance."

"On the following day, at the Battle off Samar, it would be the desperate action and great sacrifice of the much weaker force of six slow escort carriers, three destroyers, four destroyer escorts, and 400 aircraft—utterly lacking in credible weapons to sink armored ships, to stop Kurita. It also contrasts with the 527 sorties flown by the U.S. Third Fleet against Vice Admiral Ozawa's much weaker carrier decoy Northern Force on the following day."

"Vice Admiral Kurita turned his fleet around to get out of range of American aircraft, passing the crippled *Musashi* as his force retreated. Admiral Halsey assumed that this retreat signified that his threat was dealt with for the time being. Kurita, however, waited until 1715 before turning around *again* to head for the San Bernardino Strait. As a result of a momentous decision taken by Admiral Halsey and some unclear communication of his plans, Vice Admiral Kurita was able to proceed through the San Bernardino Strait during the night to make an unexpected and dramatic appearance off the coast of Samar the following morning, directly threatening the Leyte landings."

At the end of the flying day on 24 October, dive-bomber Lt.j.g. Raymond Wicklander noted in his diary, "A strike was sent out to attack the force near Mindoro, but the results were not too good.

General-purpose bombs were loaded on the planes, and there wasn't time to change them, so they didn't do much damage to the enemy's heavy ships. But our Air Group shot down a total of 61 enemy planes today!"

For combat action on 24 October, Fighting Nineteen pilots earned four Navy Crosses and five Distinguished Flying Crosses.

Bombing Nineteen pilots earned two Navy Crosses—but sadly, as has already been mentioned, their squadron commander, Cmdr. Richard S. McGowan, was lost.

Torpedo Nineteen sent 17 aircraft into the air. One reason that they didn't send more was that none of them were able to be armed with torpedoes—and level bombing using only 500-pound H.E. bombs was extremely risky to the *Avenger* aircrews for little potential gain. Thus, Ens. Warner Tyler did not fly on the 24th, nor did 13 other pilots of the squadron.

Still, three Torpedo-19 pilots earned Silver Star Medals for their efforts that day: Lt. Joe Black, Lt. Max Gregg, and Lt.j.g. Ed Schulke.

"Tonight we rendezvous with Task Groups 38.2 and 38.4," continued Lieutenant j.g. Wicklander, closing out his diary entry:

"***Tomorrow should be a big day***."

Chapter 13

Author Edwin P. Hoyt wrote that "On October 24th, according to some historians, Admiral Halsey sent orders directly to the task group commanders—bypassing Vice Admiral Mitscher, who throughout the 24th was little more than a passenger in his own task force." Interestingly, a little defensively, Halsey's later comment was that he did not bypass Mitscher "any more than was my way."

That said, at midnight on 24-25 October, Vice Adm. Marc Mitscher became the "Officer in Tactical Control" of Task Force 38, essentially making the final segment of the Leyte conflagration—the Battle off Cape Engaño—entirely his battle, rather than Admiral Halsey's. Cape Engaño is the northeast tip of the large Philippine island of Luzon, jutting into the Philippine Sea.

Task Force 38 essentially wasn't involved in the remaining segments of the huge Leyte naval battle—The Battle of Surigao Strait and The Battle off Samar.

So, at 0240 on the 25th, Admiral Mitscher moved six battleships, seven cruisers, and seventeen destroyers—formed as Task Force 34—ten miles north of the *Lexington.*

"October 25th dawned bright and clear," wrote Rear Admiral Morison, "in those northern latitudes, with only a few clouds on the horizon and a brisk (13- to 16-knot) northeast trade wind." Enemy contacts by carrier planes were at 0205 and 0235 when they saw the Main Body of the Japanese Northern Force about 200 miles east-by-north of Cape Engaño, Luzon.

"That," continued Morison, "is not what the search planes reported, probably because of an error in transmission. These contacts, bad as they were, gave at least the right direction. Mitscher ordered dawn searches to be flown from the *Lexington*, with planes to relay communications stationed at intervals from the launching point."

"The two Air Combat Intelligence officers on Admiral Mitscher's staff," wrote Pulitzer-prize winning Prof. C. Vann Woodward, "Lieutenants E. Calvert Cheston and Byron R. White, had been insisting on their belief that the Japanese carriers might now be to the *east* of the scheduled search sectors, which did not extend east of due north. They were finally given permission to try out their theory; they vectored out a division of four fighters from the *Lexington*'s CAP. One of these fighters sighted the whole, concentrated enemy force." (Mr. White would later become an Associate Justice of the U.S. Supreme Court, 1962-1993.)

Mitscher, "cannily aggressive" and trying not to waste time, hadn't waited for confirmed reports to get his attack force into the air. Thus, he commenced launching between 0540 and 0600. When the solid contact report came in about 0740, "Many surface 'gadgets,' course 015, distance 150 miles," the First Strike was already in the air about 80 miles south of the enemy, holding in formation.

"At breakfast at three o'clock a.m. on October 25, 1944," wrote fighter pilot Bill Davis, "you could feel the difference and the tension. There was no small talk. We'd been in a lot of combat by this time, but we knew this would be different. We were going against a major unit of the Japanese Fleet."

Civilians Quentin Reynolds and George Jones, embedded journalists with the Task Force, wrote in *Collier's* magazine that "before the take-offs, serious young Lt. Roger "Smiley" Boles (of Santa Paula, California) told his fighter squadron (VF-19) "We're so close to the Japanese that the torpedo planes will have to make a couple of orbits to get enough altitude for the attack!" His pilots chuckled dutifully. But then he got serious. "Take it easy, stick together, and" Boles hesitated soberly, "we'll come out all right."

"Just before 0600," continued Reynolds and Jones, "they went to their planes. The impenetrable gloom of night was beginning to lift; on the flight decks were the fighters, dive bombers, and torpedo planes of the first strike, their dark shapes motionless. As the first light of dawn came, the carriers of the task force turned eastward, into the wind, pitching and rolling slightly."

"The first *Hellcat* roared off, dipped, then soared away, clutching at the sky. Before its wheels had lifted, another *Hellcat* was in the launching spot. And so the planes took off, one by one for the attack, and another deckload of planes came up from the hangar deck in readiness for the Second Strike."

Cmdr. David McCampbell of the USS *Essex* (born in Alabama, his call sign was "*Rebel 99*") directed Vice Admiral Mitscher's first and second carrier-aircraft strikes against Vice Adm. Jisaburō Ozawa and the Japanese "Northern Force"—the "Main Body." McCampbell was a fighter pilot and the Air Group Commander of the *Essex* (CAG-15). As already mentioned, during the fighting on the day before he had personally shot down a record-setting nine enemy aircraft in his F6F *Hellcat.* McCampbell will end the war as the U.S. Navy's leading "ace" with 34 confirmed victories; he will receive the Medal of Honor, the Navy Cross, and several other high decorations.

"I didn't get the dawn strike," wrote Cmdr. Hugh Winters. "Dave McCampbell on the *Essex* 'next door' was given that first strike against the Japanese carriers. There was a rivalry between the *Lexington* and the *Essex*—there always is in any force—and that morning Dave had had his way." But still it was "like opening day of quail season; you set the alarm for 5 a.m., then you wake up at 2, 3, and 4 to see if you set the clock right. I could have had breakfast in bed had the steward's mates not been at battle stations—and if I could have slept that long. The din of slamming catapults and full-power turn-ups just a few inches of steel and wood above your head penetrates the ear."

According to the Torpedo-19 history, "Our carriers launched their aircraft at dawn on 25 October to strike the first blow against Japanese carriers since the First Battle of the Philippine Sea [19 June 1944]."

"About 16 fighters," wrote Rear Adm. Ted Sherman, "all that remained of the 116 with which Vice Admiral Ozawa had started with days before, rose to oppose the first strikes of my group. Our fighters quickly shot them down. For the rest of the day it was only intense AAA fire that hampered our pilots in their work of destroying the enemy ships. We lost ten planes from AAA during the day."

The USS *Lexington* [along with the rest of the Task Group] launched a total of five strikes, but Torpedo Squadron-19 participated in only four of them.

So, early in the morning Commander McCampbell was up in the air as Strike Leader and Air Coordinator. As mentioned, the first American strike left the carrier decks in two waves—0540 and then 0600 hours—and consisted of an impressive 140 aircraft flying from several carriers.

Circling above all the action in his *Hellcat* fighter (which he had named *Minsi III)*, Commander McCampbell directed a huge collection of aircraft from several American carriers in attacking a huge collection of desperately maneuvering Japanese ships far below. He threw some fifty American planes at the Japanese southern group, which included the light carriers *Chitose* and *Chiyoda*, and about eighty planes against the northern group, which had the large carriers *Zuikaku* and *Zuihō*. Per established doctrine *Hellcats* attacked first, then *Helldivers*, and then *Avengers*. Of course McCampbell knew that the carriers were the highest-priority targets, so he initially assigned *Essex* and *Lexington* aircraft to dive on the *Chitose*. This first strike-group of aircraft continued action until about 0900, diving on several targets. The Japanese, as the reader knows, were very short on aircraft and only had around 15 planes up as a CAP. As already discussed, Vice Admiral Ozawa's "main defense was the AAA of his ships, which was brisk and intense."

"I gave the boys assignments," McCampbell later told the *Collier's* journalists, "and they went to work. The fighters strafed the outer screen of destroyers, hoping to divert their fire so the bombers and torpedo planes could make their runs and pull out safely. It worked pretty well. The bombers from my air group went in on a carrier and laid seven 1,000-pounders right in the middle of its flight deck. That took care of her, so I sent the torpedo planes after the next one."

Back in June 1944, Commander "Smoke" Strean (later Vice Adm. Bernard M. Strean) had been C.O. of Fighting-One onboard the *Yorktown* at the First Battle of the Philippine Sea. In his 1974 Naval Institute oral history he made this interesting observation. "In a fighter, when you attacked a position on the ground or the sea, you would be continuously firing six machine guns at the target. You were in formation with others. Sometimes you would fly into the others' falling shell casings, and they would knock holes in your wings—could tear up your wings pretty badly. We would fly in formation, and we were knocking out windshields."

"So you have to set rules for things like this. You fly formation, but you fly in units of four. And, where do the others fly below you so *your* casings don't go through *their* windshields? It became doctrine in the squadrons, where you assign the wing people. We just rearranged the pattern of formation flying and took care of that."

Returning to the morning of 25 October, "The boys really went to town on that Japanese task force," Commander McCampbell wrote, "and when you get right down to it, that's the job we've really been trained for. Knocking out enemy planes is only *incidental* to us. *We were trained to go after ships*, and what happened that morning showed that we had been taught pretty well."

"Everything went by the book," added McCampbell. "First the fighters would strafe, then the dive bombers would drop their loads, and they were immediately followed by the torpedo planes. Huge columns of smoke now came from the burning ships, and the water was full of sailors."

In the "southern group" both carriers were hit. The *Chiyoda*'s damage was not significant, but the *Chitose*—hit by the *Essex* and *Lexington* aircraft—was terribly hurt. Bombing-Fifteen, from the *Essex*, appeared to drop twelve 1,000-pound bombs and claimed seven or eight hits. These claims are not quite accurate and too high, but because of three 1,000-pound bomb near-misses—one extremely close—the *Chitose* was now fully stopped and listing to port, probably due to underwater concussion damage opening seams in the hull. There also may have been one or two torpedo hits. Quickly realizing that American aircraft have likely achieved the *Chitose*'s demise and that there were many more fish to fry, Commander McCampbell—as he mentioned above—succeeded in diverting most VT-15—and most of the incoming VT-19—*Avengers* to other targets.

Around 0925 the Japanese light cruiser *Isuzu* was ordered to take the crippled *Chitose* under tow, but before those steps could be taken it became obvious that the ship was sinking.

To the north the destroyer *Akitsuki* received multiple hits in rapid succession; she burned, blew up, and went down.

Specifically regarding young Warner Tyler's squadron—Torpedo Squadron-19 of course—this "first strike" went well. However,

Ensign Tyler wasn't there. He had to force himself to keep calm and remain patient, for he personally won't join this battle until the "Fourth Strike" of the day, which will launch around 1315 in the afternoon.

In any event, preceded by Air Group-19 fighters and dive bombers—which took off around 0540 hours—Torpedo Squadron-19 launched nine of its aircraft around 0615. VT-19's squadron commander, Lt. Cmdr. Frank Perry in *Mohawk-96*, led eight of his pilots toward the enemy. Most of them were in VT-19's "First Division" according to the squadron's October tactical organization table and the radio-log entries of the day. These planes arrived over target about 0840. Along with the *Hellcats* and *Helldivers* from VF-19 and VB-19—and also accompanied by aircraft from the *Essex*'s Air Group-15—many of the *Lexington*'s planes participated in the attacks on the light carrier *Chitose*. VT-19's Lt. Len Mathias, Lt.jg. Bob Durian, Lt.jg. Morris Goebel, and Lt.jg. Ray Stacy received credit for "hits on a carrier." During this action the torpedo planes released their torpedoes when at 700 to 1,000 feet in altitude, and at ranges from 1,400 to 1,600 yards. Later bomb-damage assessments concluded that VT-19 and VB-19 scored three hits on the *Chitose*.

In addition, VT-19's Lt. Joe Black and Lt.j.g. John McDonald appeared to have torpedoed one of the "hybrid" battleships—but it wasn't clear whether it was the *Ise* or the *Hyūga*—and it was impossible to determine damage, if any. Aircraft from the *Lexington*, *Essex*, light carrier *Belleau Wood*, and light carrier *San Jacinto* also attacked a couple of light cruisers, including the *Tama*; Lt.j.g. Jim Sipprell appears to have scored a hit while Lt.j.g. Gordon Whelpley narrowly missed her. The *Tama* retired from the area, alone, and at 1150 she was given permission to head for Okinawa. She will not make it—later in the evening the submarine USS *Jallao* (on her first war cruise) will torpedo the *Tama* three times and she'll sink with all hands—450 men.

Every pilot in this early attack of Torpedo-19—except one—would be awarded a medal for hitting or pressing home an aggressive attack against his designated target ship. Ironically, the one exception was the squadron commander, Lieutenant Commander Perry. However he will redeem himself in Strike No. 4 later in the day.

Nevertheless, Mr. Perry did pen an interesting note about this morning's attack. "There was one incident involving VF support of VT that I most graphically recall personally. I had made a run on one of the Japanese carriers, dropping my 'fish' at about 500 yards, and then was just trying to get the hell out of there. On my escape route I had failed to notice one of their cruisers that had been masked from my view during the run in—now I was practically going to fly up his hawse pipes. Suddenly, to my great comfort, I noticed four VF-19 fighters, two on each of my wings, practically flying formation on me. When they cut loose with their twenty-four .50-caliber machine guns, there wasn't a single muzzle flash to be seen from the cruiser's AAA. I flew almost directly over her foc'sle, and from all appearances the enemy gunners had their helmets pulled down over they eyes—or were dead."

In the northern group the large carrier *Zuihō* was missed by *Avengers* from the *Essex* and the *Lexington*. However, she was hit amidships by a *Helldiver* from the USS *Intrepid*—though not seriously. Then an *Avenger* from either the *Intrepid* or the light-carrier *San Jacinto* hit the *Zuikaku* in the stern, which disrupted communications and caused a six-degree list with disabled propulsion and inoperative steering. As mentioned before, the *Zuikaku* was Vice Admiral Ozawa's flagship, which he reluctantly abandoned around 1100, transferring to the light cruiser *Ôyodo*.

Fighter pilot Bill Davis had attacked the *Zuikaku*, not only spraying her with his six machine guns but dropping a 500-pound bomb from his *Hellcat*. Very afraid of the ship's 112 AAA guns, he came in extremely hot to make it harder to be hit. "I had not looked at my altimeter or air speed. I was way over the red line of the aircraft, and of course I blacked out from the G forces on the pullout."

"When I could see again what I saw scared me to death. I was so low I was clipping the spray from the waves. I was also 40 knots over the maximum speed for the plane (around 460 miles per hour). And, I was heading right for the side of the *Ôyodo*, a Japanese cruiser. I couldn't gain altitude. I was going to hit the ship! At the last moment I rolled my plane on its right side and flew between the cruiser's second gun turret and the bridge. Three feet from the windows on the bridge I could see Japanese officers who were commanding the ship." There is a magnificent pencil drawing of this incident on the back cover of Davis's autobiography.

Torpedo-19 aircraft closed out their role in the day's first strike by returning to the *Lexington* around 0930.

By the way, the expressions "observed," "appears," and "claims" were used of necessity when discussing hits. When dozens of fighters, dive bombers, and torpedo bombers simultaneously attacked a ship, precise accounting of hits and any resulting damage assessment were incredibly difficult.

In order to mask her movements or her precise position, a ship could generate an enormous smoke screen—which unsurprisingly was done by creating and releasing a large quantity of smoke. One of the basic ways for a ship to do this on a large scale was by injecting fuel oil directly into the smokestack, where it evaporates into a white cloud.

In addition, a ship could put up staggering amounts of AAA fire directed against incoming aircraft. Aside from the actual lethality of this gunfire, the fire was also accompanied by significant quantities of gunsmoke. Remarkably, by this time in the war Japanese battleships averaged 120 AAA guns per ship.

Actual bomb and torpedo hits created additional fire and smoke. The near misses of large bombs (which, unlike torpedoes, often detonated when they hit the water) created huge splashes close aboard, obscuring the ship with heavy spray and further degrading visibility. Finally, all aircraft were coming in hot, concentrating on avoiding mid-air collisions, concentrating on aiming, purposefully jinking and weaving (in the case of the fighters), shaking and vibrating from AAA explosions (in the case of the bombers), and then all planes seriously jinking at full speed to get away. Thus, along with sky-high heart rates and considerable adrenaline rushing through everyone's veins, a lot of things were unclear, and accurate damage assessment could be very problematic.

In any event, what is clear is that by 0940 the light aircraft-carrier *Chitose*—crippled, burning, dead in the water, and abandoned by the other Japanese ships—succumbed to her battle damage. At this point she was 230 nautical miles east of Cape Engaño. The *Chitose* wallowed in a mass of flame, above which hung a huge and dense column of black smoke. She rolled over onto her port side, hesitated for a few moments, and then disappeared under the Philippine Sea with 903 of her crewmen.

Many of the first strike's aircraft were still airborne when the Americans began to launch more planes for a second—but much smaller—strike. The launch for this one started around 0845. This modest strike only had about fourteen *Hellcats*, six *Helldivers*, and eighteen *Avengers* from both Task Groups 38.3 (under Rear Adm. Ted Sherman, of course flying his flag in the *Essex*) and 38.4 (under Rear Adm. Ralph Davison, flying his flag in the *Franklin*). These aircraft were from the *Lexington*, *Franklin*, and *Langley*.

Thus, over the target area, the Americans' Strike No. 2 from Admiral Mitscher's carriers made its appearance, and Commander McCampbell again became insanely busy trying to coordinate them and direct targeting, furiously jotting notes and making calculations on his pilot's kneeboard. This was about 1010. Because of damage apparently resulting from catapult launching, none of the five *Langley* torpedo planes was able to make an effective attack. But McCampbell had almost 30 aircraft make runs on the carrier *Chiyoda.*

The hybrid battleship/carrier *Hyūga*, under the command of newly promoted Rear Adm. Tomekichi Nomura, had been positioned near the *Chitose* and *Chiyoda* to try to protect them with her anti-aircraft guns. Her radar had picked up the American airstrike at a range of 125 nautical miles at 0713. The carriers, of course, were the prime targets more so than was the *Hyūga*. Thus, only fragments from a few near-misses by bombs damaged the battleship's anti-torpedo blister. Although she developed a 5° list it was easily corrected. Despite the *Hyūga*'s protection, as already stated, the *Chitose* was destroyed, and the *Chiyoda* was set afire with her engines disabled.

Indeed, *Helldivers* from the *Lexington* and the *Franklin* made a number of bomb hits on the *Chiyoda*. A direct hit on her port side, aft, started large fires. Crippled by four bombs, together with several near misses, she slowed and stopped. The *Hyūga* and the light cruiser *Isuzu* attempted to take her in tow, but that effort was not successful and was soon abandoned. So, the *Chiyoda* remained dead in the water for almost eight hours. Then, much later in the afternoon, a force of two American heavy cruisers, the *Wichita* and the *New Orleans*, and two light cruisers, the *Santa Fe* and the *Mobile*, backed by nine destroyers, caught and finally sank the *Chiyoda* with gunfire—apparently she was lost with all hands, 1,470.

Once again, preceded by Air Group-19 fighters and dive bombers, Torpedo Squadron-19 put up seven of its *Avengers* around 0900. This division was led by squadron executive officer Lt. Len Prater in *Mohawk-85*. All of these aircraft made runs at the large carrier *Zuikaku*.

The hybrid battleship/carrier *Ise*, under the command of recently promoted Rear Adm. Noboru Nakase, was positioned astern of the carriers *Zuikaku* and *Zuihō* to try to protect them with her anti-aircraft guns. Her mission was very similar to her sister *Hyūga*'s task to protect the *Chitose* and *Chiyoda*. The *Ise*'s radar had picked up American aircraft at a range of 125 nautical miles at 0739. The first attack began at 0820, with the battleship engaging enemy aircraft with "Sanshiki" AAA shells from her main guns—apparently to no effect. The *Ise* herself was not heavily attacked because the carriers were the Americans' primary targets, but two bombs fell nearby. The second wave of aircraft attacked at 1005 and the ship's gunners claimed to have shot down five of the ten dive bombers. The *Ise* was near-missed eight times, although one small bomb appeared to strike her No. 2 turret. The third wave was detected by her radar at 1228, but again it did not attack the battleship, finally sinking the damaged *Zuikaku* and *Zuihō* instead. The *Ise* was able to rescue 98 survivors from the *Zuihō*.

As a side note, the "Sanshikidan" or "Sanshiki" was a Japanese Navy combined shrapnel and incendiary AAA round. These large shells were intended to be used by battleship and cruiser main guns to put up a barrage of flame through which any aircraft attempting to attack would have to navigate. However, with experience, U.S. Navy pilots had begun to consider these shells to be more of a pyrotechnics display than a competent AAA weapon. They were used here on 25 October, but actually seem to have been rarely used in combat against Allied aircraft. Indeed, for obvious reasons, the blast of the main guns turned out to disrupt the fire of a ship's smaller AAA guns. In addition, the copper drive-bands of the rounds were poorly machined and, thus, constant firing would damage the gun rifling.

In any event, Lieutenant Prater and Lt. Don McMillan closed with, but unfortunately closely missed, the *Zuikaku*. However, Lt. Jim West, Lt.j.g. Frank Fox, and Lt.j.g. Ed Myers all appear to have scored hits. According to one source, Lt.j.g. Jim Langrall hit an *Ise*-class battleship, but his subsequent award citation specifies that he hit a carrier. If it had been a battleship, it would no doubt have been the *Ise* herself which was in the vicinity of the *Zuikaku.*

"Lastly, Ens. Fred Schuler attacked the carrier, but his torpedo wouldn't release. He then looped around and tried a run against a light cruiser; this time he was rewarded with both a release and a hit. It's not clear which cruiser it was, but it likely was the *Ôyodo.*

Then the American Strike No. 3 of the day arrived on the scene, but Commander McCampbell, needing a break and needing to refuel, left the area and returned to the *Essex.* Cmdr. Hugh Winters who, as the reader well knows, was the commander of the *Lexington*'s air group, relieved Commander McCampbell as strike leader. For a time Lt. Claude O. Roberts, from the *Belleau Wood*'s Fighting-21, remained on scene observing, tracking, and reporting enemy movements, which was extremely helpful to Winters as he came on target to take over.

According to Rear Admiral Morison, Lieutenant Roberts described the 1130 "picture" to Commander Winters. "A destroyer was leading the *Zuikaku* and the *Zuihō,* steaming at around 20 knots on a course of 345^0, with three other destroyers protecting their flanks and the *Ise* in the rear. Twenty miles behind the *Ise* was the light cruiser *Tama* making ten knots and trailing oil. Five miles south of her the other hybrid battleship, the *Hyūga*, and a damaged destroyer were circling the *Chiyoda,* which was dead in the water."

Coming to the scene with Commander Winters was the largest American strike of the day—almost 200 airplanes about evenly distributed as to type—which immediately put the large carrier *Zuikaku* under a fatal hammering. Many of the American pilots were back once more, having flown in the day's Strike No. 1.

"By the time I relieved McCampbell as Strike Leader and Air Coordinator over the targets," wrote Winters, "there were only three carriers left and about two battleships and three or four cruisers. They were more or less spreading out, trying to get away...so we took our aircraft on up a little further north and hit...the *Zuikaku* and the *Zuihō* with aircraft from the *Lexington* and *Langley*." Indeed, Vice Admiral Ozawa's "Main Body," assaulted and battered by the first two strikes, was no longer an integrated force and now resembled a collection of individual targets spread out over approximately sixty miles.

"What kind of defense can be made against such an assault?" asked *Collier's* Reynolds and Jones in their January 1945 article. "It is hard for us to say, because no American seagoing force has ever been subjected to a comparable attack."

Even with only a few defending aircraft, Reynolds and Jones continued, "The enemy was not defenseless. The badgered enemy resorted to anti-aircraft fire of volcanic proportions. Fourteen-inch guns sprayed the attacking planes. The skies, as on the previous day in the Sibuyan Sea, were daubed with purple, green, and yellow bursts. Low-flying torpedo planes rocked viciously, and it was a disconcerting discovery for a pilot to feel as if a 'freight-train' had just whizzed past, and to look back on a distant explosion."

"As usual, the most accurate and therefore the most deadly weapon in the enemy arsenal consisted of his 5-inch and 40-mm bursts, which can be fired quickly and at quite a long range. Aircraft returned to American carriers with huge flak holes a foot or more in diameter, exposing their structural framework. Said one pilot: 'Walk on that AAA? Hell, I just put my plane on it and skidded in!'"

For the third strike of the day, again preceded by Air Group-19 fighters and dive bombers, Torpedo Squadron-19 launched eight of its aircraft around 1200. Lt. Fred Doll, in *Mohawk-87*, led seven of the squadron's pilots toward the enemy. Most of them were in VT-19's "Fourth Division," again according to the squadron's October tactical organization table and the daily radio log. Unlike many others in the air at this time, none of these VT-19 pilots had been on the first strike. These airplanes arrived over target sometime after 1300.

Along with the *Hellcats* and *Helldivers* from VF-19 and VB-19—and also accompanied by aircraft from other carriers—almost all of the *Lexington*'s planes participated in the attack on the *Zuikaku.*

Six Torpedo-19 *Avengers*, including Lieutenant Doll, attacked the *Zuikaku* with great success. Twelve Bombing-19 *Helldivers* had equally good fortune, planting several hits along her flight deck, as did nine *Helldivers* from the *Essex.* The *Zuikaku* was mortally wounded, apparently struck by seven torpedoes and nine large armor-piercing bombs. Though a few other planes from other American carriers joined in, the *Lexington* and Air Group-19 were given single credit for the sinking.

Those VT-19 pilots who attacked the *Zuikaku*, in addition to Lt. Fred Doll, were Lt.j.g. Ed Schulke (*Mohawk*-92), Lt.j.g. John Middleton (*Mohawk-93*), Lt. Max Gregg (*Mohawk-91*), Ens. Mercer Jackson (*Mohawk-83*), and Lt.j.g. Bill Garrett (*Mohawk-97*).

Along with aircraft from the *Essex* and the *Langley*, two of the *Lexington*'s *Avengers* attacked the *Zuihō*, apparently successfully—Lt.j.g. Irv Kramer (*Mohawk-96*), and Ens. Wally Leeker (*Mohawk-90*). On the first run, Mr. Kramer's torpedo would not release. Bravely, he tried a second run, but now he was making an individual attack—with no other aircraft joining him—in the face of intense AAA fire. Fortunately he and his aircrew in *Mohawk-96* were not hit, and this time their torpedo did release.

"Leeker's torpedo plane," wrote *Collier's* Reynolds and Jones, "sustained a hit which set a wing on fire while he was still 6,000 yards from his target, a carrier of the *Zuihō* class. He steadied his flaming aircraft on its course and closed in to 1,000 yards, where he launched his torpedo. It plowed into the carrier and Wally Leeker, wearing a satisfied grin all the way back to the *Lexington*, sped away. Miraculously the fire on his *Avenger* died out ten miles from the scene of action."

Sadly, however, *Mohawk-93* was hit by the *Zuikaku*'s formidable AAA fire and crashed into the sea. This resulted in the loss of Lt.j.g. John Middleton, ARM[1] Bill Finger, and AMM[2] Frank Caka—all are still carried as Missing in Action and non-recoverable. Mr. Middleton's posthumous Navy Cross citation reads, in part:

> Courageous and skillful in the face of enemy air opposition and extremely intense and continuous fire from hostile anti-aircraft batteries, he boldly pressed home his attack. By his superb airmanship, daring combat tactics, and courage maintained in the face of tremendous opposition, Lieutenant, Junior Grade, Middleton contributed materially to the infliction of extensive damage and destruction on the Japanese Fleet in this decisive battle, and his gallant devotion to duty throughout was in keeping with the highest traditions of the United States Naval Service.

"I had put my group, Air Group-19, on the *Zuikaku*," wrote Commander Winters, "and they really smothered her with machine-gun fire, bombs, and torpedoes. She slowly burned for about two hours. I spent six and a half hours over the target so I watched these ships sink. The *Zuikaku* sank in about two and a half hours." Winters also noted that she went down flying "a battle flag of tremendous size, perhaps fifty feet square."

"The *Zuihō*—which when translated into English is *Auspicious Phoenix*—was a little bit smaller than our *Enterprise*. She was very fast and maneuverable, so it took several strikes on her to sink her, mainly from aircraft belonging to the *Franklin*, *Enterprise*, and *San Jacinto*. Finally she rolled over and sank after about three hours of attack. She'd been hit with at least two torpedoes and six bombs. There was no explosion or going up in a mass of flames, or anything spectacular." Several American ships and their air groups officially shared credit for the *Zuihō*. She went down with about 215 of her crewmen, with around 760 survivors. All three of Admiral Ozawa's destroyers were detailed to pick up survivors, while the cruiser *Ōyodo* and the hybrid-battleship *Ise* ran from the scene under continual attack.

"An interesting note on those two enemy fast carriers," continued Winters, "two Japanese destroyers picked up the survivors from the *Zuikaku* when she sank, and I marked them to keep our eye on them for future reference." It was later determined that the *Zuikaku*'s crew had suffered 840 dead, with 860 survivors.

"So," continued Winters, "those two destroyers then went over and picked up some survivors off the *Zuihō* a while later [as did two other ships] when she sank. But we got American destroyers and cruisers on those two 'cans' ['tin cans,' USN slang for destroyers] and before the day was over, using gunfire, they set them on fire from end-to-end. I hate to say it, but the slaughter must have been terrible."

Terrible indeed, echoed Dr. H. P. Willmott. "A peculiarity of military and naval history is that usually, in the accounting, armies lose *men* and navies lose *ships*." Several destroyers had rescued about 870 officers and men from the *Zuikaku* and other ships. And, "with a crew of about 300 officers and men, the destroyer *Nowaki* may well have had perhaps 1,100 sailors packed into her when caught by the American units. In separate actions, both the *Hatsutsuki* and the *Nowaki* were lashed by protracted fire, torn apart by a hail of high-explosive hatred. God knows the scenes on board those two destroyers. We, fortunately, do not."

One of Warner Tyler's squadron-mates, Lt. Max Gregg, torpedoed the *Zuikaku* but was in turn hit by her AAA fire. He made it back to the *Lexington* and successfully landed, albeit very far aft. Mr. Gregg was badly wounded and, right after landing, passed out from loss of blood. His plane—*Mohawk-91*—began to roll backwards and was in real danger of rolling off the fantail. "Lt.j.g. Hiram Bradford—VT-19's engineering officer—was standing nearby on the flight deck and, realizing what was happening, heroically ran for the aircraft and climbed up into the cockpit. 'Brad' sat in 'Maxie's bloody lap and shoved on the brakes 'til the deck crew could chock the wheels—at which point the tail assembly was hanging over the stern-rail."

Bombing-19 pilot Lt.j.g. George Bowen wrote that "On two occasions, back when we were forming the squadron, I had to ride rear-seat facing backwards during a dive. Being in combat was a cake-walk compared to that; to volunteer to do that, you either have to be psycho or have lots of guts. So, when I think of dive-bombing combat, I generally think of my very gutsy radioman and rear gunner, Petty Officer Luther Simmons. For example, when we landed back aboard the *Lexington* after scoring a hit on the *Zuikaku*, I jumped out on the wing and, in my excitement, asked Simmons if he *wanted* to go back to the Japanese fleet again that afternoon. He replied, 'No, sir.' Feeling somewhat miffed, I icily inquired if he was *ready* to go back and, without hesitation, he replied, 'Yes, sir.' Well, you've really got to like a guy like that."

According to Rear Admiral Morison, another "young *Helldiver* pilot was so excited when landing that he immediately—and uninvited—ran up the ladders of the *Lexington*'s island and halted right in front of Vice Admiral Mitscher, shouting, 'I gotta hit on a carrier! I gotta hit on a carrier!'"

As mentioned earlier the *Zuikaku* was the last remaining carrier of the six which had attacked Pearl Harbor on 7 December 1941. She also had fought in virtually all of the Pacific War's major sea actions (the Solomons, Stewart Island, Santa Cruz, the Marianas, and the first Battle of the Philippine Sea), and of course the sinking of the previous American aircraft carrier *Lexington* (CV-2) at the Battle of the Coral Sea in 1942. Thus, it was with enormous satisfaction that the Task Force—and particularly the *Lexington* (CV-16)—made the *Zuikaku*'s career end so dramatically on this day. As Commander Winters commented, "Boy, did we in the "new" *Lexington* covet her! It was akin to pure lust."

For much of the afternoon, hoping to stay in the air and remain on station as long as he could, Winters had "throttled back to almost stalling speed and leaned out the fuel to practically a backfiring mixture." When he finally returned to the *Lexington* he and his wingman Lt. Barney Garbow "both got aboard after about seven hours on hard, lumpy seats, with only enough gas to taxi out of the arresting gear. My tanks were all sucked dry but one, and it was bouncing on 'E' for empty—but most fighter-plane fuel gauges exaggerated 'emptiness,' just like my old Ford." Winters and Garbow are probably the only men who ever actually eye-witnessed three aircraft carriers sink on the same day.

Mr. Garbow commented many years later that the "main thing I remember—other than the excitement—was sweating our fuel situation. I do remember the problems the CAG had keeping the various carriers' strike groups on the right targets. Also, I remember the CAG and I making several strafing runs while waiting for the next strike to arrive." Garbow had also been Winters' wingman on 24 October at the Sibuyan Sea. He would receive a Silver Star for his performance on 25 October.

"After finally landing," continued Winters, it was "down to the fighter ready room for a drink (I didn't have to debrief; the admiral's staff already knew the results of our strikes). Then over to the bombers to have one with them; then over to the torpeckers for the third. We all went down to dinner that night feeling just fine, and that night we slept….."

Mitscher's "Strike No. 4, with about the same number of planes as No. 2, took off around 1300 and reached the Northern Force about 1445." This attack was another modest one, bringing forth only around 35 to 40 aircraft. As already discussed, after many hours in the air Commander Winters had to return to the *Lexington*. Thus, Strike No. 4 fell under the coordinating direction of Cmdr. Malcom T. Wordell, the CAG of Air Group-44 from the light carrier USS *Langley*. And, Winters also mentioned that he had some radio "turnover" remarks with Cmdr. Dan "Dog" Smith, CAG of Air Group-20 from the USS *Enterprise*—who appeared with a strike of fighters to go after the Japanese battleships and cruisers running north.

So now, finally, torpedo plane pilot Ens. Warner W. Tyler received an invitation to this day's enormous party. At 1315 the *Lexington* launched airplanes for this Strike No. 4, again joining aircraft from several other carriers. This will be the last effort today for Torpedo Squadron-19, even though the *Lexington* and other carriers will send more planes in a fifth strike later in the afternoon.

VT-19's squadron commander, Lt. Cmdr. Frank Perry in *Mohawk-88*, led a small group of four others of his pilots. These were Lt. Richard Greer in *Mohawk-84*, Lt.j.g. Morris Goebel in *Mohawk-94*, Lt.j.g. John McDonald in *Mohawk-86*, and Ens. Warner Tyler in *Mohawk-98*. Lieutenant Commander Perry and Lieutenants junior grade Goebel and McDonald had earlier flown in Strike No. 1, at 0615, so this was their second great adventure of the day.

As the reader has already discovered in Chapter One, Ensign Tyler wrote a summary of his flight many years later, when he was a naval reserve captain.

"At this time U.S. Navy strike doctrine against large ships required sending the fighters in first. Thus, the *Hellcats* were to strafe everything in sight on the enemy ship with their six 50-caliber machine guns; this was to get the Japanese anti-aircraft gunners to hunker down and shelter—resulting in them not manning their guns. Then the torpedo planes—ideally eight, but maybe less—*Avengers* like mine, would split up into two groups, with several planes attacking on either side of the ship. As the torpedo planes maneuvered into position, the dive bombers would begin their dives as soon as the *Hellcats* 'cleared' the area."

"We in the *Avengers*," continued Tyler, "would then approach the ship outboard from the stern at 7,000 feet and an angle of about 45 degrees. This spread of aircraft was designed to minimize and/or neutralize any course changes the enemy ship might make. Whichever direction he might turn, we would still have a good angle shot—and that would also, very likely, make more effective any hits from torpedoes already in the water."

"The TBM-1C *Avenger* carried a crew of three including the pilot. A short distance behind the pilot was the ball-turret gunner, and lower down in the bomb-bay tunnel a radioman/gunner completed the crew. This airplane was highly versatile and rugged. The enclosed bomb bay could accommodate one 2,000-pound aerial torpedo, or a 2,000-pound general-purpose bomb, or two 1,000-pound general-purpose bombs, or four aerial mines, or a mix of fragmentation and various other smaller bombs."

"Despite the intense strafing attacks of our *Hellcats*, we in the *Helldivers* and the *Avengers* nevertheless expected the *flak* (enemy anti-aircraft fire) to be intense."

"In fact," Tyler went on, "the Japanese *flak* was very intense, and in addition they had developed a new AAA shell which included short lengths of stiff wire and phosphorous. This shell would be fired above the attacking aircraft and drop into the flight path of the attacker."

"The Japanese ships," added Commander Winters in his autobiography, "were using new AAA stuff with wires and burning phosphorous shells which put up all different-colored fire and smoke around our planes. It looked like Fourth of July laid on by the Chamber of Commerce at Virginia Beach—expensive! But, we had faced so *much* deadly AAA in the last three months attacking so many *lousy* targets that it didn't bother us too much now, hunting this big game."

"Moreover," continued the older Captain Tyler, "a tactic which had been adopted by the Japanese Fleet when attacked from the air was that of lobbing large caliber (16" and 18") shells out in front of, and in the flight path of, the attacking airplanes which were at 75 to 100 feet above the water. Upon impact with the sea the exploding shells would send a solid column of water over a hundred feet in the air. Flying into one of these columns at 200 knots was tantamount to flying into a steel column. A very effective technique."

"Once having dropped our aerial torpedo, the TBM-1C had thus expended its total bomb load. While still low and close to the water, everybody—who wasn't hit—then made one or two runs at units of the Japanese Fleet in order to draw fire away from those who were still making their torpedo runs. During the confusion of battle, it hopefully went unnoticed by the enemy that some of the torpedo bombers had already dropped their armament and were making dry runs. During these runs, of course, our forward-firing .50-caliber wing guns, the .50-caliber guns in the ball turret behind the cockpit, and the bomb-bay tunnel .30-caliber machine gun, were all brought to bear on the enemy ship during the run-in and during the high-speed pass over the ship. Then, as we retired from the attack, the .30-caliber in the bomb-bay tunnel, firing to the rear, would make its presence known to the enemy."

"Having dropped torpedoes from a very low altitude," Tyler continued, "the tactic was to continue straight ahead at full throttle directly at the enemy ship unit you had passed over it, and then pull up and away, jinking all the while. The reason for this maneuver was that it was designed to minimize the time spent closing on the target and to present the smallest silhouette of the airplane to the enemy gunners—notably head-on."

"An aerial-torpedo drop," Captain Tyler went on, "was a very dicey maneuver under combat conditions. It was crucial that the torpedo enter the water at the proper angle, direction, and speed in order to run hot and true. If these parameters were exceeded, there was a good chance that the torpedo would break up when it hit the water or, at the very least, broach and pursue a totally off-course heading. The airplane, once committed to the attack, needed the pilot to make every effort to hold it straight and level at a constant altitude of 100 to 150 feet until the torpedo departed the bomb bay."

"So, that afternoon off Cape Engaño, I settled my airplane down as much as possible and commenced the run-in against the enemy capital ship designated by my squadron commander. I closed to approximately 1,500 feet before dropping my torpedo. The torpedoes needed around 1,200 feet of water travel in order to arm the detonator, which upon striking the ship would ignite the explosive charge. At this time the charge consisted of 600 pounds of Torpex. Torpex was about 50 percent more powerful than TNT."

"During the attack on the target, which was one of the 'hybrid' half-battleship and half-carrier ships, I survived the incredible AAA, dropped my torpedo, and then flew directly over the enemy ship. I then came up off the water and upended on a wingtip."

"I could see back, and through the amazingly thick gunsmoke and other kinds of smoke, it appeared to me that my torpedo may have struck the enemy amidships. It also appeared to me that my wingman's torpedo might also have hit her amidships."

"Very shortly," continued Captain Tyler, "the call came from the strike coordinator to rendezvous at altitude. Once having accomplished this, we set a course to return to the Task Group—which inevitably was to be found under the nearest rain squall."

"Returning to the ship was a fairly routine matter—with the possible exception of four- or five-hour flights. Fortunately, this strike was going to clock-in at 3.3 hours; nevertheless we all paid more than routine attention to our fuel gauges. And all hands in each airplane were swiveling their heads constantly so that there would be no surprises *enroute* back to the *Lexington*."

"Shortly thereafter," Tyler went on, "we located the Task Group, checked-in by radio with the picket destroyers and also notified the Combat Air Patrol over the Group of our imminent arrival. All seriously damaged aircraft, ones with wounded aboard, or those with a questionable fuel state broke out of formation for a straight-in approach. The rest of us flew upwind past the starboard side of the *Lexington* for a mile or two, set up our time for the landing interval, and then broke off to port into the landing pattern. I trimmed the airplane: nose up with flaps and gear down, and at the same time went to high manifold pressure settings on the throttle and eased the propeller into full low pitch. I made a good pass—I took the 'cut' and engaged the No. 3 wire. Then I went to full power as the plane handler indicated, and then taxied to my assigned spot and shut the airplane down."

Lieutenant Commander Perry had led his five *Avengers*—including Ensign Tyler—into attacking the hybrid battleship/carrier *Ise*. It was not clear right then whether it was the *Ise* or her sister *Hyūga*, but after the fact it was pretty clear that the *Hyūga* had moved some distance away from where this attack occurred. Still, it remained unconfirmed for not only days but weeks, months, and then even years. In fact, it appears that for the rest of his life Warner Tyler never knew for sure what ship it really was. The citation for his medal does not specify—which is true for most everyone's award citations. This non-specificity notwithstanding, after mission de-brief transcripts were analyzed, eyewitness accounts were processed, and photographs were studied, the Torpedo-19 planes were officially declared to have made four "hits" or "probable" hits, and as a result four of the five pilots were subsequently recognized with the award of the Navy Cross medal: Lieutenant Commander Perry,

Lieutenant Greer, Lieutenant j.g. McDonald, and Ensign Tyler. The reader need not feel badly for the fifth pilot of this flight, Lieutenant j.g. Goebel; although he received no recognition for Strike No. 4, earlier in the day he had earned a Navy Cross for a probable hit on the carrier *Chitose* during Strike No. 1.

Indeed, "*Lexington* and *Langley* planes claimed several bomb and torpedo hits on the *Ise*," wrote Rear Admiral Morison, "but this old converted battleship was rugged. She put up an 'exceedingly intense AAA fire' and in reality received only four near-misses." Another historian—Paul Dull, professor emeritus of Asian history at the University of Oregon—has written that it was more like *thirty* near-misses.

So, the *Ise* had been the primary focus of this wave and thus was attacked by about 85 dive bombers and at least 11 torpedo bombers. Saved by extremely heavy AAA and expert maneuvering, the battleship dodged all the torpedoes, and was struck by only one bomb, near the port catapult. Roughly 34 near-misses damaged her hull plating near the waterline and started a leak that contaminated an oil tank and caused minor damage to the port boiler rooms. Splinters from the near-misses and the single hit killed 5 crewmen and wounded 71.

At the time several reports came streaming in indicating that the *Hyūga* and *Ise*, and some other undamaged or slightly damaged ships of the Japanese Southern Force, had abandoned the "crippled" ships and had headed north.

Moreover, "with all four aircraft carriers of the Japanese Main Body crippled or sunk," wrote Harvard historian James Field, "the battleships *Hyūga* and *Ise*—'fattest' of the remaining targets—had become the principal objects of attack. The latter, farthest to the northward, was attacked at 1500 and again about 1700. The last attack of the day went in on the *Hyūga* and the destroyer *Shimotsuki* at about 1710."

While the attacks of Strike No. 4 were still ongoing, TG 38.3 aircraft from the *Lexington* and the light carrier *Langley* were organized to join an attack built around Task Group 38.4, commanded by Rear Adm. Ralph Davison. There appeared to be time left for one more strike before sundown.

So, the final significant American air attack—of 25 October and the Battle off Cape Engaño—was launched at 1615 and reached the target areas around 1710. This Strike No. 5 included planes from the *Essex, Lexington, Langley, Franklin,* and *Enterprise*—but as mentioned earlier it did not contain any aircraft from the *Lexington*'s Torpedo Squadron-19. Commander Wordell, from the *Langley*, continued as air coordinator and ultimately remained over the targets from 1500 until after 1800.

"A total of 98 aircraft," wrote British historian Dr. H. P. Willmott, "were launched after 1600, the lateness of the hour presumably ensuring that the aircraft went forward as launched and attacked as they came upon the enemy with only minimal coordination." Fifty-two of the planes were fighters armed with bombs as well as machine guns, and ten of the thirteen torpedo planes carried one-ton general purpose bombs instead of torpedoes.

"Commander Wordell," wrote Professor Woodward, "was out to get the hybrid battleships, and directed the great bulk of the strike against those two targets now in different groups separated by about ten miles. American airmen attacked with their usual spirit, diving repeatedly into intense AAA fire and sustaining several casualties, some of them fatal." But it seems many of the later claims of hits were perhaps justifiably erroneous.

Indeed, "the air group from one carrier," continued Dr. Willmott, "was to claim no fewer than 13 hits on one battleship, and when the day's tallies were assembled it was found that one battleship had been hit no fewer than 22 times and the other 15 times—and 7 of these hits were by torpedoes. At best, three of the thirteen *Avengers* committed to this 1600 attack were actually armed with torpedoes, and with such numbers the chances of recording any significant result against the *Hyūga* and the *Ise* were slim."

Not to belabor the point, it seems that in reality "the aircraft mainly concentrated on the *Ise* but got only 34 near-misses and failed to sink that tough old 'hermaphrodite,'" wrote Admiral Morison. "She threw up a heavy AAA fire and her commanding officer, Rear Adm. Noboro Nakase, was an expert at evasive maneuvering. Moreover, as mentioned above, twenty miles away and running as fast as she could accompanied by a light cruiser and a destroyer, the *Hyūga* had seven near-misses from the aircraft that came her way."

"Shaken by countless near misses," commented Professor Field, "inundated with water, and with their anti-torpedo blisters perforated by bomb fragments, the two hybrid battleships yet escaped all serious damage. The only hit was from a bomb which detonated outboard on *Ise*'s port catapult causing about fifty casualties." Dr. Field could also have mentioned she was almost invisible underneath a prodigious smoke-screen and considerable gunsmoke. For her part, the *Hyūga* appears to have sustained only minor damage from earlier in the day.

Dive bomber Lt.j.g. Don Engen wrote that "during my takeoff for the attack on the Japanese carrier force, I looked up and saw Vice Admiral Mitscher on the flag bridge and, impulsively, I changed hands on the stick and gave him a smile and a quick salute. To my great surprise he saw me, raised his head from his cupped hand that had been supporting his chin, smiled back and returned my 'unauthorized' salute."

"That afternoon," Mr. Engen continued, "we attacked the battleship *Hyūga*. On that strike Lt. Bob Niemeyer's SB2C was hit by AAA and he and his gunner, ARM^2 Al Thorngren, were forced to land in the water. Eventually the destroyer USS *Bronson* came along and rescued them, later returning them to the *Lexington*."

"A small sixth, and final, attack," wrote Rear Admiral Morison, "of 36 planes from Admiral Davison's group took off at 1710 and claimed a few hits, but sank nothing."

"Around 1820," continued Professor Field, "the *Hyūga* and the destroyer *Shimotsuki* overhauled Vice Admiral Ozawa—in the light cruiser *Ôyodo*—and joined up with the Main Body of the Mobile Fleet. The day's air attacks were over. The Main Body, now reduced to a light cruiser, two hybrid battleships, and a destroyer, continued to run to the north toward safety."

"The action on the 25th," commented Commander Winters with not very much modesty, "impresses me as one of the most remarkable that I've ever heard about. We sank four of their carriers, including their biggest—the *Zuikaku*—corresponding to our *Essex* class, a couple of their cruisers, and three or four destroyers. We appear to have crippled two battleships…without the loss of a single American ship in that part of the battle."

"Pilot reports, substantiated by photographs, indicate that only ten Japanese vessels were still afloat: two *Ise*-class hybrid battleships; one unidentified cruiser; one *Ōyodo* or *Agano* light cruiser; one *Natori* light cruiser; one unidentified single-stack light cruiser; and three destroyers, all under way—plus the crippled *Chiyoda*-class light carrier dead in the water and abandoned by the other ships."

After every strike the air crews were required to be debriefed and mission photographs—which had been taken from the several aircraft which carried cameras—had to be analyzed by intelligence officers. As already mentioned, each squadron had an intelligence officer who handled much of this work. But, also as previously mentioned, the overall director of Air Intelligence on board the *Lexington* was Lt. E. Calvert Cheston, a lawyer from Philadelphia; his partner was another officer from Colorado: Lt. Byron "Whizzer" White.

Before the war, Mr. White had been an "all-American" college halfback at Colorado University, a Rhodes Scholar, and a professional football player with the Pittsburgh Pirates and the Detroit Lions. When the war broke out White joined the navy and went into naval intelligence. Mr. Cheston had been an attorney in Philadelphia; his fields of practice were primarily corporate, securities, and banking.

Interestingly, in the fall of 1943, Lieutenant White had been the officer who wrote the intelligence report on the sinking of future President John F. Kennedy's patrol-torpedo boat *PT-109*. As noted earlier, "Whizzer" White (who seemed to hate that nickname, picked up while playing football at Colorado University) would many years later become a U.S. Supreme Court Justice.

"It was Capt. Arleigh Burke," Justice White wrote later, "who brought me to Admiral Mitscher's staff. I had been on Burke's Destroyer Squadron-23 staff in the Solomon Islands. He had taken me on when the torpedo-boat war in the Solomons wore out."

"This was a different world entirely," continued White. "It had been something of an experience for a drylander from Colorado to end up on PT boats and destroyers with nothing but water under and around you. But that was hardly anything compared with coming to the carriers. Having wanted to fly and having been turned down because of imperfect eyes, I came to greatly admire all of those who came and went from the flight decks from day to day."

Fighter pilot Bill Davis had another nickname for Lieutenant White besides "Whizzer." There were occasional basketball games onboard the *Lexington*, and VF-19's team periodically played the team from the admiral's staff—which included "Whizzer." The pilots indeed called him something else: *The Dentist*. This was because he played hard and played tough, and "he was continually checking your teeth with his elbow."

Cheston and White were not part of the *Lexington*'s crew, nor did they belong to Air Group-Nineteen. They worked specifically for Admiral Mitscher, reporting to Mitscher's chief of staff, Captain

Burke. A superb destroyer man, Arleigh "31-Knot" Burke was another Colorado native; he would many years later become a four-star admiral and the U.S. Navy's top officer as chief of naval operations.

Lieutenants Cheston and White had an amazingly small handful of other intelligence officers to help them, including people from Mitscher's staff, the ship's company, and the *Lexington*'s flying squadrons. Even though the lieutenants worked directly for Vice Admiral Mitscher and focused upon the big picture, they had a close working relationship with Air Group-Nineteen, particularly the seven men who were the three squadrons' air combat information officers and photo officers.

The air intelligence space on board the *Lexington* was reasonably large—not so much for the debriefing sessions but, as has already been discussed, for the occasions when hundreds of 8x10 photographs had to be spread out on the deck, in overlapping strips, for minute study.

Rear Adm. Ted Sherman assessed the Battle for Cape Engaño like this: "The situation during the day had been ideal. American aircraft had wiped out the enemy air on the day before, and we had him within striking range of our aircraft. We were proceeding toward him at 25 knots, he could not get away, and a good fresh breeze for air operations was only 45 degrees on my starboard bow."

"It was a happy situation. The enemy was between 80 and 100 miles away, an ideal distance for aircraft strikes. We pounded him from dawn 'til dark with everything we had." As Rear Admiral Morison summarized: "The Americans sank 4 carriers and a destroyer, with a total of 527 plane sorties—201 of those fighter sorties."

"Since October 20th," Vice Admiral Ozawa wrote later in his after-action report, "my force had done everything in its power to prevent the enemy from going southward so as to enable our Diversion Attack Forces to gain their objectives. Our only regret is that a considerable price in ships was exacted of us."

All three of Air Group-19's squadrons were heavily engaged on 25 October during the Battle for Cape Engaño—much more than they were on 24 October.

As Commander Winters wrote, the awarding of medals is not the measure of everything, but it does give a good indication of activity. "Although medals in combat are not, and should not, be the bottom line, many awards to Carrier Air Group-19 were won in 1944 when heroes were not really needed *as badly as they were in 1942*, when morale was *really* down. Navy Crosses were given for laying torpedoes or bombs into carriers, battleships, or cruisers—or laying them very close aboard in the face of heavy AAA. Fighters received the Navy Cross for laying small bombs onto those types of ships, as well as pressing aggressive strafing attacks on them. Silver Stars were for aggressive air-to-air or air-to-surface action. Distinguished Flying Crosses were for air-to-air action."

In the case of Fighting-19, eleven Navy Crosses were awarded to pilots, to include squadron commander Lt. Roger "Smiley" Boles. It also included the former squadron commander, and now CAG, Cmdr. T. Hugh Winters.

For Bombing-19, thirty-one pilots received Navy Crosses including the squadron commander, Lt. Donald F. Banker—who also received a Silver Star. Invariably, the radioman-gunner in each airplane received the Distinguished Flying Cross.

In regard to Torpedo-19, twenty-six Navy Crosses were awarded to pilots, to include squadron commander Lieutenant Commander Perry—who also received a Distinguished Flying Cross. Fifty radiomen-gunners received the Distinguished Flying Cross.

The casualties for Air Group-19 on that day were surprisingly and mercifully light, considering the intense combat activity and the busy and complex carrier flight operations.

As the reader already knows, VT-19's torpedo plane *Mohawk-93* was hit by the carrier *Zuikaku*'s formidable AAA fire and crashed into the sea. This resulted in the loss of Lt.j.g. John Middleton, ARM[1] Bill Finger, and AMM[2] Frank Caka—all still carried as Missing in Action and non-recoverable.

Regarding VF-19, it's sad to note the loss of Ens. Francis P. "Frank" Hubbuch. The timing and details of his loss are unclear; strangely, neither air group commander Hugh Winters nor fighter pilot Bill Davis mention him in their detailed autobiographies.

But it's good to note that Bombing-19 lost neither aircraft nor any aircrew on the 25th.

Chapter 14

So, the great Battle for Leyte Gulf was over—the largest naval battle there ever was—or ever will be. What did it mean?

Well, of course, it did not end the war. It wouldn't be until the following May that Germany surrendered, and it was the following September when Japan finally ended the conflict. Perhaps there is a parallel to the great naval Battle of Trafalgar in 1805, because even though it was a staggering, colossal victory for Great Britain against the French and Spanish, the Napoleonic Wars did not end for another ten years.

Was Leyte Gulf decisive as well as huge? Rear Admiral Morison later wrote that "'Decisive' is a relative term in warfare. Leyte was not as 'decisive' as Midway, but it did decide that the United States and her allies would rule the Pacific until the end of the war, and by so doing hasten the war's end....The sacrifice of the Japanese Navy in this battle enabled the United States Navy to transport troops and base long-range bomber planes in positions so close to Japan that victory was a matter of months, even had there been no atomic bomb."

After the battle, Vice Adm. Jisaburō Ozawa wrote that "the Japanese naval surface forces became strictly auxiliary, so that we relied on land forces, special [*Kamikaze*] attack, and air power." He added a significant obituary to the navy: *"There was no further use assigned to surface vessels, with exception of some special ships."*

"Viewed in this light," wrote Prof. C. Van Woodward, "Leyte Gulf becomes more than a victorious battle or a successful campaign. In many ways it was the death struggle of the Japanese Navy. Leyte Gulf was the last battle fought between surface forces. The network of inter-island passages and seas lay open to our fleet. The command of the seas was established."

"The destruction," wrote Rear Adm. Ted Sherman, "of so much of the enemy's fighting strength in this 'Second Battle of the Philippine Sea' ushered in a new phase of the Pacific War. It put an end to any hope of future large-scale operations by the Japanese Navy."

And, "however you look at it," added Admiral Morison, "the Battle for Leyte Gulf should be an imperishable part of our national heritage."

Chapter 15

For Task Force-38, Task Group-38.3, the USS *Lexington*, and Air Group-19 the war was, most definitely, not over.

During the combat of October 25th, Admiral Halsey took the time to consider the immediate future employment and deployment of his entire Third Fleet. "Most of his ships," wrote Rear Admiral Morison, "were low on fuel yet had to be ready for any further eventuality. At noon, Admiral Halsey ordered Vice Admiral Mitscher—upon the conclusion of the battle—to set a fueling rendezvous (at a location where nine oilers were waiting) for Sherman's TG-38.3 and Davison's TG-38.4, which at that moment were doing most of the fighting. And, a second fueling rendezvous was appointed for McCain's TG-38.1, Bogan's 38.2, and Rear Adm. Oscar C. Badger's surface force TG-34.5."

So then, early on 26 October—the day following the great battle—Halsey ordered Mitscher, "with Sherman's Group 3 and Davison's Group 4 (as soon as they finished fueling later in the day) to be prepared to make strikes or furnish fighter cover over the Leyte Area if later directed."

"Task Force-38," wrote Rear Admiral Sherman, "remained off the eastern coasts of the Philippines until it was evident than no further interference by the Japanese fleet was probable."

It should be noted that Admiral Halsey was concerned about other things than fuel. "The pilots are exhausted, and the carriers are low in provisions, bombs, and torpedoes. When will land-based Army Air take over at Leyte?"

"Carrier bluejackets and aviators," wrote Admiral Morison, "had been fighting three days out of every four since 6 October." As a further illustration, TG-38.4 had been 64 days at sea on 30 October, except for 3½ days in Ulithi or other advanced bases. Over half of carrier *Franklin*'s crew was suffering from heat rash, and other crews were in a similar condition.

Indeed, echoed Admiral Sherman, "as a result of their long weeks of action, Third Fleet personnel were suffering from combat fatigue. An increasing number of pilots were unfit for further fighting and the normal level of operational accidents was rising. All echelons were weary."

Cmdr. Hugh Winters could only agree. "It was time for a pit-stop for all hands in the Task Group. Staff needed to sort things out and try to put the [enemy] pieces together and figure out our next moves. Ships needed to suck from Mother Replenishment Group: oil for the boilers, avgas and ammo for the planes, and food for everybody."

"And the Air Group was so keyed-up it needed some old Western shoot-'em-up movies to cool it down, and some letters from home, and to write some letters, and just to sleep nights for a change. It was like walking a horse after a race."

Rear Admiral Morison wrote that "On 27 October Admiral Sherman's group, in addition to sharing CAP over Leyte Gulf, sent fighter sweeps over the Visayas and southern Luzon. A dawn sweep from the *Essex* found a small troop convoy north of the Calamian Islands and scored hits, and also sank a destroyer."

This same day Ens. Warner Tyler flew—with a catapult shot—for four hours. This was a scouting and anti-submarine patrol. His crewmen were Chief Aviation Electrician's Mate E. D. Dumez as radioman and Aviation Ordnanceman 2nd Class Wilmer Dewees as gunner. Torpedo Squadron-19 had not flown at all on the 26th, but eleven aircraft, including Tyler's *Mohawk-86*, flew in three ASW patrols on the 27th. Torpedo-19 also flew one four-plane ASW patrol on the 28th, but it did not include Tyler.

Morison wrote that "Admiral Davison's Group 38.4—including the carriers *Franklin*, *Enterprise*, *San Jacinto*, and *Belleau Wood*—carried the burden of air action off Leyte on the 28th. It was a busy day. A fighter sweep was flown against shipping off Cebu. About 44 enemy planes attacked the group and 13 were shot down by the CAP. And then, around noon, TG-38.4 was under attack by submarines."

"On October 29th," wrote Sherman, "a large flight of *Kamikaze* planes struck at Bogan's Group 38.2, which included Admiral Halsey's flagship, the battleship *New Jersey*. Although the alert CAP shot down 21 of them and the ships' AAA got another, one managed to break through and crashed into the *Intrepid*, Bogan's flagship."

"The next day another *Kamikaze* group attacked Davison's carriers and hit the *Franklin* and *Belleau Wood*, killing 158 men and destroying 45 planes. On November 1st, they shifted their attack to Vice Adm. Thomas C. Kinkaid's destroyers in Leyte Gulf, sinking one and damaging five. The *Kamikazes*, the enemy's 'Special Attack Corps,' was taking a serious toll."

Rear Admiral Sherman's Task Group, now comprised of the *Essex*, *Ticonderoga*, *Langley*, *Lexington*, four battleships, two cruisers, and sixteen destroyers, joined Vice Admiral McCain's group at Ulithi on the 30th, but remained for two days only. They were able to take aboard some ammunition, provisions, and make minor repairs. The carrier *Ticonderoga* had joined TG-38.4 on 28 October, essentially replacing the *Enterprise*. The group then sailed for a new naval base at Manus, in the Admiralty Islands, on November 1st but was shortly directed to reverse course and come back to a point off the Philippines. They joined up with Task Groups- 38.1 and -38.2 and headed west to strike Manila in accordance with orders.

Vice Adm. Marc Mitscher was no longer on board the *Lexington* at this point. On 30 October, at Ulithi, Mitscher had turned over command of Task Force-38 to Vice Adm. John S. McCain.

Retired Capt. Warner Tyler wrote, exactly forty years later, that "with the departure of Admiral Mitscher the *Lexington* experienced a great loss. Admiral Mitscher was considered to be one of the finest—if not *the* finest—carrier admiral and naval air tactician that the U.S. Navy ever produced. When he left, we all felt somewhat diminished."

Mitscher's biographer, Theodore Taylor, wrote that "during the late afternoon of October 31st, word circulated about the *Lexington* that Mitscher would leave early the next morning. It was about 0400 when Mitscher made his way down through the dimly lit hangar deck. Near the after brow stood more than 100 people. Almost all of Air Group-Nineteen was assembled though most of them hadn't had a full night's sleep in weeks. CAG-Nineteen, Cmdr. Hugh Winters, had set his alarm for 0330 and then awakened his pilots—by their own request. They waited quietly, some in uniform, others in the background clad in pajamas and bathrobes."

"Mitscher glanced up and saw them." continued Taylor. "'What the devil are all these people doing here?' he asked Capt. Arleigh Burke, who'd been his chief of staff until the day before. 'I don't know, Admiral,' replied Burke. Mitscher then looked at Commander Winters who answered, 'Well, Admiral, we just wanted to be here when you left.'"

"The Admiral ducked away quickly. After he got down to his barge, chugging at the end of the gangway, they saw him take out a handkerchief."

"In due time," wrote Winters, "we were back on track and

just in time to hit the 'unsinkable' cruiser *Nachi* coming out of Manila Harbor on 5 November. Intelligence had reports on this super-cruiser (Vice Adm. Kiyohide Shima's flagship) getting minor repairs after the big Leyte Gulf battle, and being ready for sea. We later learned that she was also the fleet paymaster ship, carrying millions in yen—which were later recovered by divers and used by us in 1945, together with some top-secret war plans."

"On 5 and 6 November," according to the Torpedo-19 squadron history, "we hit Manila with three strikes." VT-19 was heavily engaged; 28 pilots flew on the 5th, and 12 more on the 6th. "Our primary targets were Nielson Field as well as Japanese naval and merchant ships in Manila Bay. On the second strike on the 5th Commander Winters, in *Mohawk-99*, directed the *Lexington*'s air group against a *Nachi*-class heavy cruiser which was making a sortie out of the bay; our attack stopped the cruiser dead in the water. The following third strike, with fourteen *Avengers* led by Lt. Cmdr. Frank Perry in *Mohawk-81*, put a final spread of fish into the cruiser and it sank shortly thereafter. Photos taken showed how accurately our 'fish' had hit their marks. Still another strike carried delay-action bombs against Japanese barges in the Lingayen Gulf area, scoring several hits."

In his autobiography, Commander Winters quoted the *Lexington*'s battle report: "Winters first directed the strike from the *Essex* to attack the cruiser, and the strike from the *Ticonderoga* to attack shipping in the inner harbor, holding the *Lexington* strike in reserve. Two or three bombs hit the cruiser, which was making about 25 knots, but it did not stop and was only slightly smoking, so Commander Winters directed the *Lexington* strike to hit her. Four bombs, four rockets, and a torpedo in the starboard bow stopped her dead in the water and she smoked heavily. But after 45 minutes the cruiser's fire went out, smoke stopped, and she got underway."

"When the next strike arrived Winters directed the *Lexington* group to hit the slowly moving heavy cruiser, the *Essex* group to hit a light cruiser in the inner harbor, and the *Ticonderoga* group to sink the circling destroyer. Five to seven bombs, four to six torpedoes, and at least two rockets went into the heavy cruiser. She broke into three pieces and slowly sank."

Ens. Warner Tyler flew in this third strike at Manila Bay. He didn't know it at the time, but it actually turned out to be his last combat mission. He flew in *Mohawk-87*, along with Petty Officers Mark Dewees and Arthur Davis. Mr. Tyler was armed with a torpedo—for only the *second time* in four months of combat flying! When they touched back down on the *Lexington* it was Tyler's 40th carrier landing.

On 5 November, fighter pilot Bill Davis flew, in *Mohawk-4*, with one other fighter as Commander Winters' wingmen. Davis' plane had fuel transfer problems, so Winters sent him and the other fighter—piloted by Lt. Barney Garbow—back to the *Lexington*.

"But this was the afternoon the ship took the *Kamikaze* hit," wrote Winters. "As they approached the Task Group the *Lexington* (*Mohawk*) was informed of their low fuel state, and Bill was given clearance for a long straight-in approach. As he entered the groove, the *Lexington* suddenly turned sharply to port and Bill's propeller stopped as he passed over the corner of the fantail. Before he hit the water he came up on the radio: '*Mohawk*, you and I are all through!' At the moment Davis didn't know that suddenly *Mohawk* was jinking, desperately trying to dodge her first *Kamikaze* attack."

Interestingly, Davis described this incident a little differently: with a fuel line cut from AAA, he tried to get back to the *Lexington* but was refused landing approach. "Negative, *Mohawk-4*, we are under attack and can't take you aboard." Davis thus ditched in the sea at quite some distance from the ship—still making the same frustrated remark over the radio—and quickly got out of his plane in pretty rough water. He thanked himself for all the hangar-deck practice of emergency egress from a plane he had put himself through back in August. He was shortly picked up by a destroyer and returned to the *Lexington* several days later.

Chief Petty Officer Bob Whitham gave a detailed account of this *Kamikaze* attack in his journal. "Today was comparatively quiet until about 1345 when a few bogies were picked up 80 miles to the west. Aircraft carrier *Hancock* was given control of the CAP as she maintained good information on the closing bogies. However, angles were unreliable for several minutes and interception was not effected despite that six fighter divisions (24 planes) were vectored out."

"The bogies quickly lost altitude," Whitham continued, "after entering our disposition, and a few seconds later two jet-black Japanese dive bombers came at us. They were headed aft on our starboard side about a half-mile apart. The leading plane was hit by gunfire just as he peeled off in his dive and he crashed into the water. The second plane made the same approach but the guns failed to hit it effectively, and the ship commenced an emergency turn to port. The plane kept coming, strafing all the way, and then it burst into flames just before crashing with its bomb into the aft end of the island structure."

"Flame and debris flew in every direction," Whitham went on. "Every man stationed on the 'island' starboard platforms and gun galleries was killed, wounded, or burned. Secondary Conn was a shambles with a score or more men lying dead, dismembered, and bleeding in the immediate vicinity of the blast. Gun mounts beneath Conn were marked by shrapnel holes, with many of their gunners dead in the gunstraps. Ready ammunition in a gun platform just outboard of the V-3 Office went off, wiping out gunners and blowing a large hole in the V-2 Office. Men came stumbling down ladders from the upper island structure with hands, arms, and legs off and bleeding profusely. Others were screaming in agony, clothes on fire. Some survivors walked by as if in a daze. Casualties numbered more than 150, and of those around 50 were dead or missing."

"Yet, we were able to continue flight operations, striking at Luzon, and then we held sea-burial services in the afternoon. We left the formation in the evening, with a three-destroyer escort, heading back to Ulithi for repairs and removal of the wounded."

Bombing-19's Lt.j.g. Wally Griffin added this account: "My division of *Helldivers* had just returned from the air group's early morning attack on shipping in Manila Harbor. During our debriefing by Lt.j.g. George Lewis, the squadron intelligence officer, the ship's P.A. system broadcast that 'Enemy Bogies' were picked up by radar and were approaching the Task Force. We knew this meant quite a show of defensive AAA. Air Group personnel did not have a specific battle station *per se*, so we were pretty much free to go topside and watch the show. During previous attacks on the Task Force many officers would climb up into the island structure and seek out a good vantage point to watch our airborne CAP and the ship's guns shoot down attacking Japanese aircraft. I had witnessed several of these attacks, and to say it was a spectacular sight would be a gross understatement. So a group of my fellow pilots headed out the hatch toward the starboard side of the ship and the long climb up several levels to get a good view of what was sure to happen. They yelled at me to follow them when I completed my report on target damage. I headed into the passageway where our mess steward informed me that he'd just finished making the ham sandwich I had requested as I hadn't anything to eat since about three in the morning prior to my flight."

"One of my squadron mates," continued Mr. Griffin, "yelled at me to 'hurry-up or you'll miss the show' as they climbed the ladder to the island structure. I thanked the steward and started for the starboard side to climb up to the island when I heard our 20mm guns open up. I knew instantly I couldn't get up the several levels in time to see anything; 20mm guns were only used when the enemy planes were right on top of you. So I turned immediately to the port side of the ship where I could stand on the catwalk right next to the flight deck and could see almost as well as being on the island. Just as I reached the catwalk I looked up to where the tracers from our guns were streaming. Not ten seconds later came the second bogey, diving straight for the 'Lady Lex.' As I stood there, munching on my sandwich, I looked up at the thousands of rounds being fired at the diving plane and knew that he too would explode any second now, because no plane could go through that wall of fire and survive. I also saw the bomb attached under the center of his fuselage. Orange flashes were coming from his guns as he was strafing the ship as he dove on us. I yelled at the men around me that he was strafing and to take cover under the edge of the flight deck."

"Almost immediately," Griffin went on, "we heard a huge explosion and the whole ship shook and shuddered as it was hit by the aircraft. The carrier then sounded its collision horn, a mournful 'mooing' sound like a dying cow. I went back up to the catwalk to see what damage we had suffered, and it was incredible. The after part of the island was in flames and huge billows of black smoke were pouring out of the island structure. Several bodies were lying on the flight deck very still. Several men were staggering around wounded and bleeding. The enemy plane had hit the ship just aft of the smokestack and directly into the ship's Secondary Control Station. When the bomb exploded it sent its force and flames all the way up the starboard side of the ship, killing almost all personnel exposed on that side forward of the center of the explosion."

"I often think of that fateful day," wrote Mr. Griffin, "when my waiting for a ham sandwich probably saved my life. However, being a man of faith, I will in no way discount the presence of a beautiful Guardian Angel and maybe a bit of Irish luck."

Indeed, of the flying squadrons onboard the *Lexington*, Bombing Nineteen was particularly devastated by this attack. Lt.j.g. Don Engen later wrote that "Lt. Bob Parker, Lt.j.g. Bob Smith, and Ensigns John Gilchrist, Bob Doyle, and Francis Jackson were missing and presumed blown over the side. Lt.j.g. Chuck Fisher was burned and later succumbed. Lt. Joe Williams, Lt.j.g. Ray Wicklander, Lt.j.g. Herb Walters, Lt.j.g. Bill Emerson, and Ens. Bob Griffin were burned about the hands and face but survived."

"All had been standing in the catwalk aft of Secondary Conn to observe what initially appeared to be what had become 'routine' afternoon attacks by Japanese aircraft."

Of course, in retrospect, this was a foolish thing to do. Yet, as Mr. Griffin and Mr. Engen pointed out, visits by enemy aircraft had become daily routine, and at this time the notion of airplanes deliberately crashing into ships was a new concept. In fact, it was only a few days before, on 29 and 30 October, that the *Intrepid*, *Franklin*, and *Belleau Wood* had been hit by *Kamikazes*—becoming the first of many fast carriers to be struck by a suicide pilot.

"On 5 November," Engen continued, "Bombing-19 lost two airplanes along with eight officers and two enlisted men killed, and we had lost the services of another five officers who were wounded." Regarding the VB-19 aircraft lost in combat that day, Lt.j.g. Engen was making reference to Lt. Cmdr. Don Banker, Lt.j.g. John Evatt, ARM^2 Jim Burns, and ARM^3 Richard Hansen.

The CAG, Commander Winters, spent time visiting the wounded later in the day. "Our group photographer, Chief Photographer's Mate Fred Burkhardt, lived 'til the next afternoon, both legs gone. He was sedated but conscious in the sick bay when I sat with him, and he said he didn't really want to go home the way he was. I couldn't cheer him up, and I confess to crying some more that night."

Winters had something else to cry about. As reported in the official VF-19 Battle Report of 5 November, "Probably the squadron's greatest loss since coming into combat came during a late afternoon fighter sweep south of Manila when the squadron commander, Lt. Roger "Smiley" Boles, was seen to crash after being hit by AAA fire. His drive and leadership, both on the ground and in the air, had endeared him as a 'captain' and friend to each man in the squadron, new and old." He had been squadron C.O. for just 24 days.

Shortly after returning to the *Lexington* after *his* combat flight to Manila Bay, Ens. Warner Tyler had seen the two Japanese *Kamikaze* aircraft approaching the ship.

"There's nowhere to run," recalled retired Captain Tyler, "or any safe haven until you know where the hit is likely to be. So I just watched." Warner was interviewed in 1995 by the Colorado Springs *Gazette-Telegraph* newspaper as part of their *WWII: They Were There* series commemorating the 50th anniversary of the end of the war. "It seemed like hours, but in point of fact it was probably only 15 or 30 seconds." The *Lexington*'s AAA guns took out one of the planes, but the other got through. "I could see the pilot. He was wearing one of those goofy fur-lined helmets the Japanese pilots wore. There was a great fireball, and the whole ship lurched and shuddered." Forty-seven men died, and 127 were injured. "We knew," Tyler continued, "that a whole new dimension had been introduced into the ferocity and intensity of naval warfare. But if anything it only stiffened our resolve. We knew we had to get the job done, and get it done quickly."

In July 1984, Captain Tyler had written an earlier essay on this subject, although it doesn't appear to have been published anywhere:

"History records a number of now-extinct civilizations who fought their wars by bodily hurling their soldiers upon the enemy, with no concern for the survival of those soldiers. The only modern-day country which has practiced this tactic as a basis for—and in many cases, instead of—tactics was Japan. During the latter part of 1944, and in 1945, the Japanese government embarked on a program known as the *Divine Wind*, better known to the U.S. Navy as the *Kamikaze*. My first experience with this tactic was the first hit which the *Lexington* withstood on 5 November 1944."

"There is no experience which is as mind-numbing as watching two inbound aircraft, loaded with high-octane fuel and high explosives, knowing full-well that the Japanese pilot who was overtaking the *Lexington* had the *entire ship* in his gunsight. In those interminable seconds before impact, you are acutely aware that there is nowhere to run or any safe haven from the fire and explosion that will follow the impact. And, of course, until it became apparent where the hit was likely to be, no direction or bulwark could guarantee that you would not be in harm's way. As it happened, the hit was made on the starboard side of the island. The 20mm-gun tub and mostly all else at that location was blasted loose in a fiery shower. Within seconds 47 men had died and 127 more were injured. The *Lexington* was badly in need of repairs and thus shortly returned to the fleet repair facility at Ulithi."

"Other ships of the fleet also experienced the terror and power of a *Kamikaze* hit."

"The attack on the *Lexington* was carried out by two *Zeke* fighter aircraft. One was blasted out of the sky by the *Lexington*'s guns but the other penetrated the starboard side of the island and exploded. Her damage was mostly confined to command and control activities, including the Secondary Conn Station, rather than structural."

"With the advent of the *Kamikaze* attacks a whole new dimension was introduced into the ferocity and intensity of naval warfare. As more and more ships of all types were subjected to these attacks it became apparent that the [conventional] naval air capability, which the Japanese had used so successfully in the early stages of the war, was now almost non-existent. Some of these *Kamikaze* aircraft were recovered, and a number of these were found to be minus their landing gear and arresting hooks. The age of the pilots who were recovered was in some cases 16 years, some of whom had as few as 25 flight hours."

"While this tactic was most effective on a spot basis, in the grand scheme of things it proved to be one of the most self-defeating aspects of the U.S. – Japanese phase of the war. In some ways the *Kamikaze* stands out as the forerunner of guided-missile warfare."

"Over the next two days," Lieutenant j.g. Engen continued in his account of the attack on the *Lexington*, "we held somber burial at sea services for the dead. As each body was consigned to the deep from the Number Two Elevator, in a white canvas bag weighted down with brass shell casings, the playing of taps and three rifle volleys from the Marine Guard marked each departure. As at every funeral we sang the *Navy Hymn*—which by now I had memorized."

As terrible as this was," wrote Rear Admiral Sherman, "the *Lexington*'s battle efficiency was not greatly affected."

Thus, "on November 6th," reported the VT-19 history, "one more strike was launched against shipping in the Manila area but AAA fire was so intense that accurate bombing was impossible." Moreover, one of the *Avengers*, *Mohawk-83*, was hit twice by AAA. "Ens. Charles J. Patterson's radioman, ARM3 William C. Lyde, was mortally wounded by shrapnel during this attack, and when still another burst crippled the plane, Ensign Patterson had to make a forced landing in the water. Patterson and the turret gunner, AMM3 R. G. La Fleur, attempted in vain to recover their dying comrade before the aircraft sank. Fortunately, Patterson and La Fleur were soon able to be rescued by the destroyer USS *Dortch*."

The VF-19 battle report from the same day was more positive. "Big news of the 6 November action was the destruction of 13 enemy fighters by Lt. Elvin 'Lin' Lindsay's and Lt. Albert Seckel, Jr.'s divisions over Clark Field." Lindsay was the new C.O. of VF-19 after the death of 'Smiley' Boles the day before. "Ens. Robert A. 'Ish' Farnsworth, in *Mohawk-27*, became the 'Divine Wind' of the squadron when he returned to the ship with five square feet of Japanese aircraft metal lodged in his wing." He had refused to break away from a 'playing chicken' incident with a Zero fighter; 'Ish' won. Fighter pilot Bill Davis wrote that this incident happened on 12 October versus 6 November, but the battle report might be more accurate.

"The day's kills brought Air Group-19's overall total to 167 Japanese aircraft shot down." A pretty successful last day of combat for the group.

"On board the *Lexington*," wrote Lt.j.g. Engen, "the burned people from the *Kamikaze* attack certainly needed better hospital care, and the ship itself needed its damage repaired. So, the Task Group headed for Ulithi."

While sailing for Ulithi the Air Group flew more anti-submarine patrols. Torpedo-19's share of this was a four-plane morning search on November 9th. This flight was actually the last one for Air Group-19 on board the *Lexington*.

Upon arrival the wounded were sent to the hospital ship *Relief*, and the repair ship *Jason* pulled alongside.

For everyone else, continued the VF-19 battle report, "Cold beer and a foot on solid ground for the first time in over seven weeks were the treats of 9 November in Ulithi Lagoon. During the next two weeks a broad athletic program, both on the ship's basketball court and around the Ulithi Bar (the officers' bar was a thoroughly converted tribal chief's thatched hut), made the time pass quickly. Many new replacement pilots required daily indoctrination lectures and checkouts as they arrived to fill our vacancies."

On 11 November the large carrier *Franklin*, and the light carrier *Belleau Wood*, joined the *Lexington* at Ulithi. As the reader knows, they also had been hit by *Kamikaze* aircraft.

Then, "a pack of Japanese two-man submarines," wrote Chief Radarman Bob Whitham, "penetrated the submarine nets in the lagoon on November 20th. This was about 0545. One sub was rammed by a destroyer outside of the nets and three were sunk by depth-charge attacks in the anchorage. One fleet tanker was hit by a torpedo just inside the anchorage and a supply ship outside of the nets was sunk. Another sub was beached a mile or so north of Mogmog. The oiler burned furiously for some time."

About this time the Air Group hosted a major awards ceremony on the flight deck. Commander Winters made the presentations on behalf of Vice Admiral Mitscher. Ens. Warner Tyler received the Navy Cross for his actions during the Battle off Cape Engaño. Standing at attention with him were Aviation Ordnanceman 2nd Class Wilmer Mark Dewees, and Aviation Radioman 3rd Class Arthur Davis. Dewees and Davis both received the Distinguished Flying Cross for that same action.

Looking closely at the photos it's amusing to discern three boxes marked in chalk on the deck in front of Winters [pilot / gunner / radioman] to ensure everyone stood in the correct place. It was a long ceremony; Winters had to pin on 67 Navy Crosses, 84 Distinguished Flying Crosses, 2 Silver Stars, and a few other awards.

The day after the awards ceremony, Commander Winters talked to the fighter pilots after dinner. According to Lt. j.g. Bill Davis, Winters stated, "Gentlemen, tomorrow morning the fleet is heading north. We're going to hit the Japanese Islands. This will be the first action against them since General Doolittle's raid on Tokyo over two years ago. We can expect very heavy opposition. We are the senior group, so we will lead the attack."

"Well, it had to come sooner or later," Mr. Davis said to himself. "Attacking the Japanese Fleet was one thing, but attacking the Japanese main islands was another. We congregated in Lt. Bill Masoner's room, but no one was saying much."

"Suddenly, Lt. John Hutto burst into the room. 'Hey fellows, there's a carrier coming in.' We all looked at each other, then jumped up as a man and ran to the flight deck. There she was, entering the lagoon." It was the *Enterprise*, recognized by all.

"Word spread around immediately. 'Her air group, AG-20, is going to relieve us. We are NOT going to Japan tomorrow; in fact, we are going home!'" Mr. Davis took a quart of bourbon he'd been saving and drank most of it by himself. Fortunately, he threw most of it up—while nearly falling overboard in so doing. As he envisioned the hundred-foot fall while puking, he thought to himself, "After what I've been through, what a way to die."

The VT-19 history reported that "Great was our joy—*and surprise*—when scuttlebutt preceded orders for our Air Group to embark in the carrier *Enterprise* for Pearl Harbor, which would be our first leg on the journey back to the States. Home for Christmas! The war, for us, was over—at least for a while."

This amazing turn of events came about very rapidly. According to Petty Officer Gerald Warnke of Bombing-19, "Somebody stuck his head into the Ready Room and announced that we had thirty minutes to pack our personal belongings and report to the quarterdeck to be transferred to the *Enterprise* for the start of our journey back to the USA. Hell, I only needed ten; I had twenty minutes to kill before our transportation arrived!"

In fact, this happened so suddenly it almost found ARM[1] Charles W. Lebkisher in trouble for "missing ship's movement." Very early on Thanksgiving Day, having heard none of this scuttlebutt, he'd gone ashore from the *Lexington* to prepare for a planned ship's beer party. After most of the day had passed, during which he saw no other Air Group-19 people, he worked himself back to the ship via several small boat rides and found not a single Air Group-19 man on board. "I rushed to my locker; the lock was snipped off and my things were gone! I discovered a landing craft being loaded for the *Enterprise*, where a ship's company seaman told me my group transferred." To his great relief, the LC delivered him to the

Enterprise and his squadron mates. He'd already been reported as "UA" (unauthorized absence), the navy version of "AWOL."

According to Mr. Davis, "After a Thanksgiving mid-day dinner, on 23 November, we took off and landed on the *Enterprise*." It's interesting that he wrote this, because naval historian Edward P. Stafford, in his wonderful book about the *Enterprise*, reported that "On the 23rd, CAG Daniel "Dog" Smith and his Air Group-Twenty embarked with their gear in landing craft and 50-foot motor launches, and crossed the anchorage to the *Lexington*, while the *Lexington*'s Air Group-Nineteen transferred to the *Enterprise* for transportation to Pearl Harbor." So, apparently, no airplanes were transferred between the ships.

Dive-bomber pilot Ens. Louis A. "Squeaky" Heilmann wrote that it was a heck of a busy day, which included "two Thanksgiving feasts—one on the '*LEX*' before the transfer, then one on the '*Big E*' afterwards."

As they departed Ulithi Lagoon, Lieutenant j.g. Davis wrote that from the *Enterprise* he stared at the *Lexington*, apparently soon to sail towards Japan. "I would have liked to have gone with them; on the other hand, there's nothing wrong with living." Right after the *Enterprise* left the *Lexington* pulled out of Ulithi for eight days' gunnery practice.

Carrier Air Group-19 had been on board the *Lexington* from 10 July 1944 to 23 November 1944; a short time for some, but an eternity for others.

The *Enterprise* sailed from 23-26 November, *en route* to Hawai'i. There wasn't a lot to do for Group-19's personnel, other than VB-19 had to fly a lot of anti-submarine patrols. The *Helldivers* left by AG-20 were the only aircraft available for such work. Someone in authority decided that they wouldn't risk married men, so the unmarried aircrews drew the duty—which created friction between the two groups of men. And, since there was apparently some sort of shortage of landing signal officers (the men who guided pilots in on their final landing approaches), the ship was using new, non-pilot officers which almost created several disasters. Lt.j.g. Wally Griffin almost punched the LSO on the flight deck after one hair-raising landing. "I was so mad to think I had come through the whole damn combat tour and now on my last flight before reaching Hawai'i this little jerk almost killed me!"

VT-19 pilot Lt. Jack Meeker later mentioned another challenge: "Being catapulted off to fly an ASP. What a short catapult! It was like being shot out of a cannon."

Other personnel viewed the trip as a vacation. Petty Officer Eno Leaf recalled that "Some enjoyable moments were playing cards in the ready room, and at times we would go on the catwalk at the bow right under the flight deck and tell sea stories. I also enjoyed watching the flying fish and porpoises swim alongside the ship."

The *Enterprise* came in to Pearl Harbor on 26 November. Then the Air Group's personnel moved directly to the escort carrier USS *Long Island* (CVE-1).

Petty Officer Warnke recalled that "We arrived in Pearl Harbor and almost immediately boarded a "Kaiser Coffin" bound for San Diego. We never really had a chance to set foot in downtown Honolulu. Oh well, 20-25 years later I made it back to Hawai'i and Maui. I found that the old NAS Kahului was now the main commercial airport on the island of Maui, NAS Pu'unene no longer existed, the road to the top of Mount Haleakalā had been paved, and the islands were overrun with tourists and hotels. I'm sure that the native Hawai'ians would rather have their homeland back the way it was prior to WWII. Such is 'progress?'"

Warnke's remark about the *Long Island* being a "Kaiser Coffin" refers to the misconception that the smaller escort carriers, many built in the shipyards of Henry J. Kaiser, suffered from a lack of seaworthiness. In reality, they proved their worth in hunting submarines and in several major actions with Axis forces.

The *Long Island* sailed on 6 December and arrived at San Diego on the 14th. Lt. Bob Niemeyer was frustrated with the voyage, later writing, "How can it take this long to get from Pearl Harbor to San Diego?" Part of the reason was that it was a trip filled with foul weather. It must have been rough. VB-19's Lt.j.g. Alvin F. Emig, who earned a Navy Cross on 5 November, mostly recalled being seasick; this is from a man who had just spent almost six months at sea and had been in more than a few noteworthy storms.

Lt. Don Engen recalled "the four-deep bunks, the long trip, and the fact that no cigarettes would be sold to 'passengers.'" Lt.j.g. Bob Duncan remembered "seeing the movie *Constant Nymph* with Charles Boyer and Joan Fontaine every single night for the entire trip." Petty Officer Ray Schoener recalled playing a number of basketball games. "I never have forgotten the helpless feeling of going up for a shot at the basket, and the ship rising on the waves at the same time, making you feel like you were glued to the deck."

Schoener also remembered "great satisfaction as we entered the harbor at San Diego and were greeted by banners and a band and many 'welcomers' at the dock. It was made even greater for me when some of us were on the catwalk, with many of that *Long Island* bunch standing on the flight deck behind us, full of puzzlement at all the celebrating, and asking each other what it was for. It was a great feeling to see their jaws drop when we turned around and informed them that it was for *us*!"

Fighter pilot Lt.j.g. Bill Davis was also pretty excited to reach San Diego. "We rounded Point Loma, and I can tell you San Diego never looked so good. We were home. We had made it. And on top of everything else it was December 17th, so we were going to be home for Christmas. Disembarking from the *Long Island* we found we were assigned quarters as there were apparently some formalities before we went on thirty-day leave." In the short run, "the party at the Hotel Del Coronado that night was a real screamer."

The formalities, it turned out, appeared as a series of interviews in front of a board—which included a psychiatrist. They wanted to see if anyone was suffering from battle fatigue, and if the pilots wanted to return to combat. At first this seemed like it might take several weeks for the group; but, fortunately, it only took three days. "The truth was that we assumed we were all going back into combat anyway, so we might as well 'game' the interviews and tell them what they wanted to hear, and thus get home for Christmas. Home for Christmas meant more that year than any other in my life." Mr. Davis saw a lot of Christmases; he made it to age 91, barely finishing his wonderful autobiography from which we've learned so much for this story.

Fortunately, Bill Davis got home in late December 1944, before his ailing father passed away. "I could tell he was proud of me, although he wouldn't put it into words. His only remark regarding my Navy Cross was, "Did you have to do something *that* brave?"

Davis also took a 60-mile drive from Philadelphia down to Atlantic City, New Jersey, to visit the parents of his *Lexington* roommate Ens. Dan G. "Duke" de Luca, Jr. As the reader already knows, "Duke" had been killed on the very first attack the Air Group made on 20 July. "I was hoping I could lessen the sorrow of 'Duke's' death. I didn't even come close. They were beyond consoling. I've never seen such pain in a family and I realized that this was being repeated in thousands of families across America. After a short time I beat a hasty retreat."

Ens. Warner W. Tyler made it home to Colorado by Christmas—not home to stay of course, but like the others he enjoyed a brief respite before moving on to his next assignment. That next move could well have been back to the Pacific with Air Group-Nineteen and Torpedo Nineteen, which he assumed would be the case—or something else not even imagined.

On 29 December 1944 he found himself in downtown Denver, at the Albany Hotel at 17th and Stout Streets. He was interviewed there by Mr. Joe W. Miller of the news staff at radio station KFEL—Denver's second oldest station.

Mr. Miller: *"Here in the studio with me tonight is Ensign Warner W. Tyler, a local boy who has just returned from ten months of duty in the Pacific. Ensign Tyler is 22 years old, and his parents live at 1345 Madison Street. He attended Denver University for about two years before enlisting in the Naval Air Corps. Ensign Tyler has been in the Navy now for some two and one-half years, and has been overseas for the past ten months as a torpedo-bomber pilot in the Pacific. For some more personal statistics, we might add that Mr. Tyler is rather tall and slender, has blond hair and blue eyes, and is married to the former Mavis Lorenzen of Denver.*

Now to get down to business. Ensign, isn't that a Navy Cross you're wearing?"

Ensign Tyler: *"That's correct."*

Mr. Miller: *"There's always an interesting story behind these awards, it seems to me, and I'm sure there is about this award. Will you tell us something about it—and about what you've been doing?"*

Ensign Tyler: *"The action occurred on the 25th of October, east of the Formosan and Philippine Islands, notably Luzon. We caught the Japanese Fleet heading south on a collision course with our forces. They were attempting to intercept and do away with what they thought was a small force of ours. After they sent out reconnaissance planes and found that we had a little larger force than they had expected to encounter, they started to head back to some of their bases north, in the Japanese homeland and Formosa. We chased them for about 24 hours; we launched our strikes and went up and caught what the Japanese sent down after us. There were a number of carriers, battleships, cruisers, and destroyers in their force.*

We went in on the ships. We got on to several carriers—two of which were sunk and several left in a sinking condition. Four of us torpedo planes went in on a battleship—it was underway at the time and had not been molested at the time we went in after it—and after working it over a little bit we did some damage to that battleship. It was last seen heading north at a very reduced speed."

Mr. Miller: *"Was that one of the* Haruna*-class battleships, one of their larger battleships?"*

Ensign Tyler: *"That's it."* [However, both Mr. Miller and Mr. Tyler were mistaken; the *Haruna* was present at Leyte Gulf, but was not at the Battle for Cape Engaño, nor were any of her sister-ships. Tyler would not have known that at the time of this interview. In fact, for the rest of his life, Mr. Tyler never learned for sure what ship he had attacked on 25 October 1944.]

Mr. Miller: *"You were on Vice Admiral Mitscher's flagship, were you not?"*

Ensign Tyler: *"That's right."*

Mr. Miller: *"I think we ought to also say that Ensign Tyler has taken part in bombing strikes against Guam, Palau, the Bonin and Volcana Islands, and at Tinian Island. That's really taken you around the Pacific, hasn't it?"*

Ensign Tyler: *"It certainly has."*

Mr. Miller: *"What do you think of the Japanese airman as a flier—is he good? We've had rather conflicting reports about him back here at home."*

Ensign Tyler: *"The Japanese airman is an excellent flier—if he has enough training. The situation recently seems to point to the fact that the Japanese are not taking time to train their pilots thoroughly. However, the training they have had seems to be producing pretty good results."*

Mr. Miller: *"During the past two or three weeks, we've been hearing a lot about the shortage of materials and supplies. How did you find that situation in the Pacific?"*

Ensign Tyler: *"At the time I was out there we noticed no glaring need for supplies on the ship. We had all that we needed. But there is undoubtedly a large problem confronting the Navy and the nation as a whole, on getting supplies out there on the long supply route. The problem is indeed one which will have to be met."*

Mr. Miller: *"In connection with supplies, how about the cigarette situation?"*

Ensign Tyler: *"Cigarettes were no problem at all at the time I was out there."*

Mr. Miller: *"Congratulations!"*

Ensign Tyler: *"Thanks!"*

Mr. Miller: *"An interview like this is never complete unless we ask the question, 'How long do you think the war in the Pacific will last?'"*

Ensign Tyler: *"Like everyone else you interview, I am only a cog in the whole setup. To start with, it seems to me there is quite a bit of fighting to be done yet in the Pacific. The Japanese are far from being beaten, but I believe that we are going along either as good as on schedule—or better than on schedule. With things keeping up the way they have in the past, I believe the end will be in sight before too many years* [!] *have passed, at least."*

Mr. Miller: *"Do you think it's possible that it might be by the end of next year—by the end of 1946?"*

Ensign Tyler: *"I think there is a possibility, although it doesn't look like a definite possibility."*

Mr. Miller: *"Thank you very much, Mr. Tyler. It's been nice having you with us tonight."*

The thirty-day leave period went by pretty quickly for the men of Carrier Air Group-Nineteen, scattered all over the United States.

"I was nearing the time," wrote Lt.j.g. Davis, "that I would leave home and rejoin Fighting Squadron-Nineteen for a brief period of refresher training, and then back to an aircraft carrier and into Pacific Theater combat. I could see the strain on my father's and mother's faces. I could only imagine them facing what 'Duke's' family had."

"I was within days of leaving when new orders arrived by wire. I was to report to the California Institute of Technology for two years of graduate school in aeronautical engineering! I was given to understand that the Navy was preparing for a possible long extension to the war, and they wanted men in the Bureau of Aeronautics who were both combat pilots *and* engineers." Mr. Davis had completed an undergraduate degree in engineering just prior to the start of the war so had a good background.

"My old squadron," he continued, "Fighting-19, did reform and eventually made it out to Maui on their way to the Pacific. They were there when the war with Japan was over. They never made it back into combat."

In Denver, Ens. Warner Tyler was also expecting orders to rejoin Torpedo-19 and Air Group-19, and to go back to the Pacific. However, as with Davis, those orders did not come. Indeed, as Mr. Davis later found out as well, by the time Nineteen got back onto a carrier—another *Essex*-class, the USS *Hornet*—it was 11 October 1945, and the war had become history.

In the case of Mr. Tyler, his new orders did not send him to college, the west coast, or out into the Pacific; rather, they sent him east for more and varied flying training. Early February 1945 found him, very briefly, at Naval Air Station Norfolk, Virginia.

NAS Norfolk's contributions to the war effort were many, but perhaps the largest contribution was in the training it provided to a wide variety of naval air units. With only a few exceptions, all navy air squadrons that fought in the war trained in Norfolk. The air station also trained numerous British fighter squadrons as well as some French and Soviet squadrons.

All that aside, Mr. Tyler's stay at Norfolk was very brief, and by February 11th he had affiliated with Bomber-Fighter Squadron-97 (VBF-97) at NAS Grosse Ile, in southeast Michigan. There, throughout the rest of February, he flew the SBD-5 Douglas *Dauntless* dive bomber. The "5" variant was the most-produced version of the *Dauntless*. All of his flights in February were for "familiarization and practice" except the last one on the 27th which was characterized as "tactical."

VBF-97 had been established in January 1945. It's interesting to note that bomber-fighter squadrons were created in an effort to reduce the fighter squadrons in an air group to an "acceptable" size; fighter squadrons had grown to be as large as 60 airplanes and 100 pilots. VBF-97 was the East Coast *Corsair* replacement training squadron.

NAS Grosse Ile was the home of a Navy base for some forty years. The naval air station opened in 1929 after three years of construction of seaplane and dirigible facilities. During World War II the naval base developed into an important center for military flight training. The base was expanded considerably to accommodate large numbers of American—and British—fliers who trained on the island. Future president George H. W. Bush was also stationed at the base for training for about two months during 1945.

On March 1, 1945, Warner was promoted to Lieutenant (junior grade) with the designator 1315—unrestricted line officer, naval reserve flying duty.

March 1st also saw his first flight in a Chance-Vought F4U-1 *Corsair*, one of the most capable carrier-based fighter-bombers of World War II. His five flights with VBF-97 that month were again for familiarization and practice—except for two in a North American Aviation Company SNJ-5 *T-6 Texan* advanced trainer for instrument flying, and two in a Brewster Aeronautical Corporation F3A-1 *Corsair* (Brewster's contract version of the F4U-1).

In mid-March Lt.j.g. Tyler transferred to Bomber-Fighter Squadron 153 at Naval Air Station Wildwood (near Cape May, New Jersey). NAS Wildwood had been established in April 1943 to provide facilities and services for the operation of fleet units under the Commander, Fleet Air Force, Atlantic Fleet.

VBF-153 operated in conjunction with Carrier Aircraft Service Unit 24 (CASU-24) at Wildwood. A number of CASUs were in the war zones, but CASUs based in the continental U.S. received new planes, trained personnel, commissioned men and planes as squadrons, and formed squadrons to go aboard carriers.

VBF-153 was established at Wildwood on 29 March 1945, with Lt. Cmdr. Hayden M. Jensen as commanding officer. Mr. Jensen personally approved and signed four pages in Mr. Tyler's flight log from this point until the end of the war. It's hard not to admire Mr. Jensen's large and flamboyant signature on those documents!

Towards the end of March, Warner piloted *Corsairs* on further familiarization and practice flights. In April he flew on fourteen days, ten times in F4-Us and four times in FG-1s—Goodyear Corporation's contract versions of the *Corsair*. Five of these flights were for gunnery training, five were "tactical," and one was for bombing.

During May Lieutenant j.g. Tyler flew 38 times, obviously more than once on some days. Almost all of these flights were in F4U *Corsairs*. The purpose of the flights varied, but included a considerable number of instrument training, night flying, and field carrier landing practices.

Mr. Tyler then moved, with VFB-153, to Naval Auxiliary Air Station Oceana at Virginia Beach, Virginia on 1 June 1945. At that time NAAS Oceana served as a useful outlying field for the still-expanding Naval Air Force operations centered at NAS Norfolk, and allowed units to work-up for deployments away from that and other crowded bases. Warner and VFB-153 stayed at Oceana through August and the end of the war.

In June, Lt.j.g. Tyler flew twenty-five times; on several days more than once. All of these flights were in an F4U-4 *Corsair*, the last *Corsair* variant to see action in World War II. These flights covered a number of training options with tactical, gunnery, and bombing being the most common.

July saw Warner fly eighteen times, all in F4U-4s. Again, he executed multiple training options, gunnery being frequent. In August he flew nineteen times, again all in the F4U-4. Tactical and gunnery were dominant for him that month.

However, the surrender of Imperial Japan was announced by Emperor Hirohito on August 15th. The emperor gave a recorded radio broadcast across the Empire. In this address, called the "Jewel Voice Broadcast," he announced to the Japanese people that the Japanese government had accepted the Potsdam Declaration—which had been issued by the United States and its allies on 26 July 1945—demanding the "unconditional" surrender of the Japanese military. As a result, in observance of the discontinuance of hostilities with Japan, all training and cross-country flying was secured for two days by the Commander, Fleet Air Force, Atlantic Fleet. Then, those two days having passed, Mr. Tyler and his cohorts were back up in the air; he flew eight more training flights before the end of the month.

At that point, like millions of other servicemen and women, he was released from active duty as the armed forces of the United States began their massive demobilization. Warner's departure from Virginia and return to Colorado probably wasn't instantaneous, but he was back in Denver by September 23rd.

Family lore says that at first he wanted to stay in the navy, unlike future Emmy-award winning actor and recording artist Dennis

Weaver, who had recently finished F4U *Corsair* training at NAS Miami, Opa-locka, Florida.

Ensign Weaver had not yet been in an operational squadron nor gone overseas, but since the war was over he immediately decided his naval career could be over as well. He had just been "assigned to a squadron and they gave me orders to go to Pearl Harbor. I first reported to San Diego, but mostly everything was shut down. I was just an Ensign, and on 'the list' of people that they felt they could 'do without,' so when they said I could get out and go home I snapped up the offer." And he was happy that, as it turned out, he hadn't had "to engage anyone in deadly combat."

Lieutenant j.g. Tyler was not of that thinking. He thought staying in the Navy sounded like a good idea. He was no doubt *not* on the list of people they could "do without." He had a good operational record and it was one which was incident- and accident-free. He had been a carrier pilot in active warfare for five months, he had racked-up over 100 hours of combat flying time, and he'd accomplished 40 successful carrier landings. He'd earned the Asiatic-Pacific Campaign Ribbon with four bronze stars—and, of course, the Navy Cross. Thus, he wanted to continue on as a navy pilot, and the Navy likely was willing to have him do just that.

However, no one had counted on Mrs. Mavis Ann Lorenzen Tyler. She had other ideas for herself and for her war-hero husband. She thought he should take the demobilization discharge from the Navy, come back to Denver, and begin a "normal" life with her and take advantage of all the promises, hopes, and opportunities that post-war America was apparently going to offer.

Thus, like millions of other servicemen and women, Lt.j.g. Warner William Tyler, USNR, was released from active duty and went home.

Chapter 16

"So, Dad returned to Denver, came off of Navy active duty, and was suddenly unemployed," writes Ms. Linda Wieland, the daughter of Warner and Mavis. "I do know that Mom's father—my grandfather—John Henry Lorenzen, shortly invited Dad to join his company, which he had started around 1942 and was then called the Solid Carbonic Company."

Linda's brother Gary Tyler isn't precisely sure when Solid Carbonic first started up. He suspects it really got going when Warner became available to help John. "The dry-ice plant took a few people to run. Someone had to cut the large blocks into smaller 50-pound blocks, wrap them in paper, deliver them to customers, do the marketing work, accounting, etc. My guess is they had three-to-four others in addition to the two of them. My grandfather was more the mechanical end with the physical plant; Dad more the business side with sales and distribution."

Linda says that, "When Dad was first an employee with our grandfather in the Solid Carbonic Company—which in 1948 became the Carb-Ice Corporation—he did much of the selling and visiting clients in Colorado and several other neighboring states. Most of these clients were 'bottlers' and purchased CO_2 from Carb-Ice, which they added to their soft drinks as carbonation." Carbonation, of course, is the addition of carbon dioxide into a liquid and is the technique that gives drinks their fizz and makes sparkling beverages possible. Carb-Ice also produced and sold other compressed gases, dry ice, and some cryogens. Cryogens, such as liquid nitrogen, were and are used for specialty chilling and freezing applications. For a number of years the company also produced ammonium nitrate fertilizer.

Thus, with Warner gainfully employed, the Tylers were soon busy with post-war life and looking forward to a bright future. Indeed, Warner and Mavis welcomed their daughter Linda in December 1945.

However, Warner was by no means finished with aviation. In fact on 23 September 1945 he was up in the air in a civilian *Piper J-3 Cub*—the same type of aircraft which he first flew in early 1943 when he undertook flying training with the Navy. That day he soloed, no doubt to make sure he still knew how to do it, and then he took up his father-in-law John Lorenzen for an hour, followed by a second flight with his parents—Warner and Jane Tyler. Flying with their favorite naval aviator hero must have been fun, for on 7 October John Lorenzen got another ride, on 14 October it was the elder Warner Tyler's turn again, and on 21 October it was Mr. Lorenzen once more. It wasn't until 28 April 1946, however, that his wife went up with her husband; his unofficial logbook entry says: "Mavis's first ride with me."

No doubt extremely busy with his developing civilian career and new role as a family man, it took Warner some time to reengage with military flying. However, after a little time had passed, he affiliated with the local Naval Air Reserve and started flying at the new Naval Air Station Denver, located at what had been the Army Air Forces's Buckley Field, just to the east of Denver.

Chapter 17

"In June, 1946," wrote U.S. Air Force historian Ms. Shawn Riem, "a Navy survey team descended on various airfields in Wyoming, Colorado, and Utah, seeking a suitable location for an inland Naval Air Reserve station. The idea was to have a base to serve the training needs of New Mexico, Colorado, Wyoming, Utah, and portions of North Dakota and Nebraska. The U.S. Army Air Forces' Buckley Field quickly emerged as the most promising site. The installation had been first established in 1938 and was named in honor of First Lieutenant John H. Buckley, a World War I army pilot. To the Navy, in 1946, this site was made even more desirable by the over 800 local ex-Navy personnel who showed an interest in joining the Naval Air Reserve."

"By January, 1947, an advance party had arrived at the site to set up shop and prepare the installation for transfer from the Army's existing Buckley Field to the Navy's new Naval Air Station Denver. Old NAS Denver lore has it that the men had to borrow a crowbar from the Colorado Air National Guard's 120th Fighter Squadron to pry open a hangar, only to find it in a state of complete disrepair and filled with surplus army equipment. The men stuck with it, set up shop, and NAS Denver was formally established on 16 February 1947. The CANG retained operational control, until 28 September

1947, while the Navy went about manning their newly created billets."

"The installation quickly filled with over 70 navy planes. SNJ *Texans*, SNB *Kansans*, and JRB *Expeditors* were used for training. In addition, TBM-3 *Avengers*, SB2c *Helldivers*, PV-2 *Harpoons*, R4D *Gooney Birds*, F8F-2 *Bearcats*, F2H-1 *Banshees*, F6F *Hellcats*, F9F-7 *Cougars*, P2V-5F *Neptunes*, and F4U *Corsairs* all graced the skies surrounding NAS Denver—but they all kept a respectful distance from nearby Stapleton International Airport."

"NAS Denver soon became known throughout the Navy as both the 'world's highest naval air station' and the NAS farthest from a major body of water. Locally, however, the installation was early known for its 'Veterans Villages.' These were five lodging areas that provided temporary shelter for returning veterans facing the housing shortage brought on by wartime restrictions in construction."

"NAS Denver leaders immediately sought to familiarize the Denver area with the installation's primary training mission and the importance of an inland naval air station. Among other things, in a successful and humorous attempt to do this, in 1954 a NAS Denver public-information officer created the 'Prairie Dog Navy.' This program ultimately boasted fourteen 'honorary admirals' over the years; these were all prominent men and women from the Denver area (such as brewer William Coors) and beyond (such as stars Jack Benny and Bob Hope)."

Chapter 18

When Lt.j.g. Warner W. Tyler, USNR, came off World War II active duty and returned from the east coast in September 1945, there was no naval air reserve organization in the Denver area for him to join.

However, when Naval Air Station Denver was established in February 1947 to support a Naval Air Reserve presence, Warner was among the first of the "local personnel" mentioned earlier to step forward. It's fair to say he was a "plank-owner" of not only the NAS, but also of the newly established air reserve organization there. A plank owner is an individual who is a member of the crew of a ship when that ship is placed in commission. It also applies to members of newly commissioned units and new bases. The origin of the term comes from the implication that a crew member was around when the ship was being built and commissioned, and therefore has bragging rights to the "ownership" of one of the original planks used in construction.

Things moved quickly, and by the next month Mr. Tyler was already back in the cockpit of a naval aircraft, flying a North American SNJ-5 *Texan* advanced trainer on 28 and 29 March.

In fact, he may have gone on some active-duty orders, because in April 1947 he flew 32 times on 12 different days spread throughout the month. On these flights he predominantly was in two types of aircraft, the *Texan* and the TBM-3 *Avenger* torpedo bomber—the *Avenger*, of course, being the aircraft with which he was particularly at home. The flights were variously categorized, but were mostly logged as "familiarization" and "tactical."

As mentioned earlier, when Warner was first an employee with his father-in-law in the Carb-Ice Corporation, he did much of the selling and visiting of clients over a several-state area. The clients were essentially bottlers who purchased CO_2 that was then added to their soft drinks as carbonation. Warner's daughter Linda writes that as time went by "My childhood friends were curious about why my brother and I were allowed to go along on some of his business trips when I told them that his job was to provide the bubbles that went into *7-UP*. For some reason it sounded so importantly mysterious and magical to Linda, the child. Our family of four spent many 'family vacations' with three of us waiting in the hot car together while he went inside the bottler facility to call on his clients. Afterwards, the 'vacation' commenced for a day or so before returning home. Later, when Dad became a full partner and sales manager with Carb-Ice, I remember thinking that his executive status sure seemed a lot less exciting than the hands-on part of manufacturing dry ice and CO_2—and the sales trips—of his early years with the company." As already discussed, in those early days it basically was just Warner and his father-in-law, John Lorenzen, on the management side of the business with just a handful of other employees. As the business grew Warner wore successive—and—simultaneous hats. Many years later Warner reflected that he was a "salesman, sales manager, treasurer, vice president and, ultimately, president of Carb-Ice as well as other companies created by merger and acquisitions."

Solid Carbonic/Carb-Ice built a plant on land leased from the Colorado Ice and Cold Storage Company, at 1700 W. Colfax Avenue, to make dry ice from steam and flue gas which they purchased from Colorado Ice. Gary Tyler mentions that, "I don't know if this was an established manufacturing technology at the time, but family lore has it that it was pretty clever."

Of course, Warner was also busy in the Naval Reserve and continued to fly. In May 1947 he flew twice in a TBM-3E *Avenger*, and in June he flew an *Avenger* in an air show at NAS Buckley and another *Avenge*r in July. He appears not to have flown at all in August and September, but in October 1947 he flew three times in an F6F *Hellcat* fighter for "familiarization and practice." This actually seems to be his last naval flight, for his official flight log ends on 18 October 1947, with a total of 777 hours.

This also looks like a significant transition point for Lieutenant j.g. Tyler—not to mention he had become a father again in November 1947 with the birth of his son, Gary. At this point Warner may have moved into a naval reserve non-flying management or leadership position. The reader will recall that Warner was promoted to Lieutenant, junior grade, on 1 March 1945, while still on active duty during the war. At that time his naval officer "designator" was 1315, which was "Naval Reserve unrestricted line officer qualified for duty, as a Naval Aviator, involving piloting heavier-than-air, or heavier and lighter-than-air types of aircraft in flying duty."

Reflecting the slow promotion times common to post-war reservists, Warner wasn't promoted to Lieutenant until 1 September 1956 with the designator of 1355, which was "Naval Reserve unrestricted line officer in the Aeronautical Organization as a Naval Aviator, but not in flying duty."

That said, there was plenty of flying still going on at NAS Buckley, it just no longer involved Warner Tyler. Official Buckley historian Shawn Riem reports that "When the call came for service members to join the fight in Korea, the men of naval fighter squadron VF-713 'Vultures' answered and served honorably as part of

Carrier Air Group-15 on board the USS *Antietam* (CV-36), flying F4U-4 *Corsairs*. Air Group-15 held a 'Denver Day' on 11 December 1951 at which simulated air strikes were flown in honor of VF-713, and much of the ordnance dropped was marked with the names of prominent Denver area organizations and activities."

"VF-713's tour ended in March 1952 when the *Philippine Sea* (CV-47) relieved the *Antietam*. VF-713 returned home to a hero's welcome and a celebration that lasted more than a week, with a 'Navy Day' at the Denver Bears baseball stadium and a formal gathering at Denver's downtown City and County Building. The homecoming was short lived, however, as the squadron deployed again less than a year later with Air Group-15 on the USS *Princeton* (CVA-37)."

"While operations continued at Naval Air Station Denver throughout the Korean War and into the post-war period, the end of NAS Denver was drawing near. The Navy, seeking to trim its budget, determined a need to close some of its nearly 30 'dedicated' Air Reserve installations and consolidate reserve activities wherever possible. Thus, NAS Denver was selected for closure in June 1959 and its units were either disbanded or transferred to other locations. Its personnel, likewise, either opted for an early-out or affiliated with other units."

"On 18 April 1960, after twelve years of ownership, NAS Denver was transferred from the U.S. Navy to the U.S. Air Force and renamed Buckley Air National Guard Base, becoming the first standalone Guard base in the Air Force."

Even though the base was now run by the Colorado Air National Guard, there did remain a "Naval Air Reserve Center Denver" located there, using a refurbished and reconstituted World War II building. The problem was that the few aviation units that remained at NARCenDen had no airplanes, and thus were strictly devoted to administration and training.

So, at this point Lt. Warner W. Tyler, wanting to stay in the more operational part of the Naval Air Reserve and around active aircraft, had to begin commuting to drill weekends out of state. He flew to NAS Dallas, Texas for some of this, but did most of it at NAS Olathe, Kansas. Fortunately, for years the Naval Reserve operated an airlift system to facilitate reservists drilling away from their places of residence. Using naval air reserve aircraft and pilots, some places were better serviced than others, but in Warner's case the Buckley-to-Olathe commute was pretty well supported, leaving in the late afternoon or early evening on Fridays and returning on Sunday evening. Flown by airline pilots who were also naval reservists executing their own weekend duty, this part of the airlift system often employed Lockheed P-3 *Orion* four-engine turboprop aircraft out of NAS Great Lakes. Other airlift aircraft included the Douglas C-118 *Liftmaster* four-engine aircraft (which the commercial airlines called a DC-6), based out of NAS Dallas. The flights were not always, but often, unpressurised which meant low-level, bumpy, and noisy.

Olathe, to the southwest of the greater Kansas City metropolitan area, might seem an odd place for a naval air station—but perhaps no more strange than was Denver. The base had opened as Naval Air Station Olathe on 1 October 1942 to be used for the Naval Air Transport Service and the Naval Air Primary Training Command. After World War II, NAS Olathe was used for flight operations by units of the Naval Air Reserve and Marine Air Reserve, as well as Naval Air Technical Training Center Olathe—a training center for active-duty Navy and Marine Corps enlisted personnel.

NAS Olathe's runways were lengthened in 1951 to accept the Navy's first tactical jets, the North American FJ-1 *Fury*. By 1954, a Jet Transition Training Unit was established at Olathe for propeller pilots making the transition to jet aircraft. And, Douglas F4D *Skyray* fighters were later operated at NAS Olathe by Naval

Air Reserve and Marine Air Reserve squadrons until 1966. Marine Reserve Training and Naval Reserve Training continued from 1966 until at least 1971.

For over 20 years, Naval Air Reservists and Marine Air Reservists from across the Midwest honed their skills and maintained their readiness with squadrons and support units at NAS Olathe. However, in a somewhat parallel scenario to NAS Denver, budgetary pressures of the Vietnam War eventually forced NAS Olathe to close. The base was decommissioned on 29 October 1969 and the air station was officially closed in July 1970. However, and similarly to Denver, the Navy was allowed to retain buildings for non-flying naval reserve aviation programs as Naval Air Reserve Center Olathe.

Thus, for about ten years, Warner Tyler commuted to drill from his home in Denver to Olathe, Kansas. At times, apparently, he commuted from Denver to drill at NAS Dallas. He was again promoted, this time to Lieutenant Commander, on 1 July 1962—retaining his 1355 designator. He achieved greater and greater responsibility in Air Reserve units, from department head to executive officer.

On 1 November 1966, still designated as a 1355, he was promoted to Commander. At this rank he became competitive to apply for "commanding officer" positions. In this he was successful and he led a couple of non-flying aviation units, including Naval Reserve Force Air Augmentation Unit 2118. Continuing at NAS Olathe, he was given a third aviation unit.

It appears he did exceptionally well at this time, because in both Fiscal Year 1969 and 1970, "under the leadership of Cmdr. Warner W. Tyler," Naval Air Reserve Division / Naval Air Reserve Training Detachment K-2, won a "Noel Davis Trophy." These trophies were awarded to the highest-ranking squadron or unit of each type in the Naval Air Reserve Force from the standpoint of readiness as determined by annual inspection. This means that Warner's unit was among the top twelve units in the NavAirResFor for two-years running.

Just as an aside, Lt. Cmdr. Noel G. Davis (1891-1927) was designated Naval Aviator No. 2944 on August 11, 1921. While still a flight student he became officer-in-charge of the ground school at Pensacola in June 1921 and authored the first manual for that school. Resigning his regular commission in July 1922 to attend Harvard Law School, he then accepted a commission in the Naval Reserve and became commanding officer of the first station for the Naval Aviation Reserve in Squantum, Massachusetts, later writing textbooks for training reserve pilots. He was killed in a flying accident preparing to compete for the Orteig Aviation Prize; the Orteig Prize was a reward offered to the first aviator(s) from an "Allied" country to fly non-stop from New York City to Paris or vice versa. Several famous aviators made unsuccessful attempts at the flight before the relatively unknown Charles Lindbergh won the prize in 1927 in his aircraft the *Spirit of St. Louis*.

Coming off his Det K-2 assignment in 1970, Commander Tyler essentially ended his many-year attachment to Naval Air, changed his designator, and affiliated with Naval Reserve intelligence. His new designator was 1635: "Naval Reserve Officer, Special Duty, Intelligence."

Chapter 19

When Lt.j.g. Tyler had come back home to Denver in September 1945, with the ending of World War II, not only did he need to find a job, but he needed to establish a home for himself and his wife. As already discussed, he immediately found good employment with his father-in-law in the compressed-gas and dry-ice business. In addition, Warner and Mavis put together a comfortable post-war home, not only for themselves but for a family—because at that point Mavis was six-months pregnant with their first child.

We've previously learned that Mavis was a person of energy, talent, and initiative. Not only had she excelled in high school and participated in many high-end extra-curricular activities, she had obtained that job with Braniff Airlines as a ground Morse code operator. She trained for six weeks at the Midland Radio Operator Specialist School in Kansas City and was then stationed in Dallas. She relayed weather reports via Morse code to Braniff crews in flight. As stated before, this was pretty adventurous; this young lady left working in her family's drapery business and quickly obtained a very technical and professional job. Moving to Kansas City and then on to Dallas was her first time away from home.

At some point after Mavis and Warner got married in February 1944, she left Braniff Airlines and returned to Denver. Her daughter

Linda believes that her grandmother, Florence Lorenzen, sold the drapery business after Mavis began college at Denver University—or at the latest when Mavis moved to Kansas City and then Dallas when she was hired with Braniff Airlines. Florence could no longer run the business without Mavis's help, particularly as her husband—John—was busy with his new dry-ice and CO_2 company.

Mavis never worked professionally after marriage. That said, Linda comments that "Mother was an accomplished seamstress, took sewing classes for many years, participated in fashion shows, and made most of my clothes until I was in junior high school. One of her artistic hobbies was making enamel jewelry. For years she wished that she had had the opportunity to become a nurse or dietitian. She volunteered at a Denver hospital for many years in a variety of roles, so at least she had the opportunity to be part of that field in that role."

As mentioned earlier, the Tylers' daughter Linda was born in December 1945 and son Gary was born in November 1947. Linda went to Montclair Elementary School in Denver for kindergarten, and then to Carson Elementary in the Hilltop neighborhood. (Interestingly, the author's mother was an elementary school teacher working at Montclair during this same time—but did not teach kindergarten). Gary also started at Carson, and then joined Linda at another school, Whiteman Elementary in the Mayfair Park area. They both attended Hill Junior High in the Hilltop area, and then George Washington High School—Linda graduating in 1963 and Gary in 1965. (Another interesting coincidence: one of the author's older cousins taught chemistry at "GW" for many years back then, but does not appear to have been either Linda's or Gary's teacher.)

Linda writes that "At that time I was one of only a few female students at George Washington with a heavy emphasis on science in high school. My one-and-only goal since the age of eight had been to become a nurse. (I also had an alternate interest and talent in vocal music in case my childhood goal didn't work out!) I often told my parents that I wanted to have ten children—bringing heart failure and migraines to both of them.

"Dad had an admirable talent for construction, machinery repair and maintenance," Linda continues. "He completely finished the unfinished basement of one of our custom homes, including a bedroom for Gary with built-in bunkbeds, desk and dressers, bookcase, and bathroom including plumbing and electricity. He taught me how to identify and use tools which have been particularly useful skills for me all of my life. Somewhat surprisingly, he allowed me to 'help' when he was building. He constructed an industrial-strength swing set and tetherball set for Gary and me in one of our backyards. Ace Hardware stores are still one of my favorite places to shop, since that had become my dad's and my Sunday-afternoon errand together. And, he was particularly skilled with stained-glass art, most of which still remains with our family. He never was interested in selling or displaying any of his creations; he just liked the fun of the hobby itself. He helped Mother's dad—John Lorenzen—with the construction of two mountain cabins which were more like year-round homes than cabins, both very carefully and professionally built."

Gary added that Warner's mother (Jane E. Darrow Tyler) had been a sculptor, and perhaps Warner inherited some of that artistic skill. "He finished a whole basement very nicely, even creating a 'Tiki Room.' He inlaid two-foot wide Naval Aviator Wings into the bar top. He also worked in wrought iron, mosaic work, stained glass, and Tiffany lamp shades."

Gary went to work for his dad and grandfather when he turned 16 and got his driver's license. In the summer of 1964 he delivered dry ice in John's Chevrolet *Corvair* compact car—since he didn't yet have a commercial license to drive a larger vehicle. In fact, Gary worked part time for several years for the company through high school and college. "I worked every summer, Christmas, spring break, St. Swithun's Day—I needed the money! It was perfect: disposable income and honest physical work for the irreverent boss's kid."

Linda went to college at the Colorado State College (now the University of Northern Colorado) in Greeley, graduating with a BSN in 1967. She became a pediatric OBGYN/Neonatal Nursery Nurse.

Gary went to Colorado State University in Fort Collins and graduated in 1969 with a degree in business administration. He writes that "I was heavily influenced by Dad to consider Naval Aviation for my military service at the height of the Vietnam War, which I did. It was the best guidance I could have been given at the time. I enlisted in the AVROC (Aviation Reserve Officer Candidate) program." On one of his USNR trips to NAS Olathe, probably in 1968, Cmdr. Warner Tyler was accompanied by Gary in order to be sworn into the Naval Reserve as an enlisted man. Gary didn't have to drill while he finished college, but shortly after graduation he traveled down to Pensacola, Florida, where he went through the 14-week Navy Aviation Officer Candidate School. He was commissioned later in 1969. "At the end of the program, Dad and Mom came down, where he swore me in. That was a pretty special day for both of us."

Actually, 1965 impacted the family more than some other years. Gary Tyler graduated from high school and went off to the university in Fort Collins—leaving Mavis and Warner as "empty nesters" since Linda Tyler was already half-way through her college experience at Northern Colorado University. The other big occurrence was that John Lorenzen retired from his Carb-Ice Corporation, which left Warner as company president.

So, as Gary comments, "Dad had the reins and was the principal player in working issues. Carb-Ice had grown to more than a handful of employees—say 15-20. Then, not long after Warner became president, Carb-Ice combined with a regional firm in El Paso, Texas. This company became S.E.C. Corporation resulting from this merger/acquisition by Schwartz-Edmunds Carbonic (S and E, with the C now standing for Carb-Ice). Apparently Carb-Ice had been visibly doing well enough that Schwartz-Edmunds saw a merger as a way to expand their reach into Colorado and even the surrounding states. This was pretty heady stuff for a small, built-from-nothing company—to be pursued by an established regional player. The company did well through this merger and acquisitions process. I don't recall," continued Gary, "that there was any discussion about whether or not Grandfather John thought it was the right move. I think everyone was relying on Dad to navigate those waters." Linda adds that "Dad had a particular talent for financial matters as well as management."

Chapter 20

So in 1971, as mentioned, Commander Warner Tyler decided to leave the naval aviation business and become an intelligence officer in the Naval Reserve.

Perhaps a little background here will be helpful. Believe it or not, looking back from where we stand today, formalized American naval reserve intelligence activity has existed for almost 100 years. In fact, the "U.S. Naval Reserve Act of 1925" created the *Naval Intelligence Volunteer Service*. Navy leadership back then had in mind this objective: to develop a nucleus of reserve officers who, by virtue of their education, training, and experience in civilian life, would be immediately available in time of national emergency to assume duties and perform the functions of Naval Intelligence Officers both at home and abroad.

Modest initial quotas for reservists gradually increased and, by 1936, they had reached 536 spread out all around the country. The regular Navy's District Intelligence Officers, and officially designated Naval Attachés posted here-and-there around the world, began estimating their wartime needs and, as a result, they established relevant reservist mobilization training plans.

This is somewhat interesting, for in those days no one in the U.S. Navy—even the regular navy—was really a permanent intelligence officer. Similarly, for that matter, no one was a permanent communications-intelligence or cryptology officer. The Office of Naval Intelligence, founded in 1882, is in fact the world's oldest continually operating intelligence agency. But—remarkably—naval intelligence as an organized operation suffered for decades: low manning, small budgets, low priority, and low (which is to say, *no*) prestige. Essentially, it would take the Second World War before "intelligence" became a true, viable career field. Hitherto, a naval officer inclined toward this business had to carefully alternate intelligence assignments with those in a "real" specialty—such as surface-ship sea duty, submarines, or aviation. Cryptology and other forms of communications intelligence suffered similarly—including the same curse of realistically being unsustainable as a career.

Be that as it may (and needless to say), almost all members of the Naval Reserve were mobilized into the active-duty Navy in World War II—certainly including reservists in the Naval Intelligence Volunteer Service.

Well, it came to pass that, after the war, the Navy modified the program and created a number of organized Naval Reserve Intelligence Units. These units were loosely put together with, at this point, a primary mission of training which was mostly managed internally. This reserve program was divided into two parts: surface intelligence and air intelligence. The surface-intelligence segment was supported by the active-duty District Intelligence Officer of each of the twenty-one U.S. Naval Districts across the country. The air-intelligence segment was similarly administered by Air Intelligence Program Officers (AIPOs).

During the 1960s the surface program was reorganized into thirteen Naval Reserve Intelligence Divisions composed of 100 Naval Reserve Units. This program contained 1,300 officer billets and a smaller number of yeoman and other enlisted support personnel. The air program consisted of twenty-five Naval Air Intelligence Reserve Units, containing 820 officer and 345 enlisted billets. And, an additional 230 officer and 100 enlisted photo-intelligence billets were scattered among other units of the Naval Air Reserve.

In the late 1960s the U.S. Department of Defense's "Total Force Policy" stipulated reliance on the organized reserve for various emergencies and required integration of active and reserve units in contingency planning. Task-performing reserve units were to be tailored to meet the emergency needs of specific naval activities. As an outgrowth of this concept, and as a result of the findings of the Reserve Analytical Studies Project begun in 1973, the Chief of Naval Reserve proposed to the Chief of Naval Operations that the air- and surface-intelligence reserve programs should be restructured. The result, outlined in OPNAVNOTE (Chief of Naval Operations Notice) 5400 of 15 May 1974—"The Restructuring of the Naval Reserve"—created the Naval Reserve Intelligence Program (NRIP), combining both surface and air programs into a single entity.

In 1974 the U.S. Navy also established a new enlisted rating, Intelligence Specialist (IS), and in particular provided for rating conversion by Photographic Intelligenceman (PT) and Yeoman (YN) personnel. Since reserve enlisted billets were only 44 percent filled that year, the NRIP placed emphasis on soliciting conversions.

The majority of NRIP personnel found placement, in 1974, with Area Analysis Units (AAUs). This concept was created by the Fleet Intelligence Center Pacific (FICPac) at Pearl Harbor, the Fleet Intelligence Center Europe and Atlantic (FICEurLant) at Norfolk, Virginia, and the Commander, Naval Intelligence Command (NIC) at Washington, D.C. The structure was also designed for both peacetime and mobilization roles. Thirty AAUs were instituted to provide geographic-area analysis for the FICs. The AAUs were subsequently renamed Fleet Intelligence Rapid Support Teams (FIRSTs) in 1976.

By the way, "task-performing" reserve units, as just mentioned above, were units that did more than train their personnel during their monthly drill weekends. In addition to administration and training (for no one and no unit *ever* escapes administration and training), some units were able and required to produce something of immediate use to the Regular Navy. In the case of intelligence units their personnel—working in secure facilities—were able to take materials securely sent to them from an active-duty command, analyze and process such materials, and send back the finished products utilizing secure and unmarked mail. Or, these personnel would work on research tasks assigned by active-duty commands, applying the expertise and knowledge they possessed and using appropriate reference materials, and again send finished products to the requester. In all such cases, obviously, the projects could not be of the highest (such as Top Secret) or first-tier priority due to the time delays and restrictions of mail involved and every reserve unit's work-month being only two days. Still, a great deal of useful intelligence production could be, and certainly was, generated.

To expand a little more on this issue of training versus production, pressure did indeed come from the commander of the Naval Reserve Force in New Orleans. As stated, most reserve units concentrated on NavResFor training and administrative activities—and, again, there were *many* such requirements. The intelligence units were further stressed in that they had full loads of intelligence production assignments from the active-duty commands to which they were organizationally tasked (such as the Fleet Intelligence Center Pacific at Pearl Harbor, or the Office of Naval Intelligence in Washington, DC). Thus, it frequently was very difficult to get it all done to everyone's satisfaction. The author, as a former intelligence unit C.O., can testify that this was still the situation as late as 2008—and no doubt is still the case now.

So, the new Naval Reserve Intelligence Program was established with an initial total allowance of 4,993 personnel: 2,940 officers and 2,053 enlisted. There were 148 authorized units of 30 different types drilling in 73 cities in the U.S., Puerto Rico, and the United Kingdom under the direction of a ready-reserve flag officer who bore the title of Director, Naval Reserve Intelligence Program (DNRIP). The units were divided, for management purposes, into nineteen Reserve Intelligence Areas. Each had a part-time Reserve Intelligence Area Coordinator (RIAC) in charge, as well as a full-time Reserve Intelligence Program Officer (RIPO) assigned for everyday area management.

In the original concept the DNRIP himself was a part-time drilling reservist, supported by a staff comprised of drilling reserve officers and enlisted personnel. Moreover, he (and indeed it was a "he," because the first female head of the program did not take charge until 2004) was also supported by a relatively small full-time staff who worked at the headquarters on a daily basis. And, in the original concept, the NRIP headquarters was located at the drilling site of the officer selected as the DNRIP. Thus, the first DNRIP, Rear Adm. Robert M. Colwell, USNR (July 1974 - September 1977) had his headquarters at NAS Alameda, California, on San Francisco Bay. Admiral Colwell's talent-laden Bay Area staff fleshed out the DNRIP concept, "putting meat on the bones," according to retired Capt. Jon Clarke, who was on the second DNRIP's staff. "Capt. Richard A. Dirks, Special Projects Officer under Admiral Caldwell, was the main actor to organize the previously randomly-scattered Naval Reserve intelligence units into a single command."

Chapter 21

Commander Warner W. Tyler had become an intelligence officer in 1971—at least by title and designator if not schooling and background. Nevertheless, due to considerable experience and grooming as a senior manager and leader, he became commanding officer of a naval reserve intelligence unit, still in Olathe, Kansas. This unit was Naval Air Intelligence Reserve Unit D-2. There were a number of other Denver-area officers that served there with Tyler, also commuting to drill via airplane.

And, at some point in 1971, and to the great relief of those air commuters, NAIRU D-2 was moved to the Naval Air Reserve Center Denver at Buckley Air National Guard Base. Of course, with the shoe now on the other foot, some Kansas and Nebraska unit members had to commute *to* Denver *from* Olathe and, to make their lives even harder, that particular airlift was discontinued so they had to drive! At Buckley all naval reserve activities were housed "topside" in the old eastern-most operations building and hangar run by the Air Guard. Then, in the mid-1970s, the whole NARCenDen moved to a reasonably refurbished World War II warehouse at the base's Sixth Avenue gate. In fact, the years 1974-75 saw a lot of change. It was then that "the NAIRU D-2 unit," writes Captain Clarke, "became Naval Reserve Area Analysis Unit 2118 when Rear Admiral

Colwell and his San Francisco staff created and organized the new Naval Reserve Intelligence Program. At that time our assigned area of production was Northeast Asia (China, parts of the USSR, and North Korea), as tasked by our gaining command, Fleet Intelligence Center Pacific, at Pearl Harbor." (The term "gaining command" refers to a reserve unit's wartime mobilization site.)

Commander Tyler, according to all accounts, was an efficient, effective, and popular commanding officer. "A favorite motivational phrase he used," writes retired Capt. Jim Vaughters, "was, 'I will drag this unit, kicking and screaming, into excellence!'" (The caption on a framed portrait from some years later quotes *Captain* Tyler as saying "If you grab 'em by the balls, their hearts and minds are sure to follow.") Captain Vaughters also relates that "John A. Love, who was the Colorado governor at the time, had been a World War II Navy seaplane pilot in the Pacific and had been awarded two Distinguished Flying Crosses. Warner and a chief petty officer obtained a vintage navy flight jacket and made an appointment to present it to him (perhaps they discovered that the governor hadn't kept his own jacket from the war). So, after a few minutes of talking and laughing about the good old days, Governor Love told his secretary to cancel the rest of his appointments for the rest of the afternoon because he was having too much fun."

"When 5:00 pm came around on drill days," writes retired Capt. Max Dodson, "Captain Tyler would have a final all-hands unit meeting and close with the remark 'there is *no* Cure like *Sea-Cure* [secure],' and that meant we were free to go. The other saying he often had was 'black shoes [surface-ship officers] are like flies, they eat shit and bother people.'" This last was said jokingly, coming from the historic black-shoe – brown-shoe rivalry. (At this time the black-shoe reservists were drilling at the Naval Reserve Center located at the Denver Federal Center, far to the west (but coincidentally also on Sixth Avenue) in the Denver suburb of Lakewood.

Just as an aside, the author was a U.S. Navy League Sea Cadet there circa 1966-67).

"I first met Cmdr. Warner Tyler when I was stationed at the Fleet Intelligence Center Europe (FICEUR) at NAS Jacksonville, Florida," writes retired Capt. Trux Simmons. "He and several of his unit members were with us doing their Active Duty for Training in 1972. In those days I presented the "Welcome Aboard" briefing to all the reserve guys checking in for their two-week duty, including a classified current-intelligence portion. After the briefing Warner approached me and asked if I could provide his Denver unit with a copy." Trux told him that he was getting off active duty soon and was going to attend graduate school in Denver, and that he wanted to affiliate with a Denver naval reserve intelligence unit.

"I told him of my desire and he said, 'I'll see that you can join our unit when you get to Denver—particularly if you can get us a copy of that current intel briefing.'" At that time there were two Denver naval intel organizations: a small black-shoe surface one at the Federal Center (part of the Commander Naval Forces Korea unit) and the brown-shoe air unit at Buckley. "Well, being an air intel guy, I wanted to affiliate with Commander Tyler at Buckley." Trux got permission from the FIC "to send a copy of the paper script, and 35mm slides, via double-wrapped registered mail to NAIRU D-2, and was in due course welcomed as its newest member that fall when I started at the University of Denver."

In 1973 newly promoted Captain Tyler (date of rank 1 June 1973) rotated out of NAIRU D-2. He then affiliated, again as commanding officer, with Naval Air Reserve Squadron D-2—a non-flying aviation staff unit at NARCenDenver. Then, in 1975, he apparently rotated into the Intelligence Voluntary Training Unit 0118. IVTU units were organizations where officers could affiliate in a non-pay status while awaiting a suitable local pay billet to open up. The advantage of being in such a unit was that an officer maintained status and career continuity, and earned retirement points, even if not just then receiving drill pay. While in the IVTU, Warner may have volunteered to be on Capt. Marty Andrew's small staff when Andrew was drilling in Denver as the first RIAC-5. Or, there is some evidence that he may have worked down the road at NORAD—the North American Air Defense Command in Cheyenne Mountain, just southeast of Colorado Springs. There was a USNR intelligence unit in place at NORAD, but Captain Tyler doesn't claim that he was part of that unit. What he does say, in a biographical essay written circa 1986, is that "I have worked closely with the Intelligence Department of NORAD and have observed and participated in several real-time exercises which NORAD conducted on a worldwide basis. I also served as a Senior Naval Observer and assisted in writing exercises to be conducted in the future."

When the second Director of the Naval Reserve Intelligence Program, Rear Adm. Martin J. Andrew, took over at the national level (October 1977 - September 1980), the NRIP headquarters moved to his drill site in Denver. This "movement of headquarters" policy remained in effect for the next two DNRIPs, but upon the headquarters' movement to Dallas in 1987 the policy was going to change—with the headquarters then remaining in Dallas into the future. That future change would require the DNRIP and reserve staff to commute monthly, but the active-duty staff remained in place in permanent, dedicated spaces.

Around 1954 Marty Andrew, also a Denver native, had come off of active duty and returned to Colorado—joining the intelligence program that existed at the time. He subsequently commanded Naval Reserve Intelligence Division 9-1 and the Intelligence Volunteer Training Unit 0118, among other organizations. As a civilian he was a practicing attorney and a partner in a mid-sized Denver law firm. Under the new NRIP structure Captain Andrew served as the first Reserve Intelligence Area Coordinator for Area Five (RIAC-5), from 1974 to 1977. Concurrently with Admiral Andrew's promotion and appointment as the DNRIP, Warner Tyler was selected as RIAC-5, continuing a relationship with Andrew—who had also been a World War II naval aviator and who had transferred to intelligence on active duty as early as 1951. In fact, Captain Tyler had been considering retirement from the Navy, but Admiral Andrew talked him into accepting one more assignment in this significant position. At that time Area Five covered Colorado, Wyoming, New Mexico, Nebraska, and Kansas—though most of the half-dozen units operated in the Denver area.

Admiral Andrew also persuaded Capt. Joe LaRocca to join his staff. Joe had been the deputy director and chief of the Naval Intelligence Branch at the joint active-duty Armed Forces Air Intelligence Training Center at Lowry Air Force Base in Denver. Capt. Jon Clarke writes that "Joe was a super nice guy and great administrator. Like Warner Tyler, Joe had also been planning to retire, but when Marty Andrew 'got the nod' to be DNRIP he persuaded Joe to stick around as his chief-of-staff." Moreover, since Rear Admiral Colwell's reservist staff stayed in the Bay area fully in accordance with the NRIP plan, "Rear Admiral Andrew recruited local intel officers, as well as those drilling in AAU 2118, to be on his DNRIP Staff. One of his oft-repeated sayings was, 'give me hungry lieutenant commanders!' and indeed there were a good number of those to be found." Of course, Capt. Warner Tyler also had a handful of such local officers, hungry and otherwise, attached to him to form his RIAC staff.

The refurbished World War II warehouse which housed Naval Air Reserve Center Denver at Buckley was a pretty good facility, but it was not overly spacious to accommodate all of the naval air and naval intelligence units situated there—as well as supply, recruiting, and administrative offices. So, the full-time RIPO-5 shared an office with the part-time RIAC-5, and the intel units had a small administrative space—as well as a reasonably good-sized secure two-room space for intelligence production. That said, there wasn't enough room for an admiral and his full-time and part-time staff. As a result, Rear Admiral Andrew and his staff occupied spaces across town at the Denver Federal Center's much larger naval reserve facility. They occasionally proceeded over to Buckley as desire and necessity dictated.

Thus, the national Naval Reserve Intelligence Program operated from its headquarters in the Denver suburb of Lakewood, 1977-1980. Admiral Andrew led the Naval Intelligence Reserve Community through some challenging times in the post-Vietnam 1970s when "budgets were paltry, the national mood was pessimistic, anti-war sentiment remained higher than desirable, and recruiting was challenging." When Admiral Andrew's tenure was up in September 1980, he not only relinquished command, he went ahead and fully retired from the naval service—along with his chief of staff, Captain LaRocca. (The author, then a petty officer third class, is proud to have served as a "sideboy" during the ceremony at Lowry Air Force Base in Denver, which was held in close proximity to a static display of a Navy A-4 *Skyhawk* aircraft.) Capt. Warner Tyler, as RIAC of Area Five, commanded the "troops"—which consisted of blocks of naval reservists drawn up in formation. The author clearly remembers Captain Tyler's full and piercing "Aye-***YI***-Sirs," responding to various orders during the event.

According to the plan, the NRIP headquarters now moved 1,700 miles east to Naval Air Reserve Training Station Willow Grove—just north of Philadelphia. Rear Adm. John W. Cronin, Jr., an insurance executive in civilian life, took over as DNRIP. Previously Cronin had been the first RIAC in Area 16 at Willow Grove.

It's fair to say that Capt. Warner Tyler had been interested in becoming the director of the reserve intelligence program, and concurrently being promoted to rear admiral. There were many people, no doubt including Warner himself, who thought that his combat award of the Navy Cross might have been a considerable ticket towards this goal—not to mention his four years in-grade as a captain, and his experience commanding four aviation and intelligence units. However, all this was likely offset by his lack of a college degree (he had never finished his initial start at the University of Denver) and that he was a relative newcomer to the intelligence business (six years in contrast to, for example, Marty Andrew's twenty-one years—and he had not been selected to be one of the initial reserve intelligence area commanders). Nevertheless, Warner handled whatever disappointment he felt, writes Capt. Jim Vaughters, "with his usual dignity and good humor and he was totally supportive of Marty for the entire three years of his command."

Captain Tyler chose not to retire, unlike Admiral Andrew and Captain LaRocca, in the fall of 1980. It's not clear why he stayed on for another year, particularly when he had been talked out of retiring in 1977. Very likely he felt that he could be effective in continuing to meet the challenges mentioned just above, and he might have wanted to see what it was like to run Area Five without being joined at the hip with the DNRIP and the DNRIP staff. He also might have had a little emotional difficulty in actually bringing his naval service—which had always meant so much to him—to a final close. Regardless, as the end of the next fiscal year approached (the Federal fiscal year for many years governed when naval reserve command tours changed out) he and Mavis decided that it was time. Thus, as the morning newspaper *The Rocky Mountain News* reported:

> More than 400 Denver area naval reservists on Saturday [19 September 1981] will participate in change-of-command ceremonies for four aviation and intelligence units based at Buckley Air National Guard Base.

> The ceremonies at 2 p.m., on the Fitzsimons Army Medical Center parade ground, will also mark the retirement of Capt. Warner W. Tyler from the Naval Reserve.
>
> Tyler, a Navy ensign during World War II, was awarded the Navy Cross for piloting his torpedo bomber through heavy enemy fire on Oct. 25, 1944 to torpedo a Japanese battleship in the Philippine Sea.
>
> After World War II, Tyler returned to Denver.
>
> The ceremony on Saturday will commemorate his [39] years of naval service.

During the change-of-command portion of the ceremonies, Captain Tyler turned over the leadership of RIA-5 to another officer who'd long been in the Denver-area naval reserve intelligence business, Capt. Joseph M. Zanetti. Commuting from New Mexico, Captain Zanetti worked as a civilian for the Sandia Laboratory and the PNM electrical public service company; for a time he'd also been president of the University of Albuquerque.

At the time of his retirement Warner Tyler's decorations and awards were as follows: Navy Cross, Air Medal, Navy Commendation Medal, Presidential Unit Citation with small bronze-star device, American Campaign Medal, Asiatic-Pacific Campaign Medal with four small bronze-star devices, World War II Victory Medal, Naval Reserve Medal, Armed Forces Reserve Medal with gold-hourglass device, Philippine Presidential Unit Citation, Philippine Liberation Medal with two small bronze-star devices, Philippine Independence Medal, and the Navy Rifle Marksman Ribbon.

Chapter 22

Only five months after Warner Tyler became RIAC-Area Five in the Naval Reserve, something huge also occurred in his civilian life. The S.E.C. Corporation was acquired by the AmeriGas Corporation in King of Prussia, Pennsylvania—headquartered just outside Philadelphia. A large company then, AmeriGas is now the largest propane marketer in the United States. S.E.C. regional vice-president Tyler was encouraged by the new owners to continue executive employment and move to Philadelphia but, according to his son Gary, "that wasn't in the cards." Thus, Warner retired from his civilian business endeavors shortly after the AmeriGas acquisition. What the original founder of the Carb-Ice Company, John Lorenzen, would have thought of this huge event isn't known, for he had passed away around a year earlier, in May 1977. No doubt he would have been impressed to see the company now pursued by a very large, established, and national-level corporation.

By this time Mavis and Warner—having become empty-nesters some years earlier—had moved to Perry Park, Colorado. From 1945 to 1975 they had lived in several homes in the Denver area, but now they moved a little south—to south-central Douglas County at the foot of the Rampart Range, the eastern edge of the Rocky Mountains in this area. Perry Park is 15 miles southwest of Castle Rock;

during this time their mailing address was Larkspur, Colorado. It was a very nice home associated with a golf course, clubhouse, and a couple of tennis courts.

Their son Gary writes, "Mother and Dad were pretty comfortable while living well-within their means. They educated both my sister Linda and me, they lived in increasingly nice homes, they had nice cars, and they traveled pretty widely as long as their health held together. For a while they belonged to the Wolhurst Country Club. I think that by all measures Dad was a successful guy."

In fact, Gary Tyler continues, that success was rooted in a number of factors, not the least of which was that "Dad always worked hard, he always treated his employees well, and he continuously earned their loyalty. As just one example, I specifically recall that he went in to work on one Christmas Day to cut and deliver dry ice so that one of his employees could stay home with his family. Not an uncommon happening for him; he did things like that continuously."

This might be a good place to discuss Captain Tyler's nickname of "Captain Chaos," which is how he became known among almost everyone who knew him in the Denver area reserve naval air and naval intelligence communities. This *nom de guerre*, if you will, doesn't appear to have attached itself to him *too* far back in his history and, after all, he was only promoted to captain in 1973. Moreover, while he always exhibited a certain amount of playfulness and constantly presented a wonderful sense of humor, he was always a practical, effective, efficient, professional, and high-performing leader and manager whether one cares to consider either his naval or civilian career. As Rear Adm. Bruce Black wrote in his foreword to this book, "I'm not exactly sure why we all affectionately called him "Captain Chaos"—and still refer to him as such even to the present day." Admiral Black thinks that it might have been based on an earlier nickname Warner had earned from his World War II flying days in the Pacific and some of the "chaos" that he and his colleagues had unleashed upon the Japanese army and navy. That would make sense, but there doesn't appear to be any evidence. However, there's no question that Warner's wonderful and often-irreverent sense of humor, his irrepressible center-stage personality, and his "frequent hi-jinx during the many navy social occasions he attended—often with Mavis—both before and after his retirement from the navy certainly sustained this reputation among all of us who admired the man he was." Indeed, for a good number of years it was a rare Denver-area navy social event where the Tylers were not in attendance. Flamboyant might be too strong of a word to describe "Captain Chaos," but he was certainly and consistently lively, dashing, colorful, jaunty, and exuberant.

For many years Warner's best friend in the reserve community was Capt. William Collins (1926-2009). Bill was another Denver native who—particularly in later years—was one of the rare people in the reserve group who was close to Warner's age. Bill had also been a World War II veteran—enlisting as a seaman recruit in 1944 on the day he turned eighteen. For decades Collins ran an East Colfax Avenue bicycle shop that his father had founded and which is still in business. Coincidentally, as a young kid, retired Capt. Jon Clarke was an occasional customer at this shop. Retired Capt. Max Dodson writes that "Bill was a wonderful, thoughtful person and his wife was a hoot." Admiral Black recalls that he "thought Warner and Bill were very different kinds of people and that it was a little surprising that they were friends." But retired Capt. Trux Simmons commented that in fact the two were thick as thieves, always in cahoots, and that "It's just too bad that you didn't get a chance to speak with Bill for he would have been 'the real source' for Warner Tyler stories. I think he and Warner were both what we call in the navy 'liberty risks,' really enjoying themselves at social events and out on the town." It's fair to say that if Bill Collins wasn't an active contributor to Warner's "Captain Chaos" reputation, he certainly wasn't an impediment. It's also fair to say that their hi-jinxes were nothing more than good clean fun—nothing sordid, illegal, nor embarrassing.

Mavis and Warner did a good deal of traveling all over the world, during their life together, both before and after retirement. Their daughter Linda wrote that "They enjoyed Mexico very much, even learning a bit of Spanish to be able to better enjoy the culture. I think Dad was more fluent and able to coach Mother a bit while they visited the country." Back in 1940 Warner had been in the Spanish Club at East High School and, 45 years later, wrote, "I am reasonably conversant in Spanish, and at one time had business dealings in Mexico City."

Linda also wrote that "One time Mother and Dad flew on a Concorde supersonic passenger airliner, home from Paris, during early flights offered to the public—as I recall they weren't too impressed. Some of their traveling was as part of his naval reserve activities; sometimes he was allowed to take Mother along."

"I have travelled extensively throughout the world as a civilian," Warner himself wrote. He also made this intriguing comment, in 1986, with no elaboration or other confirmation: "During the course of my travels I was asked by the Central Intelligence Agency to perform certain tasks for them in both Bangkok and Paris."

No one should think for a minute that his family, his civilian business, and his participation in the naval reserve were his only activities and interests—whether one considers his life before or after retirement. In an autobiographical essay he wrote late in life he gave us a glimpse of a few of those things.

> "I have a commercial pilot's license and am a Fellow of the American Institute of Management. I'm a Past-President of the Denver Round Table organization, Past-President of the National Sojourners (Fitzsimons Army Medical Center

Chapter), the Mayor's Traffic Committee, a past-member of the Perry Park Water and Sanitation District's Board, and a past-member of the Douglas County Library Board."

"I have been a six-year member of the Colorado Chapter of the Employer Support of the Guard and Reserve organization (the Defense Department program promoting cooperation and understanding between civilian employers and their National Guard and Reserve employees), and I have been the ESGR Executive Director for Colorado for 5 years."

In regard to the ESGR, retired Capt. Jon Clarke recalls that "in 1981 a leadership vacancy occurred in the Colorado Chapter. I was then executive officer of the IVTU and a very junior commander. However, I had the opportunity to inform the departing ESGR director (a Marine colonel) that there were a couple of senior navy captains available who were 'perfect for the job.' My commanding officer was then Capt. Bill Collins who thus volunteered and secured the vacancy. One part of the job—escorting senior business leaders on DoD inspection tours of CONUS (continental U.S.) and Hawaiian military facilities—turned out to be extremely time-intensive for the sole proprietor of a small business. So Bill then recruited Warner Tyler and, for a while, they shared the job. Bill shortly had to completely stand down but, fortunately, Warner was doing such a stellar job he easily rose to the occasion and superbly ran the whole Colorado ESGR show for several years."

In fact, the author still has a copy of the February 1986 "Reserve Intelligence Area Five Newsletter." Significantly, it contains an article in which retired Capt. Warner Tyler volunteers his services to any and all who might be having any problems with their employer regarding conflicts or complications with drills or active duty for training.

In the early 1990s Warner was diagnosed with Parkinson's disease, the neurological movement disorder. In 1992 Mavis and

Warner moved from Perry Park further south to the state's second-largest city, Colorado Springs—a little over an hour's drive from Denver on Interstate 25. "I think his Parkinson's diagnosis drove them to be closer to more robust medical care," wrote their son Gary. "And the property at Perry Park required a lot of maintenance that he wasn't going to be able to manage going forward. They were not the kind of people who would hire ongoing yard help, etc., so the move to Colorado Springs, into a townhouse community where the outside stuff was dealt with, made a lot of sense. Today we call such moves 'downsizing,' and they were the right age to do that notwithstanding his medical condition. Also, for some time his tennis activities were centered down there. However, sad to say, with the Parkinson's his tennis days were winding to a close."

A good number of people, certainly including his children, have commented on Warner's love and proficiency to tennis over a several-decade period. While he doesn't appear to have played on high school teams (and East High had winning teams in those years), "Dad was a pretty good tennis player even into his later years," writes his daughter Linda. "He had a particular friend and partner and they entered many tournaments together." "I think that friend may have been Frank Thomson," writes son Gary. "He had a tennis court in his backyard and lived a block or so away from the house they had on Oneida Way. I don't remember the name of a particular partner when they lived in Perry Park or Colorado Springs." According to a RIA-5 colleague Warner played at various locales while living in the Denver area, and played "some serious tennis" during his Perry Park years.

Of particular note, in November 1994, Warner and Mavis took a trip to Corpus Christi, Texas; Captain Tyler was invited to be a speaker on board his old ship. This was part of ceremonies opening the USS *Lexington* Museum's exhibit on the November 1944 *Kamikaze* strike on the carrier. As noted elsewhere, the *Lexington* was decommissioned in 1991, having contributed an active-service life longer than any other *Essex*-class ship. Following her decommissioning she was donated for use as a museum ship at Corpus Christi.

No one should think that age and illness diminished the spirit of "Captain Chaos." For example, retired Capt. Jim Vaughters wrote that "When Rear Adm. Marty Andrew died in December 1995, Rear Adm. Gene Dickey came up from Texas to the funeral, and Rear Adm. Bruce Black came up from New Mexico. The funeral was held at the St. Vincent de Paul Catholic Church in Denver. After the service we navy folks made two long lines along the sidewalk outside to escort him down to the hearse. Well, we waited—and waited—and waited, with the intention that we would all salute as he passed by. We were all rigged out in our service dress blue uniforms. I stood right beside Captain Tyler. Finally, after a long, long time Warner broke the silence and said, rather loudly, 'You know, we have *three admirals* here. You would *think* we could start this on time!' Only Warner could say something like that, at such a time, with his particular sense of humor. We were still trying to stop laughing when the casket was finally rolled past us."

Of course, inevitably, Captain Tyler's illness progressed. When he really got sick in the later years, Mrs. Tyler cared for him at home as long as she possibly could. He ultimately had to go into assisted care, but he didn't linger there for very long.

On Wednesday, 9 September 1998, he passed away from complications of Parkinson's disease at a Colorado Springs care facility. He was 75 years old. Services were held at the Shrine of Remembrance "America the Beautiful" chapel on the following Saturday, and he was buried in a private ceremony at Olinger Chapel Hill Cemetery in the Denver suburb of Littleton (now Centennial). He was survived, of course, by Mavis, as well as his two children, five grandchildren, and one great-grandchild.

Chapter 23

Mrs. Mavis A. Tyler continued to live in Colorado Springs until 2005, when she became ill herself and decided she should be nearer to family. Thus, she moved to Loveland, Colorado, fifty miles north of Denver, to be close to her daughter, Linda, and son-in-law, Dave.

As noted earlier, Mavis was a skilled homemaker, prolific seamstress, and successful gardener. She was an ace bowler, adapting her skills to the Wii bowling game in her later years. She knitted, crocheted, and embroidered with precision. She played the piano, Hawaiian guitar, and harmonica and also sang in a lovely alto voice. She was a committed and consistent coupon clipper, revered for her thriftiness and bargain-hunting by her family. Mavis made many life-long friends everywhere she lived, and was usually looked at as the "social-director" in any group of which she became a part. She was proud to be a Red Hatter. She later became a bridge player—as well as bingo, dominoes, and any board game within reach—and actively sought out worthy opponents among neighbors, family, and friends.

As with her husband before her, Parkinson's disease found a formidable and determined foe in Mavis. Linda worked admirably as her advocate, friend, and dedicated, loving daughter. Over a period of years Mavis inevitably progressed from independent living to assisted living and, finally, to skilled nursing.

And, like her husband, she persisted with enviable grace, strength, and dignity. She passed away on 16 October 2016 in Loveland, age 93. Mavis is survived by a daughter, son-in-law, son, daughter-in-law, five grandchildren and eight great-grandchildren.

Illustrations

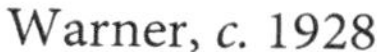

Warner, *c.* 1928

Warner / Mavis: East High School, Denver, 1940

Initial flying training: *Piper J3 Cub*, Boulder, Colorado, 1943

Warner and Mavis *c.* 1943

"Wings of Gold," 1943

Air Group-19

Fighting-19

Bombing-19

Torpedo-19

Little lioness Cleo, 2-months old and briefly Torpedo-19's mascot, with her caretaker Ens. Edward H. Schulke, supposedly awaiting takeoff in California [*Look* magazine, April 1944]

Air Group-19 leaders, April 1944: [l-r] Lt. Cmdr. David Dressendorfer, Lt. Cmdr. Richard McGowan, Lt. Cmdr. Hugh Winters, and Cmdr. Karl Jung [USN]

Mrs. Tyler, Morse Code operator, Braniff Airlines, 1944

Ens. Tyler, new at Group-19 and Torpedo-19, Maui [USN]

The CAG, Cmdr. Karl Jung, inspecting AG-19, 3 June 1944, at NAS Kahului, Maui [USN]

The USS *Lexington*, or, *"Mohawk."* They have moved an aircraft "pack" forward to facilitate recovering aircraft at the stern. [USN]

(l) Curtiss SB2C-1 *Helldiver* [http://wpalette.com/en/pictures/27759].
(r) *Mohawk-99*, "Hangar Lily," F6F *Hellcat*, CAG-19
[www.markstyling.com/F6F.15.htm]

Mohawk-91, a TBF-1, VT-19, USS *Lexington*, October 1944
[www.pmcn.de/English/USN%20Markings%20II/USN%20
Markings%20II.htm]

Avengers returning home [USN]

Hellcats landing, February 1944 [USN]

Ensign Tyler, ready to go [USN]

Lexington, 12 October 44, VT-19 *Avengers* [www.navsource.org]

Grumman TBF *Avenger* [USN]

Carrier "Ready Room," squadron unspecified [USN]

Battle for Leyte Gulf: Oct. 23-26, 1944

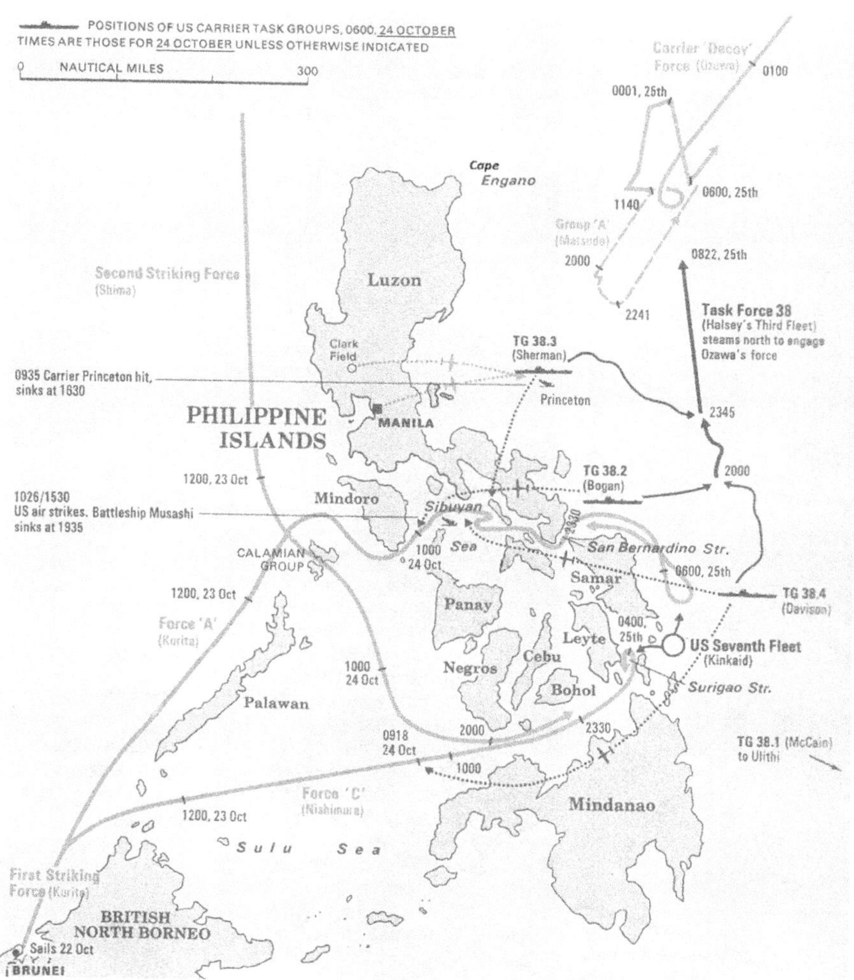

"Battle for Leyte Gulf," focusing on 24 October 1944 [Humble, *Aircraft Carriers: the Illustrated History*, with modifications]

Battle for Leyte Gulf: Oct. 24-25, 1944

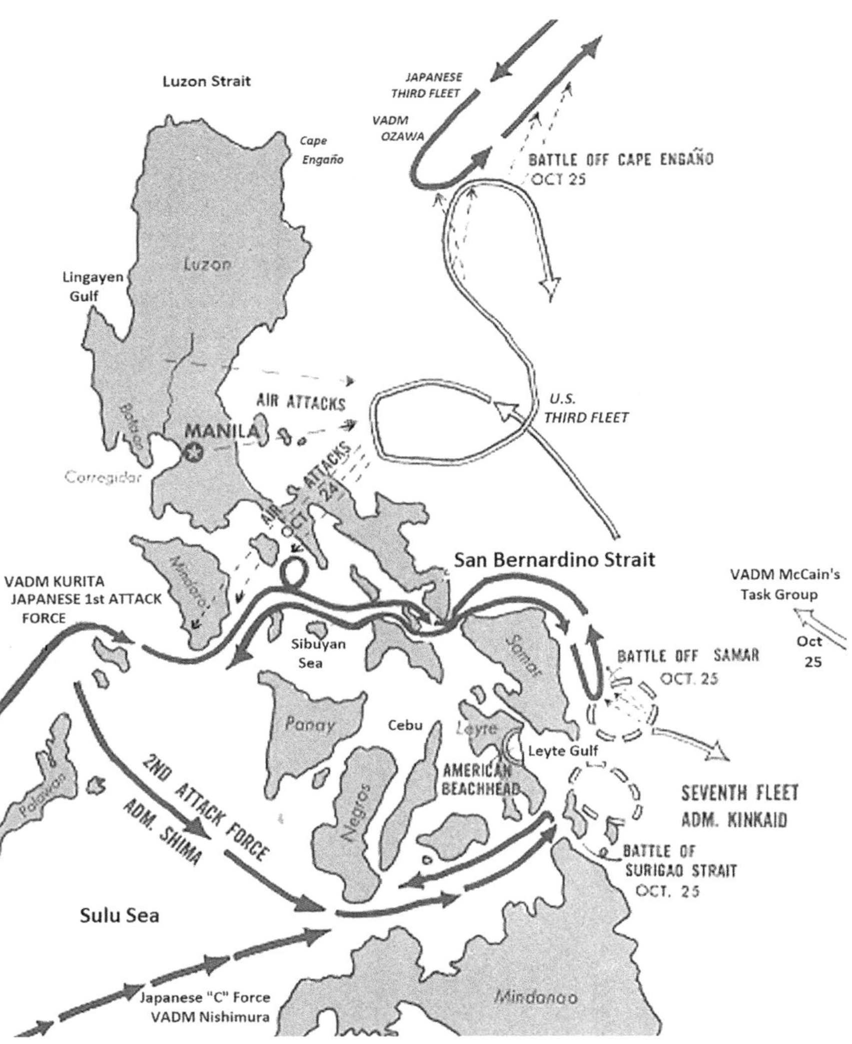

ONWAR.com Maps of World War II 1939-1945
www.onwar.com/wwii/maps/pacific/17pacific.html

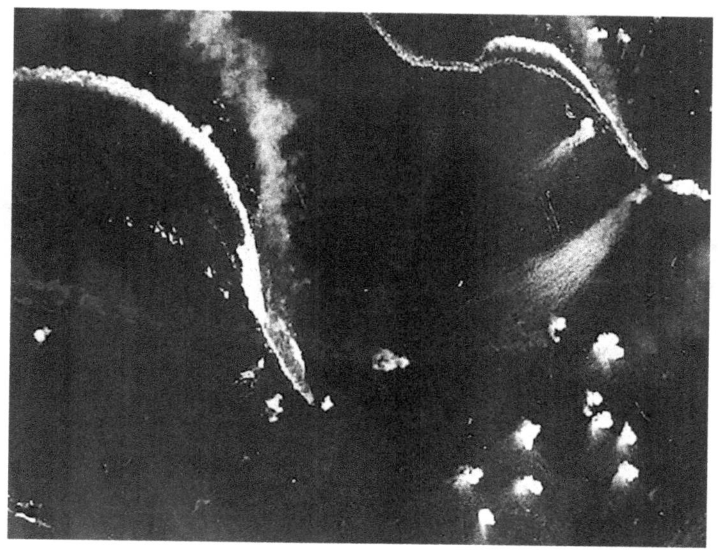

Carriers *Zuikaku* and *Zuiho* under attack, 25 Nov 44 [Nat. Archives]

William F. Halsey
C.O. U.S. 3rd Fleet

Marc A. Mitscher
C.O. Task Force 38

Frederick C. Sherman
C.O. Task Group 38.3

T. Hugh Winters
C.O. Air Group-19

Arleigh A. Burke
Chief of Staff, TF 38

Frank C. Perry
C.O. Torpedo-19

Byron R. White
Intel. Officer TF 38

William E. Davis
Pilot VF-19

Ozawa Jisaburō
C.O. Northern Force

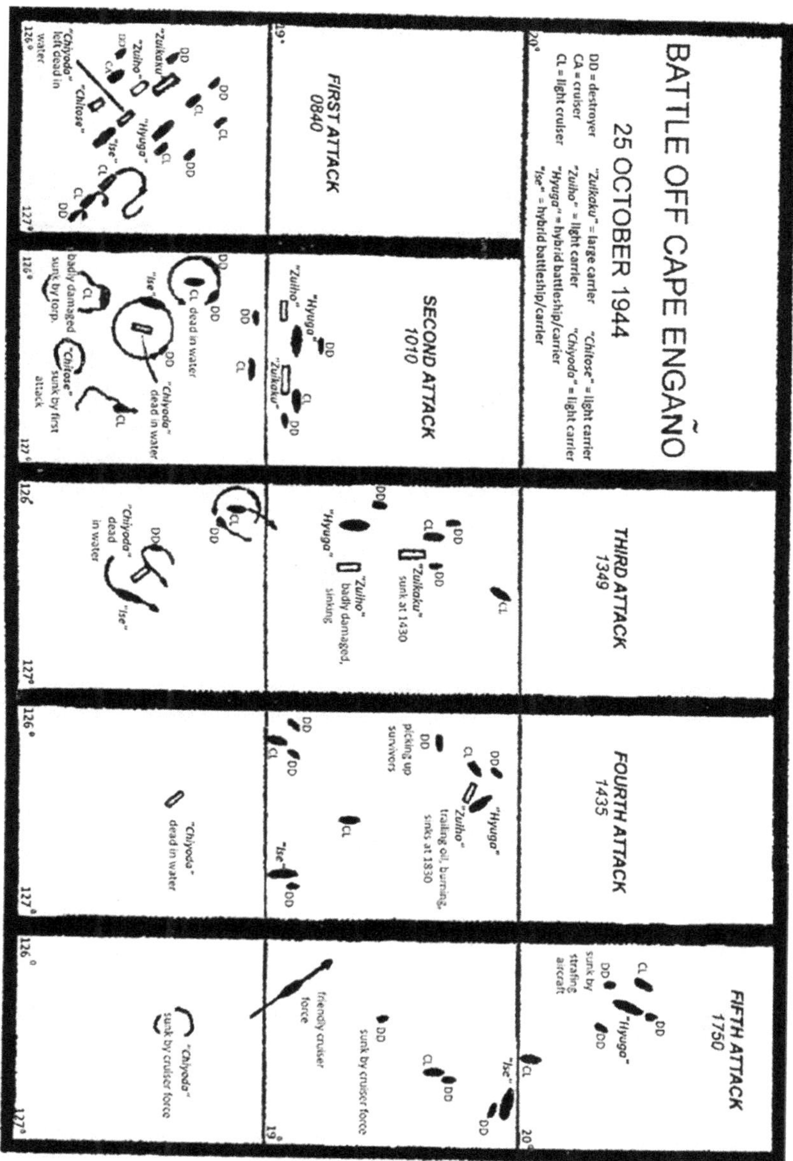

Chart, (modified) courtesy Dr. C. Vann Woodward, 1947. "Progress of the battle as our pilots reported it and as they identified the ships.…*It is of value in spite of errors.*"

Hybrid battleship/carrier *Ise* [IJN]

Ise under attack, photo from a USS *Essex* aircraft [U.S. National Museum of Naval Aviation]

Ise. Most of the smoke is her AAA gunfire [National Archives]

Ise firing AAA, including the large guns of her main battery [National Archives]

Near miss, *Ise* [National Archives]

Just how dangerous was torpedo-bombing? INCREDIBLY, whether you were USN or IJN. <u>Note</u>: *this* photo is of a Japanese Nakajima *B6N "Jill"* torpedo bomber unsuccessfully attacking the USS *Yorktown*, off Truk Atoll, 29 April 1944. It was shot down seconds later [UPI]

Ens. Warner Tyler, AOM^2 Wilmer Dewees, and ARM^3 Arthur Davis on their torpedo run against the IJN battleship/carrier *Ise*, 25 October 1944. The painting is by Rear Adm. Bruce A. Black, USN, Ret. This evocative painting was done for Tyler's naval reserve retirement in September 1981. It currently is on display in the captain's cabin onboard the USS *Lexington* at Corpus Christi, Texas. Admiral Black placed Air Group-19's number on this *Avenger*, but Tyler's airplane that day actually displayed "98" (*Mohawk-98*) as its individual number.

Kamikaze hit on the *Lexington*, 5 Nov 1944.
47 men killed; 127 wounded. [USN]

Mr. Tyler, P.O. Dewees, and P.O. Davis receiving medals for the Battle off Cape Engaño. This was part of a huge awards ceremony held on the *Lexington*'s flight deck, on or about 22 November 1944.
The CAG, Cmdr. Hugh Winters, made the presentations on behalf of Vice Adm. Mitscher [USN]

"Aviation Working Green"

Lt.j.g. and Mrs., 1945

Chance-Vought F4U *Corsair* fighter
[https://airpages.ru/eng/us/cors.shtml]

Mom and Dad with baby Linda, Jan. 1946

NAS Denver (Buckley), February 1948 [USN]

Mavis, Linda, Gary, and Warner, *c.* 1952

Lieutenant, *c.* 1959

Warner, Mavis, Gary, and Linda *c.* 1964

Commander Warner W. Tyler commissioning his son, Ensign Gary L. Tyler, at Gary's Aviation Officer Candidate School graduation, NAS Pensacola, Florida, 1969

Lt. Cmdr., *c.* 1964

Commander, *c.* 1969

Cmdr. and Mrs., *c.* 1971

Commander, *c.* 1971

Vice Pres., S.E.C., 1970

Captain, *c.* 1979

RIAC-5 inspecting NR Fleet Intelligence Rapid Support Team Pacific 0571, NARCen Denver, *c.* 1980

CAG-19 reunion, Sep. 1981

Captain Tyler's Naval Reserve retirement, September 19, 1981, at the parade ground of the old Fitzsimons Army Medical Center, Aurora, Colorado

RIA-5 "Dining Out," Denver, 1985. The author as "Mr. Vice" is sampling the beef (to "ensure fitness for human consumption") to everyone's amusement—except, apparently, Capt. Tyler (lower left). [USN]

The author's promotion party (to Lt.), July 1986, Denver. Mrs. Tyler (left); Capt. Tyler (right); then-Capt. Bruce Black (center); the author (with back to the camera).

RIA-5 "*lū'au*" party, Lowry AFB Officers' Club, Denver, *c.* 1988. The author's wife, Rhonda, is immediately behind Warner.

Perry Park, Colorado, *c.* 1990.

On board the *Lexington*, November 1994, Corpus Christi. Warner was a speaker at the opening of the museum's exhibit regarding the November 1944 *Kamikaze* strike on the *Lexington.*

Mavis in Loveland, Colorado, 2011

Grave marker, Warner and Mavis, Olinger Chapel Hill Cemetery, Centennial, Colorado

Afterword

"I know what you're thinking." These were the frequent words of actor Tom Selleck, playing Honolulu private investigator Thomas Magnum (television's fictional former U.S. Navy SEAL. Oh, and Magnum was also an Annapolis graduate and former Fleet Intelligence Center Pacific intelligence officer). At times he'd say those words, looking right at the camera, before he'd comment on some glaring or at least curious plot issue in that night's episode.

What *I* think *you* might be thinking is this: with all the detail that Captain Maffeo found regarding the history of Carrier Air Group Nineteen for almost twelve months, and all the extensive first-person accounts of a considerable number of people in the group, why don't we have more specific detail about Ensign Warner Tyler, and why don't we have more of his "voice" as opposed to all those others?

Well, many World War II veterans kept diaries during the war. Many wrote letters home. Some (such as Cmdr. Hugh Winters and Lt.j.g. Bill Davis—not to mention army Maj. Dick Winters, U.S. Marine Corporal Eugene Sledge and U.S. Marine Private Robert Leckie) later wrote amazing autobiographies. Some (such as Rear Adm. "Ted" Sherman and Mrs. Lee Fleming Reese) later authored superb historical books with considerable first-person perspectives.

Some units (such as Bombing Squadron Nineteen) for many years maintained reunion groups which gathered and published superb first-person accounts of wartime experiences.

Alas, it appears that Ens. Warner Tyler did not keep a diary and if he wrote letters home they no longer exist. Later in life he wrote a few insightful but very short essays about his wartime experiences; yet, he authored neither autobiography nor historical book. As far as can be determined *no one* in Torpedo Squadron Nineteen wrote an autobiography or a book. And, apparently, VT-19 put together no reunion group. As a result, in my book here, you have considerable commentary and voices from people in VF-19 and VB-19, but very little from VT-19. That said, such commentary from the other squadrons is highly valuable and relevant to VT-19 and people in VT-19, for the three squadrons—and the air group to which they belonged, and the aircraft carrier from which they flew—were all intertwined, so any information on any of their activities and experiences was to a huge degree closely shared.

***

You might be also thinking, "with all the detail that Captain Maffeo found about the Battle for Leyte Gulf, the Battle for Cape Engaño, Carrier Air Group Nineteen, and Torpedo Squadron Nineteen, why doesn't he seem to have a better, specific handle on what ships were hit during the last strike of the day—and by which pilot—causing what kind of damage?" Well, I have wondered that too, spending an enormous amount of time reading many, many historical accounts—as well as reading over sixty citations for Navy Crosses awarded to those pilots for the action on October 25, 1944. *It's just not specifically clear.* It is clear what the Japanese order-of-battle was early that morning. But, in the words of prominent British historian Dr. H. P. (Ned) Willmott (who was a specialist in

Japanese sea power and who, sad to say, just passed away in June 2000):

> The order-of-battle, it would seem, would be about the only aspect of the Cape Engaño action that can be stated with any certainty. This action is seldom afforded much consideration in the various histories that have been written. The American attacks have *never been afforded detailed accounts* of the numbers of aircraft, their parent carriers, *and a detailed analysis of their attacks relative to individual Japanese ships.*

***

Of course, another prominent thing you could be thinking is, "where were the Japanese carrier aircraft? Why didn't they attack the American aircraft as they approached the Japanese fleet, and why didn't they mount their own strong attacks against the American carriers? Why wasn't this battle more like the Battle of Midway was, with very many airplanes of both sides all over the place?" Well, I'm glad you asked—or at least were thinking about asking. Even Admiral Halsey was puzzled about that at the time. As mentioned earlier, what wasn't entirely clear to the Americans was that the Japanese carriers had lost "most" of their planes in the first Battle of the Philippine Sea in June 1944 and, according to Prof. E. B. Potter, "any Japanese fleet aviators who had attained proficiency *after* that time had been sacrificed in trying to protect the Formosan bases from [the American] carrier attacks."

***

All that aside, at least two more things have to be said about the War in the Pacific. "Naval pilots," wrote the editors of *American*

Heritage, "were a new breed of American fighting men; their courage and superior skill finally blasted the enemy out of the air. And, aircraft carriers and carriers, and more carriers, produced in such numbers by American shipyards that at the war's end there were *nearly a hundred* of them paving the way to the surrender ceremony in Tokyo Bay."

This last sentence reminds me of the drunken American soldier towards the end of the movie *Band of Brothers*, who shouts at a group of German prisoners-of-war, "*What were you thinking!?* Did you not know you were up against *General Ford*!? And *General Motors*!?" (Similarly, we could add "Generals" Newport News Shipbuilding, Fore River Shipyard, Norfolk Navy Yard, New York Navy Yard, Grumman Aircraft, Douglas Aircraft, Curtiss-Wright Aircraft, Springfield Armory, Colt Firearms, and *countless* other American and Allied industrial manufacturers.) It's amazing to realize, as Prof. Victor Davis Hanson writes, that "During the four years of the war the Americans constructed *sixteen* major warships for every *one* the Japanese built."

***

A couple of "technical" notes:

I've used abbreviations for rank or grade that are more in conformance with those used in the 1940s than those used today; for example, Capt. or Cmdr. rather than CAPT or CDR.

At times I've also referred to junior officers as "Mr." rather than by their actual rank. Not terribly common today, this convention was widely used for centuries in the British and American navies, and was certainly in play during World War II. For example, Mr. Tyler versus Ensign Tyler.

Moreover, unlike today's common usage, the bulk of the literature (as well as many peoples' memories) supports a preceding article used more often than not in most of the twentieth century (not to mention earlier centuries), so I have proceeded accordingly. For example, "he transferred to the *Lexington*" versus "he transferred to *Lexington.*"

I've used the expression "naval reserve" versus "navy reserve" throughout this story. "U.S. Navy Reserve" might be current usage, but it was the U.S. Naval Reserve from 1915 to 2005. The word "naval" is a perfectly good and elegant adjective that has no equivalent in the other services and it's too bad, in my opinion, that we're pretty much giving it up. I've been proud to be a naval officer and was proud to be in the naval reserve—and I dare say Captain Tyler was too.

Lastly, I had hoped to get a copy of Warner Tyler's service record from the National Personnel Records Center in St. Louis, Missouri. However that has not come to fruition, even though Warner's son Gary made such an official request almost a year and a half ago. Apparently the Center essentially shut down for a whole year due to Covid, and now is horribly backlogged with requests. Currently they are focused upon serving high-priority requests associated with medical treatments, burials, and homeless veterans trying to gain admittance to shelters—thus "routine" requests remain low priority. Nevertheless I feel pretty confident, drawing upon a multitude of other sources, that I've captured Warner's wartime and later service pretty accurately and completely.

There's no way a person can review the complexities of another person in just a few minutes or in just a few pages. It's difficult to distill an extremely active life of three-quarters of a century into a relatively small document. And, you have to be very careful of anecdotes; displaying too *few* can lend inordinate weight to what you include and give them importance beyond their true merit. On the other hand, displaying too *many* might confuse or muddle the story and diminish the broader scope. That said, I feel reasonably comfortable that I've captured the essence of Warner Tyler fairly and accurately.

***

So, this little biography has been a special effort to honor one of those men—and certainly his wartime comrades—so rightfully extolled above by the *American Heritage* editors. As Leyte historian Thomas Cutler wrote, "Thousands ... are to be honored ... for being there at Leyte Gulf....[T]he sands have swallowed their footprints and the waters show no trace of their wakes. But the glory of their deeds will never be tarnished by time."

Warner William Tyler and Mavis Ann Lorenzen Tyler—among *so many* others—were truly great people belonging indeed to the "Greatest Generation."

Acknowledgements

A goodly number of people have put their shoulders behind my wheels—or, perhaps more appropriately, air under my wings—on this project. I am incredibly grateful for them all. Firstly, the book could not have gotten airborne at all without the extremely active support and contributions of Warner's and Mavis's children, Ms. Linda Tyler Wieland of Loveland, Colorado, and retired naval aviator Lt. Cmdr. Gary L. Tyler of Southport, North Carolina. Additionally, Gary's wife Sue and Linda's husband Dave smartly stepped forward, cracking open some genealogical sources as well as providing good family information. A couple of grandchildren and great-grandchildren have also materially contributed, such as Kevin Wieland and Aiden Kibler. As the reader might imagine, all of their efforts to provide information, photos, documents, reminiscences, general support, and huge enthusiasm have been priceless.

A 21-gun salute certainly goes to Ms. Melanie Templin, the Historian/Registrar of the USS *Lexington* Museum in Corpus Christi, Texas. Her unfailing, constant, and enthusiastic research, support, and initiative were key throughout the process. She dug up countless documents and pictures, photographed and scanned them, and wore out her computer emailing them to me. She never appeared to become tired of my emails which invariably began, "Hey Melanie, just one more thing……" and I am terribly grateful. Moreover, also at the *Lexington* museum, I can't overlook the solid help of Ms. Templin's assistant historian, Mr. Robert Kymes.

A full-throated "Attention on Deck!" must go to recognize retired Rear Adm. Bruce Black and Capt. Michael Waldron for not only their magnificently written forewords but also their interest in, and enthusiasm for, the project. And, of course, Admiral Black's original painting on the book's cover is simply amazing.

I must mention a number of old colleagues from Naval Reserve Intelligence Area Five, and Naval Air Reserve Center Denver (at the former Buckley Air National Guard Base), who also knew "Captain Chaos" and gave me great anecdotes, historical references, encouragement, and enthusiasm. (By the way, the reader needs to know that *no one* who knew him speaks about Captain Chaos without admiration and a smile on their face!) At huge risk I'll overlook someone, these folks include retired Captains Charlie Tennyson and Max Dodson as well as Commander Suzanne Brannon. Additionally, I'm particularly indebted to retired Captains Jon Clarke, Trux Simmons, and Jim Vaughters for above-and-beyond amounts of insights and information. Among these, I really have to say that Captain Clarke has put in a truly remarkable amount of time and effort in helping me.

A last-minute contributor has been Mr. Andrew Grosheider, son of one of my former COs, Capt. Art Grosheider, who sent me some great photographs *circa* 1979-1980. Another has been Major Jim Yagmin, a retired USAF intelligence officer, Vietnam-veteran, good friend, and docent at the *National Museum of World War II Aviation* in Colorado Springs. With him I got to get up close and personal with the museum's two pristine and flyable TBM *Avengers* and its equally flyable F4U *Corsair* and SBD-4 *Dauntless*—as well as its mid-restoration SB2C *Helldiver*.

My wife, Rhonda, also knew Captain and Mrs. Tyler and contributed some good memories—and helped me delve into further online genealogical sources. Interestingly, Rhonda's great uncle, Lt.j.g. John A. Zehrung, Jr., was also a Pacific Theater *Avenger* torpedo bomber and like Warner Tyler frequently carried bombs and depth charges to share with the enemy. Alas, he and his air crewmen ARM^2 Norman F. Gaffney and AMM^2 Jesse R. Manning (the latter from Colorado Springs) were killed in a carrier landing accident on 20 March 1944, on board the USS *Coral Sea* (CVE-57).

As it turns out, an old friend and neighbor was also at the Battle for Cape Engaño. Ensign Joseph P. Natale, Supply Corps, USNR, was on board the destroyer USS *Charrette* while she escorted the *Lexington* and other carriers as they launched their strikes on 25 October 1944. I knew Mr. Natale pretty well; he was a wonderful man. He had been born in Denver, graduated from North High School in 1940, and later earned bachelor's and master's degrees from Denver University. His lovely wife, Kaye Duncan Natale, another Denver native whom I also knew very well, graduated from East High in 1941 and then earned a BA from DU. At this point we will never know, but it's very possible she knew Mavis Lorenzen and Warner Tyler, at East High, before the war.

Thanks once again to Mr. Tony Mauro for a fabulous cover design and to Ms. Stephanee Killen for marvelous interior structure and software support. Thanks also to retired Commander Steve Phillips, owner of Focsle LLP and a great colleague from our days on faculty at the National Defense Intelligence College.

Lastly, and as always, I'm grateful for the information gleaned from the U.S. Air Force Academy's McDermott (Cadet) Library (and for great help from recently retired reference librarian Ms. Frances K. Scott). It has always impressed me that the tremendous holdings of that *Air Force* library have superbly supported my *naval* historical research—for *multiple* projects—over the last 25 years.

Appendix 1

Colleagues of Ensign Warner Tyler, in "Fighting Nineteen," who did not make it home *

Name / Hometown	Location	Date
Ens. Dan G. "Duke" de Luca, Jr. Atlantic City, New Jersey	Guam	20 Jul 44
Lt. Howard R. "Redbird" Burnett Coldwater, Kansas	Bonin	4 Aug 44
Ens. Blair M. "Bob" Wakefield Long Beach, California	Bonin	4 Aug 44
Lt.j.g. Joseph "Joe" Kelley Milwaukee, Wisconsin	Bonin	5 Aug 44
Lt.j.g. John H. Morrison Laurel Hill, North Carolina	Sea crash vic. the *Lexington*	31 Aug 44
Ens. Alfred N. "Ruff" Ruffcorn San Diego, California	Mindinao	10 Sep 44
Lt. Donald K. "Doc" Tripp San Diego, California	Luzon	12 Oct 44
Lt. Cmdr. Franklin E. "Toby" Cook San Diego, California	Formosa	12 Oct 44

Lt. Warren H. Abercrombie Ossining, New York	Sea crash vic. the *Lexington*	21 Sep 44
Lt.j.g. Robert W. "Bob" Blakeslee Kalamazoo, Michigan	Off Formosa	4 Oct 44
Lt.j.g. Clarence E. Bartlett Dove Creek, Colorado	Formosa	14 Oct 44
Ens. Francis P. "Frank" Hubbuch Chattanooga, Tennessee	Off Cape Engaño	25 Oct 44
Lt. Roger S. "Smiley" Boles Santa Paula, California	Manila	5 Nov 44
Lt. Robert S. "Knobby" Felt ** Billings, Montana	Sea crash vic. the *Lexington*	8 Nov 44

* CAG Cmdr. Hugh Winters wrote in 1985 that "The life of a naval aviator operating at sea is chancy. Add a war into the mix and the odds go down even more." He estimated VF-19 losses were almost 50%; however, it seems this list reflects a figure more like 26%. Either way, it's terrible.

** According to the Bureau of Naval Personnel's compilation of World War II casualties, "Knobby" Felt was lost on 2 June 1944. *However*, fighter pilot Bill Davis, apparently a close friend, asserts that "Knobby" crashed into the ocean, close to the *Lexington*, on or about 8 November 1944. I'm inclined to accept Mr. Davis' frequent accounts of flying and living with Mr. Felt during July through October.

Appendix 2

Colleagues of Ensign Warner Tyler, in "Bombing Nineteen," who did not make it home

Ens. Franklin P. Hart Illinois	Seal Beach, Calif.	16 Nov 43
ARM^3 Theodore G. Scheck Oregon	Seal Beach, Calif.	16 Nov 43
Ens. Paul A. Gevelinger Mineral Point, Wisconsin	Takeoff crash into the sea	20 Jul 44
ARM^3 Louis O. Nitchman Santa Rosa, California	Takeoff crash into the sea	20 Jul 44
Ens. Roy F. Majors West Palm Beach, Florida	Iwo Jima	4 Aug 44
ARM^2 Edward R. Albini Valley Ford, California	Iwo Jima	4 Aug 44
Ens. John A. Cavanaugh, Jr. Philadelphia, Pennsylvania	Ha Ha Jima	5 Aug 44
ARM^1 Michael M. Blazevich Waukegan, Illinois	Ha Ha Jima	5 Aug 44

ARM[2] John R. Snow, Jr. Denver, Colorado	Ha Ha Jima	5 Aug 44
Cmdr. Richard S. McGowan Montclair, New Jersey	Ditched into the sea vic. the *Lexington*	24 Oct 44
Lt. Cmdr. Donald F. Banker Duluth, Minnesota	Luzon	5 Nov 44
Lt.j.g. John W. Evatt Long Beach, California	Luzon	5 Nov 44
ARM[2] James J. Burns Brooklyn, New York	Luzon	5 Nov 44
ARM[3] Richard E. Hansen Reno, Nevada	Luzon	5 Nov 44
Lt. Robert B. Parker Troupe, Texas	*Kamikaze* strike on the *Lexington*	5 Nov 44
Lt.j.g. Charles F. Fisher Fresno, California	*Kamikaze*	5 Nov 44
Lt.j.g. Robert G. Smith Indianapolis, Indiana	*Kamikaze*	5 Nov 44
Ens. Robert W. Doyle Rochester, New York	*Kamikaze*	5 Nov 44
Ens. John W. Gilchrist Satanta, Kansas	*Kamikaze*	5 Nov 44
Ens. Francis O. Jackson San Bernardino, California	*Kamikaze*	5 Nov 44

Appendix 3

DEPARTMENT OF THE NAVY
RESERVE INTELLIGENCE AREA COORDINATOR
PROGRAM AREA FIVE
Naval Air Reserve Center Denver
Buckley Air National Guard Base
Aurora, Colorado 80011

DBK:gs
1800
19 September 1981

From: Reserve Intelligence Area Coordinator, Program Area FIVE, Naval Air Reserve Center, Denver
To: Captain Warner William TYLER, USNR-R, xxx-xx-xxxx/1635

Subj: Letter of Appreciation

1. Upon this, the occasion of your retirement from the United States Naval Reserve, and your transfer to the Retired Reserve after 39 years of distinguished naval service, I am honored to be able to take this time to express the Navy's sincere appreciation

for your service and your diligence to duty. You willingly took upon yourself the responsibility of defending this country, a calling which you did not take lightly, and for which you and your family can be justifiably proud.

2. You began your naval service, during World War II, on 8 August 1942 as a student pilot at NAS Corpus Christi, Texas. Following pilot training you were commissioned Ensign and designated a Naval Aviator on 16 November 1943. You were then assigned to Torpedo Squadron 19 and reported for duty aboard the USS "Lexington," an aircraft carrier in the Pacific Theater. During this assignment you participated in numerous campaigns against Japanese Fleet Units flying combat strikes as a torpedo and bomber pilot in the TBM "Avenger" aircraft. On 25 October 1944, during a campaign in the Philippine Sea, you skillfully and courageously piloted your aircraft against major enemy units including aircraft carriers, battleships, cruisers, and destroyers. During this action you made a determined attack, in the face of intense anti-aircraft fire, against an enemy battleship, scoring a direct hit with a torpedo, causing the enemy vessel to sink.[1] You were subsequently awarded the Navy Cross for this action. The Navy Cross is this nation's second-highest award for heroism of its fighting men. You were then transferred to Bomber-Fighter Squadron 153 at NAAS Oceana, Virginia, flying the Navy "Corsair" aircraft. Following the end of World War II you were released from active duty, moved back to Denver, Colorado, and entered the dry ice and compressed gas industry. Then, in 1947, you joined the Naval Reserve and became a "plank owner" of Naval Air Station Buckley. Since then you have served with various units at Buckley, NAS Olathe, Kansas, and NAS Dallas, Texas. You have had the privilege of being commanding officer of both aviation and intelligence

units, including Naval Air Reserve Division / Naval Air Reserve Training Detachment K-2, Naval Air Intelligence Reserve Unit D-2, Naval Air Reserve Squadron D-2, and Naval Reserve Force Air Augmentation Unit 2118. During the years 1969 and 1970, while commanding officer of NARDIV/NARTD K-2, your unit was awarded the "Noel Davis Trophy." This trophy is awarded annually to the most efficient aviation division of the United States Naval Reserve. Then, on 1 October 1977, you commenced your final tour of duty as Naval Reserve Intelligence Coordinator for Area FIVE.

3. By virtue of your service, you are entitled to wear the Navy Cross, the Air Medal, the Navy Commendation Medal, the United States Presidential Unit Citation (with 1 small bronze-star device), the American Campaign Medal, the Asiatic-Pacific Campaign Medal (with 4 small bronze-star devices), the World War II Victory Medal, the Naval Reserve Medal, the Armed Forces Reserve Medal with gold hourglass-device, the Philippine Presidential Unit Citation, the Philippine Liberation Medal (with 2 small bronze-star devices), the Philippine Independence Medal, and the Navy Rifle Marksman Ribbon.

4. Throughout your naval career your performance and attention to duty has been consistently commendable. Your fulfillment of your obligations as a citizen of this country, your unswerving dedication to duty, and your thoroughgoing professionalism have gained you the trust, admiration, and respect of all your associates, of the United States Navy, and of this grateful nation.

5. On behalf of the Department of the Navy, and from those whom you have known and influenced, I extend a hearty "well

done," and wish you the best of luck and happiness in your future endeavors. May you always enjoy smooth sailing, fair winds, and following seas.

J. M. ZANETTI

[1] Of course, this action was the Battle off Cape Engaño—which was part of the largest sea battle in history, the Battle for Leyte Gulf. And, as we now know, the battleship in question was not actually torpedoed by *anyone* that day, and it did not sink during *this* action.

Appendix 4

Linda Tyler Wieland

Our parents, Warner and Mavis, were both only children, so we all have always lamented the lack of cousins and aunts and uncles.

Knowing your parents only as parents, and then youngish adults, and then maturing and aging adults, gives you a whole different perspective as to who they really were. I think of my parents both as having very strong personalities and the expectations for their lives that fit perfectly into the society and period of time they found themselves. Each had a strong sense of role models, followed precisely without apology. Factoring personal involvement in a war into their very early relationship (as have many of us in every generation), then parenthood very soon thereafter, adds a sense of undeniable subjectivity to my experience as their child.

As Steve mentioned in the text, both my brother Gary and I were born and raised in Denver, and we both attended George Washington High School. I am the eldest, exhibiting all of the predictable rule-following, respectful, careful, precision, and conflict-avoidance traits in the personality book. I graduated in 1967 from the University of Northern Colorado in Greeley (well, it's UNC now, but it still was Colorado State College in 1967) as one of the first class of eight students to complete all four years from the newly accredited BSN program. So, with my Bachelor of Science in Nursing degree I became a pediatric/OBGYN/Neonatal Nursery Nurse. Dad and Mother strongly encouraged me to graduate but were not so much in favor of my ever being employed. At that time, women were usually encouraged to use any further education as a "backup" plan after marriage.

My husband, Dave, was born and raised on a dry-land wheat farm in eastern Colorado. We met at the wedding of college dorm-mates of each of us at CSC, not knowing each other at that time. Dave was the last groomsman of five, I the last bridesmaid of five, each of us being the shortest in the lineup! We walked down the aisle together as partners that day, and have been together ever since, evidently deciding that was truly a life's omen to be followed without question! We married in 1966. Dave graduated from CSC the year ahead of me, with a BA in Business Administration, right at the apex of the Vietnam War. Almost immediately he was accepted into the Air Force Officer Training School at Lackland AFB in San Antonio, Texas. This was doubtless in lieu of being drafted and probably having no choice of service or training. He spent his first two years as an administrative officer in a Civil Engineering unit belonging to the Military Airlift Command. This was at Norton AFB in San Bernardino, California.

As soon as I graduated from CSC, in 1967, I moved to Norton as well. In July, 1968, our first child was born. As a complete surprise a few days later, Dad flew into southern California on a Navy flight, then on a 2-engine puddle-jumper to Norton, completely off-grid and in uniform. There he was greeted by a formal welcoming committee after they were informed that the flight had an "O6" on board. Having no idea who this "O6" was, or why he was arriving, they saluted, he saluted, and he then was greeted by Dave and transported to our apartment to say hello to his newborn first grandson. Even my mother didn't know of this plan as she had come a few days earlier to help me and meet our new son. We never were told the complete and unedited version of how this visit came to be! And, likely, neither was the Norton duty officer that day.

After spending two years at Norton AFB, Dave received orders to report to Clark AFB, in the Philippines, as Admin Officer with the MAC unit for C-141 aircraft travel and maintenance. Our five-month-old son and I were shortly allowed to join Dave as it was to be a two-year accompanied tour. Mother and Dad traveled to Manila and then to Clark, as part of a Far East tour, for a visit with us while we were stationed there. I can hardly imagine the range of emotions they must have felt during that holiday. I must admit that I find it particularly poignant that Dave and I spent two years stationed on an island that, a generation before, my Dad had helped to free—and upon which he'd dropped a lot of bombs.

Dad was quite instrumental in assisting me with the initial legal and military requirements of traveling overseas alone with an infant. We never would have been able to join Dave as soon as we did had it not been for Captain Tyler's expertise and intervention. We have always been grateful for his support during this chaotic portion of the Vietnam War—particularly following the TET offensive that had occurred earlier that year.

We lived off-base due to the gigantic population housed on-base there during that war. I worked part-time at the Clark AFB hospital in the psychiatric unit. After two years, when we returned back to Denver after Dave's commitment, he was hired by Eastman Kodak Company, where he stayed for almost 35 years as a financial analyst.

Dave and I had three children, two boys and a girl, and fostered thirteen newborns over five years in preparation for their adoption. Needless to say, Mother and Dad were terrified that we intended to adopt every one of them ourselves! Actually our intention was to give them the best newborn start that they each deserved so they could eventually bond appropriately with their adoptive parents, or be in better health if they returned to their birth mother. Dave and I and our kids are all extremely proud to have had the opportunity to accomplish that goal for those infants, plus giving our own children a real-life opportunity to see how much of an enormous responsibility parenting can be. I retired clinically in 1996, then consulted with daycare facilities for six more years.

Dave and I have five grandkids. Lianna belongs to son Kevin and Andrea. Isabel belongs to son Ty and Quoc. Kyle, Cameron and Emily belong to daughter Kendra and Bill Silver. Our grandchildren are our blessings and challenges, to say the least. The best part of having them has definitely been their unique abilities to keep us active, interested, loved, surprised, part of their lives, amazed, proud, intellectually stimulated, and fortunate. They coach us to stay aware of technology (I would never be able to describe us as completely literate, however), with humor and patience.

We enjoyed several years of traveling both overseas and in the U.S., with lots more in the planning stages until Covid cut it short. We are mostly now at home trying to stay healthy and safe and helping our kids do the same.

This turned into more personal biography than I planned since Steve's main objective was my dad's life and naval career. That's the penalty you pay when you ask a woman to describe her family and give her a chance to prattle on-and-on!

It's been a joy to read Steve's discoveries about Warner W. Tyler, many of which we had never heard. Now we have a whole added perspective on Dad's military contributions to the country—particularly his wartime ones. As everyone knows, military stories don't often get shared, even (or maybe especially) to family, for a myriad of reasons. Now there are some that have been shared.

Thanks to Steve for this gift which has offered a new introduction of my father—to me and my family—and expanding the narrow perspective that a child has of a parent.

Appendix 5

Gary L. Tyler

I graduated from Denver's George Washington High School in 1965 and was a very average student. When I spoke of college, Mom and Dad agreed to let me attend anything in state I could get into—*except* the University of Colorado at Boulder. They thought it was too much of a "party school" and, knowing my proclivities, that was probably a good call. I was accepted by Colorado State University in Fort Collins, and enrolled in the fall of 1965. I met my wife-to-be, Sue Amos, on registration day through a common acquaintance. She was born in Houston, came to Denver with her parents when she was three or four, and graduated from Abraham Lincoln High School in 1965. Sue was a very strong student and challenged me to be the same. I got onto the very good side of the GPA curve which gave me a lot of "political capital" with Dad. We became very close from that point forward for the rest of his life. A pretty magical time for me, and I think for him, too.

Sue and I both graduated from CSU with honors in 1969, she with a BA in History and I with a BS in Business Administration. We dated throughout our college years and married on 23 November 1968. Mom and Dad were not happy about our marriage before graduating and, in fact, made us pay our remaining tuition through the next June. We picked our wedding date to be *after* our 21st birthdays so I wouldn't have to ask permission.

I went through Aviation Officer Candidate School and flight school; Sue pinned on my wings in May 1971. I was a "distinguished naval graduate" and was offered and accepted a commission in the regular Navy. Following training in the Replacement Air Group in Jacksonville, Florida, I joined VA-72, flying A-7 *Corsair II* light attack aircraft off the carrier USS *John F. Kennedy*. I made two deployments to the Mediterranean (very lucky) and enjoyed the entire military experience thoroughly. I also had a collateral job as a Squadron Legal Officer following Naval Justice School in Newport, Rhode Island.

When it looked like I was going to get my wings and have a job, Sue and I started our family with Amy, born in March of 1972. She was joined by her sister, Alisa, in September of 1974.

I finished my active duty in December of 1974 and joined Air Products and Chemicals, Inc., in Allentown, Pennsylvania in January of the following year. I was in the human resources business and IT systems integration with them for around 28 years, retiring in 2003. I then joined KPMG Consulting in systems integration for another five years and then finally gave it up. While I was dealing with my career, Sue worked primarily in medical billing for a local practice in Allentown and managed the formidable job of running our family and raising our daughters. After our retirements we moved to North Carolina where we now live in Southport, south of Wilmington. We've travelled fairly extensively and both enjoy the exquisite pain of golf.

We have four grandkids. Will, Aidan, and Olivia belong to Amy and her husband, Joe Kibler. Kate is Alisa and Tommy Evans' daughter. Amy is an occupational therapist and Joe is a foot-and-ankle surgeon, all living in Southport. Alisa works for Bank of America and Tommy is a consultant, both in the IT end of the business; they live on Mountain Island Lake northwest of Charlotte, North Carolina.

Mom and Dad fit my understanding of what a post-war young family looked like. They worked hard, saved what they could, and built a sound future for their family and the generation to come. They instilled good values but also struggled with the challenges life throws at all of us.

I was surely the more difficult kid to raise. I got in my share of trouble and frequently conflicted with Dad when my trajectory got out of tolerance. He was tough but fair and, importantly, consistent in his view of the world. Those traits seemed to serve him well throughout his career and life. Mom was the buffer between me and Dad and frequently struggled during my teen years as the family referee. As it turned out, she backed him all the way. That said, she was caring, loving, and always had forgiveness in her heart. When Dad got sick in the later years, she cared for him at home as long as she possibly could. What a killer it was to see him go into assisted care. Makes me cry right now. The good news was that he didn't linger there for a long while.

When Mom got sick she moved to Loveland to be close to Linda who did yeoman's duty as her advocate, friend, and dedicated, loving daughter. Over a period of years Mom progressed from independent living to assisted living and, finally, to skilled nursing.

She was at that stage much longer than she wanted, I'm sure. But through it all I never heard a complaint. Linda may have since she was with her frequently, but I tend to doubt it. Mom was stoic, taking what was coming her way. She made me proud of her courage and composure through it all. Linda, Dave, Sue, and I were in the room with her when she passed. We were lucky to have such great parents.

Hopefully this will give the reader a sense of the fabric of their lives. Dust off your copy of *The Greatest Generation* and you'll get a good picture of who they were.

Sources

All of the sources listed below were of great value in the composition of this story, and I certainly recommend them to you. That said, there are five publications that were of *incredible* value: Lt. Bill Davis's autobiography *Sinking the Rising Sun*; Lt.j.g. Bill and Kathy Emerson's *The Voices of Bombing Nineteen*; Mrs. Lee Reese's *Men of the Blue Ghost*; Cmdr. Hugh Winters's autobiography *Skipper*; and Admiral Sherman's *Combat Command*. Even though I have quoted extensively from them and brought to you many gems from each, I enthusiastically recommend that you look for each one and dig further into each for many more amazing insights into the World War II *Lexington*, Carrier Air Group Nineteen, and the Battle for Leyte Gulf.

Aviation Archeological Investigation and Research. *USN Overseas Aircraft Loss List September 1944*. www.aviationarchaeology.com/src/USN/LLSep44.htm.

"Battle of Leyte Gulf." *Wikipedia: the Free Encyclopedia*. Accessed 24 February 2021. https://en.wikipedia.org/wiki/Battle_of_Leyte_Gulf.

Beauchamp, Lt. Paul R. "The Lake of the Sun and the Moon." Fighter pilot, VF-19, July-November 1944. Typewritten story dated 13 May 1980, as found in Reese, *Men of the Blue Ghost*, pp.215-221.

Cammeron, Eugene. Battle off Cape Engaño, 25 October 1944. *NavWeaps: Naval Weapons, Naval Technology, and Naval Reunions.* www.navweaps.com/index_oob/OOB_WWII_Pacific/OOB_WWII_Cape_Engano.php.

Cutler, Thomas J. *The Battle of Leyte Gulf, 23-26 October 1944: The Dramatic Full Story, Based on the Latest Research, of the Greatest Naval Battle in History*. New York: HarperCollins, 1994.

Davis, Lt. William E., III. *Sinking the Rising Sun: Dog Fighting & Dive Bombing in World War II—A Navy Fighter Pilot's Story*. Monee, Illinois: CreateSpace, 2010.

Dull, Paul S. *A Battle History of the Imperial Japanese Navy: 1941-1945*. Annapolis: Naval Institute Press, 1978.

Dupuy, Col. R. Ernest and Col. Trevor N. Dupuy. *The Encyclopedia of Military History from 3500 B.C. to the Present.* New York: Harper & Row, 1970.

Emerson, Lt.j.g. William and Kathy Emerson. *The Voices of Bombing Nineteen: The Stories of the Men of Bombing Nineteen in their Own Words*. 2nd ed., August 1995. ww.emersonguys.com/bill/vb19.htm.

Ewing, Steve. *The "Lady Lex" and the "Blue Ghost": A Pictorial History of the USS* Lexingtons *CV-2 and CV-16*. Missoula, Montana: Pictorial Histories Publishing, 1983.

Field, James A., Jr. *The Japanese at Leyte Gulf: The Shō Operation*. Princeton: University Press, 1947.

Hanson, Victor Davis. *Carnage and Culture: Landmark Battles in the Rise of Western Power*. New York: Anchor Books, 2002.

Home of Heroes. *Major Military Award List Online*. https://homeofheroes.com/.

Hoyt, Edwin P. *The Battle of Leyte Gulf: The Death Knell of the Japanese Fleet*. New York: Weybright and Talley, 1972.

Humble, Richard. *Aircraft Carriers: The Illustrated History*. Herts, England: Winchmore Publishing, 1982.

Jentschura, Hansgeorg, Dieter Jung, and Peter Mickel. *Warships of the Imperial Japanese Navy, 1869-1945*. Annapolis: Naval Institute Press, 1977.

King, Fleet Adm. Ernest J. and Cmdr. Walter M. Whitehill. *Fleet Admiral King: A Naval Record*. New York: W.W. Norton, 1952.

Lawson, Robert and Barrett Tillman. *World War II U.S. Navy Air Combat*. Ann Arbor: Lowe & B. Hould Publishers, 2002.

Macintyre, Capt. Donald. *Leyte Gulf: Armada in the Pacific*. New York: Ballantine, 1969.

Military Times. *Hall of Valor: The Military Medals Database.* https://valor.militarytimes.com/.

Morison, Rear Adm. Samuel Eliot. *Leyte: June 1944 – January 1945.* "The History of United States Naval Operations in World War II," Vol. XII. Boston: Little, Brown and Co., 1958.

NAS Kahului. http://hiavps.com/Kahului.htm.

Perry, Lt. Cmdr. Frank C. *History of Torpedo Squadron Nineteen, 15 August 1943 – 14 December 1944.* U.S. Pacific Fleet. Air Force. Torpedo Squadron Nineteen, 1945. In the collection of the USS *Lexington* Museum, donation of Lt. Donald W. McMillan; Accession No. 1997.062.024.

Potter, E. B. *Nimitz.* Annapolis: Naval Institute Press, 1976.

Potter, E. B., *et al. Sea Power: A Naval History.* 2nd ed. Annapolis: Naval Institute Press, 1981.

Powers, Chief Aviation Radioman W. Ernest. *Radio Squawks VT-19: Radio Logbook.* Torpedo Squadron Nineteen, USS *Lexington*: 15 July – 9 November, 1944. In the collection of the USS *Lexington* Museum, donation of Lt. Donald W. McMillan; Accession No. 1997.062.024.

Reed, Richard and James Van Westering. *Floyd Bennett Field: Naval Aviation's Home in Brooklyn.* National Park Service. https://www.nps.gov/articles/floyd-bennett-field-naval-aviation-s-home-in-brooklyn-teaching-with-historic-places.htm.

Reese, Lee Fleming, comp. *Men of the Blue Ghost (USS Lexington CV-16): Historic Events of World War II in the Pacific as Told by the Men Who Lived Them, 1943 – 1946*. San Diego: Lexington Book Co., 1982.

Reynolds, Clark G. and the Editors of Time-Life Books. *The Carrier War*. Revised ed. Alexandria, Virginia: Time-Life Books, 1987.

Reynolds, Quentin, George Jones, Frank Morris, and Ralph Teatsorth. "America's Greatest Naval Battle," *Collier's*, three-part series, Jan. 13, 1945, p. 11; Jan. 20, 1945, p. 18; Jan. 27, 1945, p. 18.

Riem, Shawn. *Naval Air Station (NAS) Denver Has Proud, Long History*. 460th Space Wing History Office. Aurora, Colorado: Buckley Air Force Base, 7 February 2011. https://www.buckley.af.mil/News/Article-Display/Article/322920/nas-denver-has-proud-long-history/.

Sears, Stephen W. and the Editors of "American Heritage: The Magazine of History." *Carrier War in the Pacific*. New York: American Heritage Publishing, 1966.

Sherman, Adm. Frederick C. *Combat Command: The American Aircraft Carriers in the Pacific War*. Originally published in 1950. New York: Bantam Books, 1982.

Stafford, Edward P. *The Big E: The Story of the USS Enterprise*. Annapolis: Naval Institute Press, 1962.

Stille, Mark. *Imperial Japanese Navy Battleships, 1941-1945*. New York: Osprey, 2008.

Stubblebine, David. *Barbers Point Naval Air Station*. https://ww2db.com/facility/Barbers_Point_Naval_Air_Station.

Stubblebine, David. *Kahului Naval Air Station*. https://ww2db.com/facility/Kahului_Naval_Air_Station.

Taylor, Theodore. *The Magnificent Mitscher*. Originally published in 1954. Annapolis: Naval Institute Press, 1991.

Tillman, Barrett. "The Navy's Aerial Arsenal at Leyte Gulf." *Naval History*. Annapolis: U.S. Naval Institute. October 2019, pp. 20-25.

Tyler, Ens. Warner W. *Aviator's Flight Log Book*. February 1944 – October 1947.

Tyler, Capt. Warner W. *Biographical Resumé*. Date *circa* 1986.

Tyler, Capt. Warner W. *Second Battle of the Philippines, 25 October 1944: Strike Narrative*. Date unspecified but no earlier than 1973.

U.S. Navy. Bureau of Personnel. *World War 2 - United States Navy at War. United States Navy Casualties, Bureau of Naval Personnel Entries by Name*. https://www.naval-history.net/WW2UScasaaDB-USNBPbyNameD.htm.

U.S. Navy. *Dictionary of American Naval Fighting Ships*. "Lexington (CV-16)." Washington: Naval History and Heritage

Command. https://www.history.navy.mil/research/histories/ship-histories/danfs/l/lexington-cv-16-v.html.

U.S. Navy. *Dictionary of American Naval Fighting Ships.* "Nehenta Bay (CVE-74)." Washington: Naval History and Heritage Command. https://www.history.navy.mil/research/histories/ship-histories/danfs/n/nehenta-bay.html.

U.S. Navy. *Register of Commissioned and Warrant Officers of the United States Naval Reserve.* Washington: U.S. Government Printing Office, July 1944.

U.S. Pacific Fleet. Air Force. Torpedo Squadron Nineteen. *Tactical Organization.* Undated; pen-and-ink notation states "about late Oct 44."

Weaver, Dennis. *All the World's a Stage.* Newburyport, Massachusetts: Hampton Roads, 2001.

Whitham, Chief Radarman Robert O., "*Action Starboard – Action Port: USS* Lexington, *CV-16, September 1, 1943 – March 20, 1945.*" Typed manuscript as found in Reese, *Men of the Blue Ghost.*

Willmott, H. P. *The Battle of Leyte Gulf: The Last Fleet Action.* Bloomington: Indiana University Press, 2005.

Winters, Cmdr. T. Hugh. *Recollections of Events Leading Up to and During the Carrier Air Action in the Battle for Leyte Gulf, 24th and 25th October, 1944, by Commander T. Hugh Winters, USN, Commander Air Group 19, Strike Leader, and Target*

Coordinator. Narrative, dated 1945, as found in Reese, *Men of the Blue Ghost*.

Winters, Capt. T. Hugh. *Skipper: Confessions of a Fighter Squadron Commander*. Mesa, Arizona: Champlin Fighter Museum Press, 1985.

Woodward, C. Vann. *The Battle for Leyte Gulf: The Incredible Story of World War II's Largest Naval Battle*. Originally published New York: Ballantine Books, 1947. New edition New York: Skyhorse Publishing, 2017.

Note on *Wikipedia*: While I do make reference to specific *Wikipedia* articles a few times in the list above, the reality is that I checked a huge number of facts and copied several score of comments from multiple *Wikipedia* articles (not to mention other web sources). Citing each article would have been very cumbersome for me and for the reader; thus, I haven't. Moreover, while many academics disparage *Wikipedia* as a solid source, my experience over many years is that it is often a *very* solid source—as long as the subject isn't political or otherwise "controversial."

What happened to...

Buckley Air National Guard Base: The regular Air Force took over the installation on 1 October 2000, renaming it Buckley Air Force Base versus Air National Guard Base. Following the establishment of the United States Space Force, in June 2021, the base was renamed Buckley Space Force Base. However, Naval Reserve intelligence activities remain strong on site. Indeed, the Navy has maintained a constant presence as a tenant unit since relinquishing administrative control of the installation, first as Naval Air Reserve Center Denver and, currently, as Navy Operational Support Center Denver. Somewhat ironically, as of this writing, scuttlebutt has it that the NOSC Denver name will shortly be changed *back* to NAR-Cen Denver.

Lieutenant, junior grade, William E. Davis, III (1921-2012): Mr. Davis, even before the war ended, was sent by the Navy to CalTech for two years of graduate work in aeronautical engineering. After that he went to work for Bell Aircraft as a design engineer and test pilot. During World War II he became a fighter ace, shooting down seven Japanese aircraft, and was the recipient of the Navy Cross.

Lieutenant, junior grade, Donald D. Engen (1924-1999): Mr. Engen, a pilot in VB-19, stayed in the navy and in aviation, later commanding VF-21, Air Group 11, USS *Mount Katmai*, the carrier USS *America*, and Carrier Division 4. His final position was Deputy CINC of the U.S. Atlantic Command, and he retired as a vice admiral. He later headed the Federal Aviation Administration and was also Director of the National Air and Space Museum. Ironically, he was killed in an experimental glider accident. His awards included the Navy Cross and the Distinguished Flying Cross.

Commander David S. McCampbell (1910-1996): Commander McCampbell was promoted to Captain in 1952, and held several important assignments including commanding officer of the carrier USS *Bon Homme Richard*. He retired from the navy in 1964 with 31 years of service. McCampbell is the U.S. Navy's all-time leading fighter ace with 34 aerial victories. He was the recipient of the Medal of Honor, Navy Cross, Silver Star, and the Legion of Merit with Combat "V" Device.

Vice Admiral Marc A. "Pete" Mitscher (1887-1947): Vice Adm. Mitscher (U.S. Naval Aviator No. 33) later became commander of the 8th Fleet and then, in March 1946, became commander-in-chief of the Atlantic Fleet with promotion to full Admiral. He was the recipient of three Navy Crosses, three Distinguished Service Medals, and the Legion of Merit with Combat "V" Device.

Rear Admiral Frederick C. "Ted" Sherman (1888-1957): Rear Adm. Sherman was promoted to Vice Admiral in July 1945 and became commander of the 5th Fleet. He then was appointed a full Admiral when he retired in March 1947. He was the recipient of three Navy Crosses, three Distinguished Service Medals, and the Legion of Merit with Combat "V" Device.

Commander Theodore Hugh Winters, Jr. (1913-2008): Commander Winters was a fighter ace with eight confirmed World War II air-to-air victories. After the war he was instrumental in the establishment of the Navy's "Blue Angels" flight demonstration team. He was promoted to Captain in 1956, and commanded the carrier *Franklin D. Roosevelt*. He was the recipient of two Navy Crosses and three Silver Stars.

USS *Lexington*: For her World War II service the aircraft carrier *Lexington* was the recipient of 11 battle stars and a Presidential Unit Citation. Following the war the *Lexington* was decommissioned but then was modernized and reactivated in the early 1950s, being reclassified as an attack carrier (CVA). Later she was reclassified again as an antisubmarine warfare carrier (CVS). In her second career she operated both in the Atlantic/Mediterranean as well as the Pacific. She then spent a considerable amount of time, nearly 30 years, in Pensacola, Florida, as a training carrier (CVT). The *Lexington* was decommissioned, in 1991, with an active service life longer than any other *Essex*-class ship. Following her decommissioning she was donated for use as a museum ship at Corpus Christi, Texas. In 2003 the *Lexington* was designated a National Historic Landmark. Her World War II Presidential Unit Citation reads:

"For extraordinary heroism in action against enemy Japanese forces in the air, ashore, and afloat in the Pacific War Area from September 18, 1943, to August 15, 1945. Spearheading our concentrated carrier-warfare in the most forward areas, the U.S.S. *Lexington* and her air groups struck crushing blows toward annihilating Japanese fighting power."

Mohawk-98: The airplane which Ensign Warner Tyler flew from the *Lexington* on 25 October 1944. It was a TBM-1C *Avenger*, BuNo 16922, later transferred to VT-45. It was sadly blown off the deck of the light carrier USS *San Jacinto* (CVL-30) in a Philippine Sea typhoon, 18 December 1944. Mr. Tyler had flown it once before, on 24 September, during an attack against Cebu in the Philippines.

About the Author

Photo: U.S. Navy

A third-generation Denver native, Steve Maffeo attained the rank of Eagle Scout in 1969 and graduated from Thomas Jefferson High School in 1972. He is also a graduate of the University of Colorado (B.A.), the University of Denver (M.A.L.S.), and the Joint Military Intelligence College (M.S.S.I.). As a civilian, Steve served as the associate director of the academic library at the U.S. Air Force Academy from 1998 to 2015. In 2008 he retired after 31 years in the Colorado Army National Guard (Signal Corps), the U.S. Navy, and the U.S. Naval Reserve. Captain Maffeo commanded three reserve shore-based naval and joint-service intelligence units in Salt Lake City, Denver, and Washington, D.C. His final reserve assignment was as director of the 'history of intelligence' course, and as the director of part-time programs, at the National Defense Intelligence College in Washington.

Steve now writes books on naval history and the history of intelligence. He tinkers with his two '60s muscle cars, is a recreational shooter, and for several years has been a volunteer "commissioner" at the local Boy Scout summer camp. He lives in Colorado Springs with his wife, Rhonda, a retired computer programmer and software project lead. Their son Micah (also an Eagle Scout) was a district executive for the Boy Scouts, is active in developing real estate, and is a military intelligence officer in the U.S. Army Reserve. (Coincidentally, Micah's current army intelligence unit operates out of secure spaces in the Naval Air Reserve Center building at Buckley Space Force Base).

***

"Historians keep moments from becoming
'lost in time, like tears in rain.'"

— Rutger Hauer and Andrew Grosheider